Church Planting in Europe

Church Planting in Europe

Connecting to Society, Learning from Experience

edited by

EVERT VAN DE POLL
JOANNE APPLETON

WIPF & STOCK · Eugene, Oregon

CHURCH PLANTING IN EUROPE
Connecting to Society, Learning from Experience

Wipf & Stock
An Imprint of Wipf and Stock Publishers
199 W. 8th Ave., Suite 3
Eugene, OR 97401

www.wipfandstock.com

ISBN 13: 978-1-4982-0199-5   04.27.2015

Manufactured in the U.S.A.

CONTENTS

PART III   CHURCH PLANTERS

PART IV   CASE STUDIES

ILLUSTRATIONS

PREFACE

THIS PUBLICATION IS THE outcome of a significant and valuable symposium held in Leuven, Belgium, in July 2014, on the theme, "Mission in Europe: Developing New and Existing Churches Connected to Society." The following chapters are based on the lectures, case studies, workshops, and group discussions from that event.

Sponsored by European Christian Mission International (ECMI), the Evangelical Theological Faculty (ETF), and the Leuven Centre for Christian Studies (LCCS), this symposium brought together theologians, church leaders, and mission workers from over twenty-five European countries, all of whom are involved in planting new churches in some way.

We would like to thank ECMI and the ETF for having taken the initiative of the symposium, and the LCCS for hosting this event. While acknowledging the important role played by all the members of the preparation committee, we would like to particularly mention its chairman, Johan Lukasse. Not only did he bring vision for the process, but his network of contacts and his perseverance proved to be essential in realizing the idea of this important event.

We also extend our thanks to all the speakers for their contributions, and to the participants for their input in the discussions. The speakers have put in much effort to rework the text of their presentations for publication in this book. In addition, the co-editor listened through the recordings of the group discussions that took place after each presentation and summarized them in an additional "Discussion Highlights" section at the end of many of the chapters. This makes the book even more practical, as readers will be able to identify with those who put forth questions during the sessions.

The publication itself has been enabled through the preparatory financial support of the ETF, and the efficient cooperation of Laura Poncy at Wipf & Stock during all stages of editing, formatting, and printing the manuscript.

We would like to say a very special word of thanks to Stephanie Shackelford, PA to Johan Lukasse, for all the precious work she has put into this project. Not only did she take care that the speakers hand in their text on time, and that all their necessary paperwork was signed and returned, she also spent countless hours of concentrated proofreading through the chapters that we had initially edited. You did a marvelous job, Stephanie. With your eye for detail and linguistic skills, you have contributed enormously to the project.

Finally, we would like to express our gratitude to the various churches and church planting teams with which the authors of this book are involved. What could they have said without the experience of working and sharing with so many brothers and sisters all over Europe? For this reality we can ultimately only thank the Author of Life, who continues building his Church.

Evert Van de Poll, editor
Joanne Appleton, co-editor

1

INTRODUCTION

*The Ongoing Challenge of Church Planting
in Europe*

EVERT VAN DE POLL

FROM THE 1980S ONWARDS, the development of new churches has become a major objective of denominations and mission organizations in Europe—not only in Evangelical Free churches and independent charismatic circles that are always prone to start new local communities, but also in Anglican, Reformed, and Lutheran churches.

There are several church planting networks on a European scale, and countless seminars, as well as a growing amount of literature on church planting, mainly of a practical, theological nature. Church leaders are drawing up plans for pioneer projects, and are aiming to connect with a section of the population that is out of touch with existing churches. Teams are continually taking off to start new Christian groups and assemblies in virtually every European country. Theological institutions offer master's diplomas in church planting, and dissertations are being published on the subject.

Sadly, quite a few initiatives in preceding decades have not born lasting fruit in the form of churches that survive and continue to develop. Some observers have perceived a weakening in the wave of church planting as a result of the lack of lasting fruit.[1] While these efforts are still definitely taking place, there seems to be more caution than before. There

---

1. Reimer, *Die Welt umarmen*, 13–15.

are growing questions about which approaches are to be avoided and what kind of churches we need in Europe today. Organizations, churches, and groups of concerned Christians planning to start new churches are increasingly reflecting on preceding experiences on the field, on biblical foundations and ecclesiology, and on the possibilities to collaborate with others.

The authors of this book share these concerns. They consider church planting as an ongoing task, but they want to learn from recent developments and identify the challenges posed by the changing socio-cultural context. Coming from a variety of backgrounds and countries, they share their insights and experiences here. Moreover, as they come from and work in Europe, they write with a knowledgeable view on the European situation. Many publications on church planting, especially those with a practical approach, stem from other contexts—often North America. That does not disqualify them as such for European readers, but there is a cultural distance. When it comes to mission, evangelization, and church development, things do not work the same way here in Europe as they do elsewhere.

The purpose of this publication is twofold:

1. To equip readers for a ministry of church planting and, where needed, church restoration.

2. To relate this ministry to the spiritual needs and opportunities in multicultural and postmodern Europe.

Missionary church planting

The theological identity of the authors can be described as Evangelical Protestant, but that does not in itself imply a particular form of church planting. In order to be clear, Stuart Murray's table of different types of church planting is often quoted. He distinguishes the following:

- *Pioneer* church planting in areas where there is not yet a church, or among "unreached" peoples and people groups.

- *Replacement* church planting in areas where there have been churches in the past that no longer exist.

- *Contrast* church planting refers to new churches created in contrast to existing ones. They differ from the latter in doctrine, form of worship, and/or lifestyle. (Murray calls it "sectarian," in the socio-logical meaning of the term.)

- *Saturation* church planting is the creation of new churches in areas where churches already exist. This is not done in contrast to them, but in order to reach and attract more people.[2]

In the European situation, the first type of church planting, *pioneer planting*, is needed among sections of the population emerging from recent immigration flows. One thinks in particular of the various Muslim communities in Western Europe. Here is a major challenge for church planting!

The second category, replacement planting, has unfortunately become a necessity in Europe, and increasingly so. As a result of secularization, there are now "spiritual deserts" all over the continent, where church buildings have been demolished or turned into shops or apartments, and where there is no longer a clear witness to the Gospel. Clearly, there is a need to start new and viable church communities in such areas. Many church planting teams are needed, as their ministry will not come by way of existing churches.

What about areas where churches already exist? That is invariably the case in Europe, which brings us to the third and fourth types of church planting mentioned by Murray. In fact, there are several means of starting new churches that are deliberately different from existing churches in the same area, or among the same population. Let us refine Murray's table and make a distinction between several options.

- *Culturally sensitive* church planting is a response to the particular situation in which migrants find themselves. New fellowships are created in which the cultural background of the original country is perpetuated to a certain extent.

- *Denominational* church planting results as members of a particular denomination settle in new towns and new suburbs, or it is due to a policy to implant the denomination in areas where it is not yet represented—considering that its particular doctrine or church style is a complement to other existing churches.

- *Split-off* church planting is the consequence of conflict and disagreement, not only about doctrine or ethical matters, but also about

2. Murray, *Church Planting*, 87–95.

worship style, leadership, or finances. The points of conflict then become the distinguishing mark of the split-off.

We are not taking sides in the discussion as to whether these forms of church planting are needed, but we do want to point out another form that is of the utmost importance in Europe today:

- *Missionary (or missional)* church planting. In the extensive study and analysis of recent new church initiatives in the Netherlands, Gert Noort and others make the important remark that not all church planting is driven by missionary motives. Sometimes the motive is to create a new pastoral post for the denomination; at other times it is to spread a certain model of church life that attracts believers who are dissatisfied with their actual church experience.[3]

We already noted a few of the various motives involved in a split-off. All these motivations can be discussed, but they should be distinguished from the purpose behind a "missionary initiative," which can be defined as follows:

> A missionary initiative is primarily outward looking. In this context, it is not suspect to "win people." Here we see the old missiological relation between "conversion" and "church planting." There is also the notion of "being sent." The church planters are related to and supported by an organization, a network, a church denomination or a local church. Even though we do not disqualify all sorts of work done from personal initiative, without being commissioned by someone else, we believe that "missionary" implies "being sent." Those who are sent should be prepared to share their experiences with a mother church or a sending agency, and be accountable to them.[4]

We find this description most helpful, because it is exactly what we are dealing with in our book: missionary church planting.

Biblical Reflections

The following chapters are arranged in four sections. In the first section, we will look at some biblical foundations for the work of church planting.

---

3. Noort et al, *Als een kerk opnieuw begint*, 15.
4. Ibid.

Chapter 2: Chris Wigram will be taking us to the *Bible*, the essential foundation of any church planting ministry. On the basis of a well-known passage, "All Scripture is God-breathed and is useful for teaching, rebuking, correcting and training in righteousness . . ." (2 Tim 3:16), he gives valuable advice and shows how to apply biblical principles today.

Chapter 3: Boris Paschke concentrates on the *prayer life* of church planters, and shares insights from those in the New Testament who planted churches. What was the power and influence of prayer in their ministry? As he answers this question in a very thorough manner, he challenges us to place prayer at the center of church planting today.

Chapter 4: Dietrich Schindler reveals that the ultimate point of reference for a church planter is not Paul, nor the apostles, as important as those examples are, but in our Lord Jesus himself. He describes *the ministry of Jesus as a model* for planting multiplying churches.

Connecting to Society

As authors of this book, we are concerned that churches be connected to society in Europe. What use is there in multiplying the number of churches when they do not relate to the concerns of our fellow Europeans? And when they do not influence developments in society? We can state and commend the faith only in so far as we put ourselves inside the doubts of the doubters, the questions of the questioners, and the loneliness of those who have lost their way. The days in which unbelievers come to faith are not over, thank God. But this often occurs in new and unexpected ways. Churches must adapt to the fact that conversion is now usually a long process. People need time to find out what the Christian faith means in their life situation. In this respect, John Stott calls for "double listening." He explains,

> The voices of our contemporaries may take the form of shrill and strident protest. They are now querulous, now appealing, and now aggressive in tone. There are also the anguished cries of those who are suffering, and the pain, doubt, anger, alienation and even despair of those who are estranged from God. We listen to the Word with humble reverence, anxious to understand it, and resolved to believe and obey what we come to understand. We listen to the world with critical alertness, anxious to understand it too, and resolved not necessarily to believe and

obey it, but to sympathize with it and to seek grace to discover how the gospel relates to it.[5]

This is the task of every church that endeavors to be true to its missionary calling to communicate good news to the postmodern man in Europe, and it calls for a thorough reflection.

Church in Europe

The challenge to plant churches connected to society is taken up in the second part of our book.

Chapter 5: Johannes Reimer discusses the unique and necessary relationship between the Gospel and the culture in which we want to develop existing and new churches.

Chapter 6: Reimer further applies the above general theory to the context. What does it mean for a local church in Europe to be culturally relevant? How can we embrace society without losing our specific identity?

Chapter 7: Jeff Fountain focuses our attention on Europe itself. This is a very specific context for the communication of the Gospel, as it is unlike any other region in the world. Fountain offers several keys to understanding Europe today, and discusses different Christian expectations for the future. How can we offer hope to the peoples of this continent?

Chapter 8: Evert Van de Poll pursues the reflection of what makes Europe such a specific context. A symbol of the message that has brought Europeans together in a common cultural zone is the Cross, which has important implications for evangelical church planting.

Chapter 9: Van de Poll goes on to consider the paradox of Europe. It has been influenced by the Bible more than any other part of the world, but at the same time is marked by the abandonment of Christianity and the emergence of alternative secular lifestyles and ideologies.

Chapter 10: David Brown takes up the question, "What kind of church for postmodern Europeans?" He identifies a number of communication bridges, and delves into ways that local churches can use them effectively.

Chapter 11: Andre Pownall discusses the place of the church in a multicultural society, which describes much of Europe today. His

5. Stott, *The Contemporary Christian*, 27–28.

observations are very relevant to any European country, and he offers valuable practical insights into what it means to be a multicultural church.

Chapter 12: Ishak Ghatas takes the reader to the particular situation in which Muslim Europeans find themselves. He concentrates on the question of what kind of churches are most suitable to reach out to Muslim citizens, and to make them welcome in the body of Christ.

Church Planters

The third section of this book deals with people who are involved in the ministry of starting new churches as they share the Gospel with those not connected to a community of believers. Today, much attention is paid to being a missional church, living a missional lifestyle, and so on. "Missional" has become a new buzz word that seems to indicate that mission should not be seen as one of the *activities* of the church, but that the *church is an aspect* of God's mission to realize his plan in the world. "Missional" refers to the awareness that the life of a church, and that of the individual believer, is intrinsically linked with mission. So what does this mean in practice?

Chapter 13: Joanne Appleton shares from a survey taken among young European Christians who are exploring being involved in mission. What is their spirituality? What are their experiences and ideas about spiritual life? And what does that imply for the kind of churches we are aiming to plant?

Chapter 14: Jim Memory asks a question that is not often dealt with, even though it touches on an important aspect of any service in God's Kingdom. How can we measure the effectiveness of church planting; how do we know we are on the right track? The answer depends on how we perceive this ministry in the wider context of mission.

Chapter 15: Ron Anderson addresses another facet of church planting, which is a ministry that should not be limited to a special category of "missionaries." We must discover how best to involve lay people, and practical advice is offered on this topic.

Chapter 16: Johan Lukasse has exceptional amounts of experience in church planting and therefore is well placed to speak on the subject. After many decades of involvement in church planting in Belgium and elsewhere in Europe, he brings together what he has learned and observed, and describes workable ways to start healthy, reproducible churches.

Case studies

Finally, we turn to the practice of church planting. Among the countless initiatives that could be mentioned, we have selected three case studies. While some newly established churches follow a traditional format, others cultivate new forms of worship and language, and develop creative ways of linking into society. They are listed by a host of names, including missional churches, emerging churches, simple churches, mission-shaped churches, virtual churches, network churches, multiplying churches, mobilizing churches, transformational churches, youth churches, night churches, motorway churches, and many other so called "fresh expressions" of church—not to mention the host of non-local language variants. In the multicultural societies of today that are characterized by the postmodern mindset, the idea of "being a church" seems to be continually reinvented.

The creativity and energy of church leaders and church planters deserves respect. This also reveals a partial explanation for the rapid multiplication and diversity of these new forms of church. The methods adopted are clearly attractive to some Europeans and are frequently touted by their advocates as the best way of reaching societies which are increasingly diverse, even fragmented.

Chapter 17: Eric Zander gives a description of a rather successful experiment in French speaking Belgium. After years of involvement with more traditional kinds of church planting, he felt the need to "throw the nets on the other side of the boat." Along with a number of others, he developed an unconventional kind of church called *Autre Rive* ("the other side").

Chapter 18: Jim Memory talks about an interesting collaborative church planting initiative taken by a mission agency in the Cordoba area in southern Spain. There, churches of different persuasions succeeded in coming together in joint efforts to create new churches.

Chapter 19: Stephen Bell is the coordinator of the Balkan Project, which was launched by European Christian Mission in partnership with local churches in Zagreb, the capital of Croatia. It is a telling example of the multiplier effect; a team collaborates with one community to create another one nearby. This case study makes us aware of the missionary potential of even a small local church.

As we look at these case studies and compare them to the situations in which we find ourselves, we should keep in mind that there are special windows of opportunity to go forward in certain places at certain times. At other times and in other places, the process might be more difficult, or proceed in a different way. Every comparison has its limits. We can learn from examples, and we can apply certain aspects, but we should not be discouraged by the specific difficulties we are faced with. There is a time to sow—often with tears—and there is a time to harvest. However, it is *always* time to trust the Lord that he will continue to build his Church.

I

BIBLICAL REFLECTIONS

2

THE ESSENTIAL FOUNDATION

The Bible and Church Planting

CHRIS WIGRAM

"YOU, HOWEVER, KNOW ALL about my teaching, my way of life, my purpose, faith, patience, love, endurance, persecutions, sufferings—what kinds of things happened to me in Antioch, Iconium and Lystra, the persecutions I endured. Yet the Lord rescued me from all of them. In fact, everyone who wants to live a godly life in Christ Jesus will be persecuted, while evildoers and impostors will go from bad to worse, deceiving and being deceived. But as for you, continue in what you have learned and have become convinced of, because you know those from whom you learned it, and how from infancy you have known the holy Scriptures, which are able to make you wise for salvation through faith in Christ Jesus. All Scripture is God-breathed and is useful for teaching, rebuking, correcting and training in righteousness, so that the servant of God may be thoroughly equipped for every good work" (2 Tim 3:10–17).

There is nothing more fundamental to church planting in the name of the Lord Jesus Christ than giving serious attention to the texts that show us all we need to know about him. Church history makes it clear that when the Bible has been given prominence it has led to the *inception* of the church as well as the *renewing* of the church. As a leader of European Christian Mission (ECM), I have always asserted that our church planting operations should be "theologically conservative but ecclesiologically adventurous." What do I mean by that? Well, it is very simple, and we are not developing a post-biblical theology.

In 2 Timothy 3:10, Paul notes that Timothy knows about his teaching and the way of life that flows from that teaching. Paul is realistic. His faithfulness to the Bible, the Old Testament, has led him into conflict in various places (v 11), yet God has delivered him from them all. Here we have the divine combination that is so powerful in teaching the Christian hope. We see the necessary connection between teaching and experience, and that both are vital in establishing churches. We do not want people to worship the Bible; we are advocating the worship of the Lord Jesus Christ and to live in relationship with him. That is experience based on what the Bible teaches about Jesus Christ. So it is not surprising that Paul writes of Scripture as being "God breathed." Paul has deep roots and is well equipped to deal with those false teachers who are abusing scripture to their own and others' detriment (v 13). Timothy had wise parents (v 15). Bear in mind that a Jewish parent had to instruct his or her son in the Law from the age of five. Timothy's Jewish mother was a believer in Jesus, so her tutelage made Timothy acquainted with the Lord Jesus Christ. At any rate, he was his disciple.

I want to consider these words of Paul and focus on four ways from 2 Timothy 3:16 in which Scripture is useful in church planting situations.

Teaching

Timothy is a church planter in Ephesus. He has taken over the responsibility for the running of the church, and teaching is one of his main tasks (1 Tim 4:6, 13, 16; 6:3). Timothy has what he needs to teach the church; the Scriptures inspired by God, and the gift of the Holy Spirit to help him. So both the Scripture and the church planter are inspired by the Spirit of God.

What does it mean to use the word inspire? It is helpful to use the three "I's" when talking about preaching. Our task as preachers is to inform (teaching), interest (pedagogy), and inspire (Holy Spirit). For the church planter, the Bible must be in the driving seat. It is essential for the shaping of the church and the leaders and members of the church. If the Bible is not central to church planting, then we will be doing it by our own reason.

How does this work out in practice? Paul showed his motivation in his instructions to Timothy, and also in Colossians 1:28–29. He wanted to make the Word fully known. This is hard work. When Paul arrived in

Thessalonica he went into the synagogue (Acts 17). There he reasoned with the people about who the Lord Jesus Christ is, through showing how the Old Testament pointed to a suffering Messiah rather than the various possible Jewish viewpoints of the Messiah's identity. Paul said Jesus is the Messiah. This produced fruit (v 4) followed by opposition (v 5).

Paul had the same approach in Corinth (Acts 18:4), but this time Greeks were included in the proclamation. In Ephesus he preached about the kingdom of God (Acts 19:8). So if we as church planters are to teach the Bible as a priority, what will happen?

- *It will establish the authority of God over the believers' minds and spirits.* God will begin to reign over their thoughts and actions. It will show to them that the pastor, too, is under the authority of the Word of God.

- *It will exalt the Lordship of Christ over his church.* We have already seen how Paul suffered in his ministry. Indeed, many people have suffered for their commitment to the Bible. Think of the fate of William Tyndale or John Huss who agreed with Wycliffe that believers were the Church, and that Christ, not the Pope, was the head of it. Huss was burned at the stake, but stated that someone would come after him who they could not silence. He was one of Martin Luther's heroes because he had criticized indulgences one hundred years before Luther. Huss died singing songs of praise to the God he had learned about from the Bible.

- *It will determine our ecclesiology.* Here we seem to find flexibility. Church history shows this. We find biblical principles for setting up a new community of believers in a particular context with the emphasis on relationships and the efficient working of the body of Christ.

- *It will provide the context for the Holy Spirit to work.* People will be saved. Believers will be sanctified. If we exposit the Bible faithfully we will cover all that God wants a new church to know. We are forced to deal with issues which we would prefer to ignore and do not find easy to teach.

The Bible has created, sustained, directed, reformed, united, and revived the Church in history. We need to thank God every day for grace to study his Word and to be taught by it.

Rebuking

Secondly, we come to a less welcome aspect of church planting: the necessity of rebuking. There are so many ways of looking at this issue. In one way we were all rebuked when we decided to follow Christ and put aside our previously held views and life in order to follow Jesus. Our task is to see this issue in the context of church planting, and it is an important matter. It is not enough for preachers to tell people the truth; this is only part of the task of preaching and teaching. They must also refute error in order for there to be a basis for reform in the church. When leaders have had the courage to present the "whole counsel of God," they have laid the foundation for necessary change.

Second Timothy 3:16 is in the Pastoral Epistles. These letters particularly deal with the life of a leader in the church and his or her responsibilities. In 2 Timothy 4:2–3, Timothy is reminded to rebuke when necessary. Titus, too, is told very clearly that he needs to deal with the false teachers (Titus 1:13; 2:15).

We must also note that in the two exhortations to Timothy and Titus the word "encourage" is alongside "rebuke." As leaders in the church it is important that we do the ministry of rebuking where necessary. But it is also important *how* we rebuke. According to Paul, it is alongside encouraging. In the current climate in Europe, we face the political incorrectness and the ethical implications of our preaching the gospel and planting biblically-based churches. We have to fight for the Bible to be heard, but we also have to be wise in how we do this. We need to rebuke with encouragement where possible.

Martin Lloyd-Jones wrote,

> One of the first things you are to learn in this Christian life and warfare is that, if you go wrong in doctrine you will go wrong in all aspects of your life. You will probably go wrong in your practice and behavior and you will certainly go wrong in your experience.[1]

We also face another reality in church planting. Many of us think that if we preach, people will come. Yes, some will come, but some will leave as well. There is an inherent offense to the Gospel, in particular to its implications for purity of life, its challenge to mission, and the need to deny self. Many will be attracted by the freshness and purity of the

---

1. Lloyd-Jones, "Heresies."

message of Jesus, and many will be detracted by the implications of what it means to truly follow him. You know you are preaching the Gospel when people are coming because of it and people are leaving because of it.

When we look into the Bible there are many examples of the rebuking ministry. God often rebuked his people for a lack of faithfulness. Here are two examples.

Jonah

Jonah is called by God to preach to Nineveh, but he rebels and runs away from the task God has given him. His action endangers other people, and a great storm results in him being thrown into the sea where he is swallowed by a large fish and preserved within the fish with a hymn of praise from the Psalms. Then he is sent back to Nineveh and preaches to them with amazing results. They turn from their wicked ways and repent. What is Jonah's reaction? He gets angry and sulks because God is merciful. Jonah is so different from the traditional prophets in that he is angry at the success of his preaching.

The book of Jonah includes God's rebuke of Jonah. Jonah preaches a message of judgment (Jonah 3:4). Warning is a part of the gospel, but what about the second half of the message? God gives time for a response. They listen and respond, and in Jonah 3:10, God shows compassion. Is this not what Jonah wanted? Why then is Jonah so disillusioned with the success of his preaching? The answer is that he is selfish about grace. God has changed his mind, and Jonah is angry that God is not validating his message to the Ninevites with judgment.

In Jonah 4:2–3, Jonah tells us that he knows God is gracious, compassionate, and slow to anger. God is being consistent with his character as expressed by Jonah, which in itself is a description of God from other parts of the Old Testament. God is free to do what he wants. Despite Jonah's orthodoxy and knowledge of God, he shows what he really thinks of the situation. He wants judgment, and God wants grace. Sometimes what we really think comes out, usually in unguarded moments. Jonah is indignant with a God who shows mercy to those who deserve judgment. This has happened before.

Jonah had already brought a message of judgment to Israel at a time of moral and spiritual decay, but in 2 Kings 14:23–25 we see God acting in mercy toward Israel. Jonah is perplexed. How can God act in mercy toward a people to whom he is preaching judgment?

God rebukes Jonah with a visual aid in Jonah 4. The vine is a gift from God, and Jonah is happy. But when God takes it away, he is angry again and almost suicidal. God points out his inconsistency. Does Jonah have the right to be angry about the vine? If that is the case, then surely God has the right to care for the people of Nineveh (Jonah 4:10). He rebukes Jonah through the comparison of the people of Nineveh with the vine, which does not last long and is an unimportant plant.

Peter

The second example comes from the New Testament. The book of Acts records that the apostles were reluctant to leave Jerusalem permanently. They even remained there after the persecution caused by Stephen's death (Acts 8). In Acts 10, Peter is directed by God to meet Cornelius, the Roman centurion. God needs to rebuke Peter over the Jewish view of the Gentile as unclean. Jews did not associate with Gentiles. Peter needs a lesson in this. When Peter has his initial vision in Acts 10:11–14, he refuses to eat unclean food according to his custom. However, since the coming of Christ and the New Covenant, things are different. Jesus taught about what is clean and unclean, and now Peter must discover the implications of this teaching because it actually hides a much more important issue (see Acts 10:28).

What is the evidence that Peter has learned from this rebuke? He is now open to hospitality from a Gentile (Acts 10:23, 27), and eventually stays with them for a few days. He brings what he has learned to the wider discussion of the early church, thus benefiting others (Acts 15:9). As believers, we, too, have the ministry of the Holy Spirit, who from time to time rebukes us when we are not listening to him.

We can be confident that if we are open to God's rebuke it will benefit the church. Professor Gwatkin, an English historian and theologian of the nineteenth century wrote,

> Four times, in four distant ages the truth of Christ has had to be defended from a great and deadly enemy inside his church. Every time the Spirit of Christ has pointed away from a church entangled in traditionalism to the living voice of scripture; and at each instance fresh strength has come from a fresh revelation of the ever-living person of whom scripture speaks. The first of

these crises was the contest with Gnosticism, the second with Arianism, the Reformation was the third; the fourth is the great scientific controversy opened by the Deists, which seems to be gathering to its hottest battle in our own time.[2]

We have to be aware of the vulnerabilities of evangelical church planting. The often entrepreneurial nature of the task, and those who are most successful at it, can foster human vanity, which risks exalting the personality of the church planter or leader. It is easy to get into a position where power can be abused. The Roman Catholic priest officiating at the altar has little opportunity to express himself, but the Charismatic pastor is in a very different position. Without adequate accountability structures, he can easily lord over his dependents and provide an unhealthy model for others to follow.

We end this point with Proverbs 13:1. "A wise son heeds his father's instruction, but a mocker does not listen to rebuke."

Correcting

The idea of correcting, which relates to ethics and behavior, is the more positive side of rebuking, and deals with false teachers and confusion. The admonition to correct only comes here in the New Testament. However, the idea pervades the whole of the Bible in that, as fallen human beings made in the image of God, we are continually in need of correction in order to learn how to live the Christian life.

It is a reality of our life as church planters that our ministry and the church we plant will act as an incubator for our own shortcomings. The pressures of the work constantly push, prod, and expose them, and they affect the impact our leadership has on other people.

After a while in church planting we come to realize that we are gifted in areas that we were unaware of, and also discover that we are far more inadequate in other areas that maybe we thought we were good at. Whatever our situation is, our need for correction will be highlighted in cross-cultural ministry. In church planting, our personality, character, theology, emotional stability, and physical health is scrutinized on every level. God will use this experience to correct us and make us the people that He wants us to be.

2. Broomhall, *Hudson Taylor's Legacy,* 129.

One way to look at correction is to see how the life and teaching of Jesus was passed down through the apostle Paul to those he mentored. In my research, I came across this quote from Luke Johnson,

> The human faith of the man Jesus is the pattern of faith of the Christian.[3]

Johnson also maintained that neglecting the faith of Jesus has had negative effects on the development of Christian spirituality. Hebrews 2:17–18 shows us that Christ had to be made like us in order to make atonement for us. This is why the apostle Paul issues a command to the Corinthians. "Follow my example, as I follow the example of Christ" (1 Cor 11:1). In church history, there has always been a healthy emphasis on the imitation of Christ, but our contemporary church has not made much of it. Perhaps this is because it is such an infinite concept. Imitate Paul as he imitated Christ? This statement is such a staggering challenge that in some ways we do not know where to start. How does it work? The idea remains infinite unless we give it some teeth, which Paul does in the New Testament. While Paul may issue such a command to the Corinthians, he also puts it into practice himself in his mentoring ministry of those like Timothy and Titus that he raised up into church leadership.

The setting for correction is in relationships. This should not surprise us, as we see in Mark 3:14. Jesus himself called the disciples that they "might be with him." Note that this is *before* he sends them out. Being with Jesus was essential. So it is with Paul.

- *Paul had a relationship with those who were to imitate him.* In 1 Corinthians 4:17, he sends Timothy to them to "remind you of my way of life . . ." Paul is saying that observing his life will correct them—it was all they needed. This immediately reminds us that a skilled church planter is weak unless he forms the relationships that will become the foundation of the church. To the Philippians, Paul talks of Timothy as "my true son, who has served with me in the preaching of the gospel." This idea of son-ship, the passing on of ministry from Paul to Timothy, is common in the language he uses in his greetings in 1 and 2 Timothy. Timothy is "my son" and a fellow believer who shares in grace.

- *It is likely that Timothy was converted under Paul's ministry at Lystra in Acts 14.* Here we have the foundation for a mentoring relationship

---

3. Johnson, *Living Jesus*, 57–76.

within the local church. The church planter's responsibility is for those who have responded to the gospel. In Acts 15:36, Paul and Barnabas decide to make a ministry trip to visit those who had become believers. The correction of the believers in their ethics and personal behavior are also gospel issues.

- *Timothy becomes a trusted emissary to other churches.* We have already seen how Timothy was sent to Corinth, but he also went to Philippi and Thessalonica (Phil 2:19–20; 1 Thess 3:6). This was the result of imitation (2 Tim 3:10–11).

- *Paul remained involved with those who he sent into ministry.* It is very revealing that in Titus 2:7–8, Paul writes to Titus and ends up with the word "us." He depends on his disciples, and what they do reflects on him. There is personal risk and accountability and that reflects on his work.

- *Paul expects the same imitation in those who became believers (Phil 3:17; 1 Thess 1:6).* In summary, what can we say about this aspect of the ministry of mentoring? The central idea is that Paul passed on a way of life to Timothy (1 Tim 4:12). It was passing on life with all its fullness and complexities. And, as it was ultimately about following Jesus, it included the acceptance of hostility and rejection, embracing a self-sacrificial path of suffering and mistreatment for the sake of others. It was counter-cultural. It was ethical.

Let us flesh out this idea of imitation a little more. Jesus was not the first Christian! He was not a sinner saved by grace. We cannot imitate Christ in being a single male Jew, becoming a carpenter, performing miracles, being celibate, or dying on a cross. However, if the same Spirit that is at work in Jesus has been given to us, and he enables us to say "yes" to the Father, then it follows that we can look at Christ as the exemplar of our faith. Johnson adds,

> The point of the human faith of Jesus is not that his faith is like ours but that, by the gift of his Spirit, ours might become like his (1 Pet 2:21).[4]

The vital importance of showing to new believers that we all sit under the authority of the Bible helps us here. It is important not to create an "us-and-them" mentality in our new churches. The vulnerability of Paul's

4. Ibid.

relationship with Timothy and Titus, amongst others, presumably means that they were allowed to input into Paul's life. From the beginning it is so important to show that it is the Word of God that drives us all. We should encourage people who wish to make observations about those who are in leadership because we need the rest of the body to point out what we do not see.

As John Stott writes in *God's New Society*,

> One of our chief evangelical blind spots has been to overlook the central impotence of the Church. We tend to proclaim individual salvation without moving on to the saved community. We emphasize that Christ died for us to "redeem us from all iniquity" rather than to "purify for himself a people for his own." We think of ourselves more as Christians than as churchmen, and our message is more good news of a new life than of a new society.[5]

Training in Righteousness

We need to be aware that the word "righteousness" has a number of meanings in the Bible. In Genesis 15:6, righteousness is what God gives to Abraham. Righteousness is also something that God wants from his people (Ezek 18:5–9; Amos 5:24; and exemplified in David in 2 Sam 22:21–25). In the New Testament righteousness makes us saints (Rom 1:7), and comes to the believer through the work of the perfect man, the Lord Jesus Christ (Rom 3:21–22). In the Gospels, righteousness is moral purity (Matt 1:19, 27:19; Mark 6:20; Luke 1:6; 2:25; 23:47, 50). Paul writes about moral righteousness (2 Cor 9:10; Eph 5:9; 1 Tim 1:9) and mentions a legalistic righteousness (Phil 3:6, 9).

We have looked at the imitation of Christ reflected through Paul's letters to many of the believers in the New Testament, and particularly in his relationship with Timothy and Titus. We summarized this imitation as "passing on life in all its fullness." When we talk of training in righteousness, we can get the flavor from some surrounding texts. It is clear from 2 Timothy 2:22 that we are talking about the need for change in our lives which repudiates evil in all its forms. This pursuit of righteousness is a communal affair (v 22b).

---

5. Stott, *God's New Society*, 49.

We are often intimidated by the challenges of the Christian life because we tend to think that we are alone in this pursuit. We are not. Just about all of the exhortations in the New Testament are sent to communities, and we need the rest of the body in order to live the new life.

In 2 Timothy 2:25, we also see the need for the fruit of righteousness to be a part of the way in which Christian leaders work with those who oppose them. Titus 2:12 shows us what is meant here as well. This is the positive side of the Christian life. It teaches us to say no to things that will damage us. Notice there is a motivation for it in the following verse (Titus 2:13). We do this while we wait for the return of Christ.

The best way to teach about the need for righteousness in the Christian life, which we can also call the pursuit of holiness, is to teach the whole counsel of God. This shows the flow of Scripture and the plan of salvation that God has worked out in the world. As we see how God works in the world we are encouraged that it is all worth it.

In 1 Timothy 6:11, Timothy is told to pursue righteousness. In Romans, Paul expresses it theologically when he reminds the Romans that they, if they are in fact believers, are now dead to sin but alive to God in Christ Jesus because of what the kingdom of God is (Rom 14:17). We are therefore to live as children of light (Eph 5:9). So we can say that training in righteousness includes holiness for his people, and God's central desire is to find his people holy. We need to think about this and wonder again—how can we, such sinful beings, be in relationship with the God who is holy, and what are the implications for church planting?

Why is this important? One commentator on evangelicalism thinks that holiness is slipping from the grasp of born-again believers today. He writes,

> The loss of the traditional vision of God as holy is now manifest everywhere in the evangelical world. It is the key to understanding why sin and grace have become such empty terms. What depth and meaning can these have divorced from a holy God? Divorced from the holiness of God, sin is merely self-defeating behavior or a breach in etiquette. Divorced from the holiness of God, grace is merely empty rhetoric, pious window dressing for the modern technique by which sinners work out their own salvation. Divorced from the holiness of God, our gospel becomes indistinguishable from any of a host of alternative self-help doctrines. Divorced from the holiness of God, our public morality is reduced to little more than an accumulation of trade-offs between competing private interests. Divorced from

the holiness of God, our worship becomes mere entertainment. The holiness of God is the very cornerstone of Christian faith, for it is the foundation of reality. Sin is defiance of God's holiness, the Cross is the outworking and victory of God's holiness and faith is the recognition of God's holiness. Knowing that God is holy is therefore the key to knowing life as it truly is, knowing Christ as he truly is, knowing why he came and knowing how life will end.[6]

The UK-based research leaflet *Quadrant* gives a contemporary example, reporting that holiness is no longer on the agenda for many Christians. Just 21 percent consider themselves to be holy, and only 35 percent believe that God expects Christians to be holy.[7]

Why are we reluctant to be holy? Is it a fear of legalism, or just one more aspect of our Christian lives to mourn about? Are we afraid that striving for holiness puts the emphasis on our effort rather than the work of the Holy Spirit? That we might appear unspiritual or are afraid to try hard in case we fail? The problem is clear; too few Christians look like Christ, and too many do not seem all that concerned! What will training in righteousness look like in church planting?

- *It means that every church plant is a work of integrity.* There will be no underhanded methods in dealing with the people. As the apostle Paul says in 2 Corinthians 4:1–2, we will be open about what we are doing. The character of the worker will work out within the church plant at every level.

- *Relationships are vital.* Relationships are the furnace in which we are trained in righteousness. In reality we have to work very hard in how we deal with people. There must be no secular/sacred divide. We cannot be a different person within the church than we are at the market or when playing football. We also want to prevent setting up a difference between the clergy and the laity. It is easy for us to be the professionals who are trained and experienced in church planting which somehow absolves us from getting close to those we are working with. There is a UK church plant that expects the church planter to be pastored by his congregation. He described when he mentioned to one of the members that he had been in the church office for fifteen hours in one day, expecting some kind of admiration

6. Wells, *No Place for Truth*, 300.

7. Quadrant, "2002 Christian Research".

from them for his dedication. However, the member raised their eyebrows at him and gently rebuked him for being so self-absorbed and a workaholic! We must create a culture where this is so; this is training in righteousness and it brings accountability.

- *There will be an intention to make the Bible central to every part of church life.* While there is a lot to learn from people who have pioneered different church planting strategies, there is nothing other than the Bible to direct all aspects of the church plant. The Bible will be the foundation for discipleship training, mentoring, and the equipping of the church. There will be an emphasis on raising a new generation of leaders (Matt 9:38) who will understand biblical teaching and what training in righteousness means in reality. This will include the church planter taking adequate time off from the work, which has to be planned into the schedule and made clear to everyone.

- *We will allow the Holy Spirit to work within the community and the individual.* We will show how the Word and the Spirit work together. What might a church that prioritizes training in righteousness look like? In Acts 2:46–47, we see a church trained for every good work. This was a church that met together to celebrate the work of the gospel and it had four characteristics.

  - It was a church with communal celebrations and small cell groups.
  - It was a church that put God in his rightful place for worship and adoration.
  - It was a church that "had favor with all the people."
  - It was a growing church with new believers added "day by day."

What might the words "day by day" say to us as church planters? They help us to understand the beauty of this first church in Jerusalem. It was not, as can happen in some church plants, a "Sunday" meeting church. In many cultures, Sunday is the day for church services and activities, with some other church activities taking place during the week. We cannot deny that Sunday, the first day of the week, is a special day, the "Lord's Day," as is reflected in the narrative of Acts as well as in Paul's epistles and Revelation.

The text says clearly that the believers in the first church did two things "day by day": they fellowshipped in the temple, and together in home groups. The result was that they saw the Lord adding to their number daily. They did not "go to church" as we so often hear today when people talk about gathering for worship on Sunday. Instead of "going to church" they *were* the church (gathering) wherever they were. Scholar F. F. Bruce states that the words "day by day" are applicable as far as the whole sentence flows up until "with all the people."[8] This means that the larger meeting together at the temple, the breaking bread in their homes, the praising of God, and the favor of the early believers among the general population were a day by day experience. Their Christian experience was tied into every day of their lives. C. K. Barrett comments on the expression "day by day."

> So that the meals referred to later in the verse were not weekly celebrations of the Lord's resurrection but, much more probably, the necessary daily meals, which the believers took in common.[9]

The New Testament house church furthered this holistic approach to Christianity where the church was among the people and not a sacred building that one went into. The result was that the church truly became the incarnate body of Christ, drawing people not into a building but into a life that was very present amongst all people.

There are many historical examples of the effect of people who lived a righteousness life. Holy Trinity Church, Clapham, in South London, was the base of the Clapham Sect, and the Reverend John Venn was one of the leaders. He was devoted to the church, fervent in prayer, generous with time and money, and inspired by the Bible. He wrote to his children,

> You can all bear witness that I have never represented religion as a gloomy thing, I have never said that you must do this or you will go to hell, but I have set it before you as a scene of happiness and joy unspeakable.[10]

What did he and the Clapham Sect achieve? They fought slavery, fostered evangelical faith, supported world mission, and encouraged good administration in India and Sierra Leone. They supported widespread

---

8. Bruce, *The Acts of the Apostles*, 101.

9. Barrett, *A Critical and Exegetical Commentary on the Acts of the Apostles*, 170.

10. Clay, *Disciples and Citizens*, 132–33.

education and backed Robert Raikes's Sunday schools and the Factory Act. They made provision for the poor and attacked blood sports, dueling, and gambling because they hurt the poor. They set high standards for morality in public life, and even higher standards for those with active concerns in politics. In short, they trained people in righteousness.

Conclusion

When we emphasize the four areas that come from the use of the Bible in church planting we will avoid giving the impression to people that we are just another sub-set of religion. We are here to bring people into freedom in Christ, not to observe religious rituals. We live in a world that is besotted by religion, but Paul is very clear in Colossians 2:23. If we attend faithfully to the scriptures we will prevent ourselves from falling into legalism.

When we study these verses of the apostle Paul to Timothy we see their value when applied to church planting. Keeping the four realities of teaching, rebuking, correcting, and training in righteousness in the forefront of our praxis will help us to lay a solid foundation for new forms of church across Europe who prioritize the Bible over any particular church structure.

3

PRAYER IN THE MINISTRY AND LIFE OF A CHURCH PLANTER

New Testament Insights

Boris Paschke

THIS CHAPTER PROVIDES NEW Testament insights regarding the influence of prayer in the ministry and life of a church planter. The order for this chapter is as follows: in section one we will (1) define the terms "church planter" and "prayer"; (2) select the relevant New Testament material; and (3) give a short overview of the history of research on the subject matter. Sections two through four offer a study on some of the relevant New Testament texts in detail. Section five briefly provides additional insights from New Testament texts that, even though relevant only to a limited degree, nevertheless contain worthwhile examples of prayers of church planters. The sixth and final section bundles together the findings of the study. It is my hope and prayer that these New Testament texts might be an inspiration and motivation for today's church planters ministering in Europe or elsewhere.

Definitions

Church Planter

Theological literature contains various definitions for "church planting" and "church planter." A rather narrow and specific definition is used, for example, in the Anglican Church. In his seminal publications on the topic, Bob Hopkins understands "church planting" as the taking of a whole group of people from an existing larger church and planting it, as an offshoot, as a house church in new soil.[1]

We will use a somewhat broader definition here of "church planter" that is based on 1 Corinthians 3:6–10, where the apostle Paul states,

> I planted the seed, Apollos watered it, but God has been making it grow . . . For we are co-workers in God's service; you are God's field, God's building. By the grace God has given me, I laid a foundation as a wise builder, and someone else is building on it.

In these verses, the images of planting and building are juxtaposed. I thus use the terms "church planter" and "church founder" interchangeably. On the basis of these verses in 1 Corinthians, this study considers a church planter as being anyone who—as individual or within a group—starts a church. In the New Testament, the following four church planters are mentioned:

- Paul (and his co-workers) founded the churches in Philippi (Acts 16:11-12; Phil 4:15), Thessalonica (1 Thess 1:9; 2:2), Corinth (Acts 18:5, 11; 1 Cor 3:6, 10; 15:1), and Galatia (Acts 16:6; 18:23; Gal 4:13), just to name a few.[2]

- Peter, even though he is not a church planter in the strict sense of the word, might be considered the founder of the churches in Jerusalem (Acts 2) and Caesarea (Acts 10). Martin Hengel explains that Peter "certainly played not only a role, but actually *the* most significant role in consolidating the as-yet unorganized movement of the followers of Jesus (and the Baptist?) in the motherland after Easter."[3]

---

1. Cf. Möller, s.v., Gemeindeaufbau.
2. Cf. Hanges, *Paul, Founder of Churches*.
3. Hengel, *Saint Peter*, 90.

- Philippus also might be considered the founder of the church in Caesarea (Acts 8:40; 21:8).[4]

- Epaphras could have been the founder of the church in Colossae (Col 1:7),[5] and perhaps also of the churches in Laodicea and Hierapolis.[6]

In addition, Apollos could perhaps be thought of as the ultimate founder of the church in Ephesus (Acts 18:24–26).

Prayer

Prayer is defined here as an address of God the Father or Jesus Christ in the second person singular. Accordingly, a hymn that glorifies God the Father or Jesus Christ in the third person singular is not considered a prayer. In agreement with the so-called "Our Father" in Matthew 6:9–13, most prayers in the New Testament are addressed to God the Father. While very few New Testament prayers are addressed to Jesus Christ (Acts 7:59–60; Rev 22:20)[7], the New Testament does not contain any prayers to the Holy Spirit.[8]

This present study distinguishes between intercessory, communal, and personal prayers, i.e., between (1) prayers *for* the church planter; (2) prayers *with* the church planter; and (3) prayers *of* the church planter, respectively. Of course, these three categories are not clear-cut, and might overlap at times. A further distinction concerns quoted and reported prayers. Although some New Testament passages provide the wording of a prayer in direct speech (e.g., Acts 4:24–30), other New Testament texts either summarize the prayer in indirect speech (2 Cor 12:8), or merely report that a prayer is spoken without providing its content (e.g., Acts 12:5).

With regard to prayer, important New Testament Greek terms are the nouns *proseuchē* and *deēsis*, and the respective verbs *proseuchomai* and *deomai*.

---

4. Ibid., 91.

5. Schnelle, *The History and Theology of the New Testament Writings*, 289.

6. Gnilka, *Der Kolosserbrief*.

7. Cf. Boris Paschke, "Prayer to Jesus in the Canonical and in the Apocryphal Acts of the Apostles."

8. Cf. Boris Paschke, "Praying to the Holy Spirit in Early Christianity."

Selection of the material

With regard to the identification of the New Testament texts that are relevant, only those prayers that particularly relate to church planting or the church planter will be taken into account. Of course, general statements or promises concerning prayer, even those found in the Old Testament, can be applied to all believers, and thus also concern the church planter. To look at all these prayer texts, however, would go beyond the scope of this study. Therefore, we will concentrate on prayers that are expressly related to church planting. With regard to the New Testament books that contain such prayers, the following remarks are crucial.

The four gospels are relevant here only to a very limited degree since they do not often refer to the church, let alone to church planting. In the gospels, the New Testament Greek term for the Christian church, *ekklēsia*, is only found in two verses of the Gospel of Matthew; namely Matthew 16:18 and 18:17.[9] Nevertheless, the Gospel of Luke does narrate one prayer that is particularly applicable here (i.e., Luke 22:31–32).

In contrast to the four gospels, the book of Acts is very significant in this regard, and there are three crucial reasons for this. First, the entire book is on church planting. Bruce Wilkinson and Kenneth Boa state, "Acts . . . traces the beginning and growth of the New Testament church."[10] Second, the book contains numerous prayers. Joel B. Green writes, "Over thirty times in the Acts of the Apostles, Luke characterizes Jesus's followers as being at prayer or narrates episodes of prayer."[11] Similarly, Darrell L. Bock states, "This noun [*proseuchē*] appears thirty-six times in the NT, twelve of which are in Luke-Acts and nine of which are in Acts . . . Of eighty-five NT occurrences, the verb 'pray' (. . . *proseuchomai*) appears thirty-four times in Luke-Acts, sixteen of which are in Acts."[12] Third, because the book of Acts is a narrative, a story, it is especially relevant for this study that focuses on the *influence* of prayer in the ministry and life of a church planter. Quite often in the book of Acts, both the prayer and its *outcome* are narrated.

The New Testament letters are also limited in their relevance. While they contain numerous references to prayers (e.g., Paul's prayer reports), they usually do not talk about the *outcome* of a reported prayer. As a

9. Cf. Hengel, *Peter*, 3.

10. Wilkinson and Boa, *Talk Thru the Bible*, 354.

11. Green, "Persevering Together in Prayer," 184.

12. Bock, *Acts*, 151.

reader of the letters of Paul, for example, one does know that Paul often prayed, but with only a few exceptions (i.e., 2 Cor 12:8–9; Rom 1:10), one is not informed about the outcome of his prayers.

Revelation also contains several prayers. Some of these are crucial with regard to certain research questions, for example "Amen. Come, Lord Jesus." (22:20). This prayer is one of the very few New Testament prayers to Jesus Christ, and thus important for the study of early Christian prayer to Jesus Christ. However, when re-reading the book of Revelation for the present research, I did not find any prayer that might be relevant for the subject matter of this chapter.

History of research

From a short history of research on New Testament and early Christian prayer it becomes clear that the relationship between New Testament prayer and church planting has been neglected in these specialized studies.

In the first volume of his seminal study, *La prière*, the French patristic scholar Adalbert Gautier Hamman provides a thorough investigation of New Testament prayer that I still consider one of the finest and best works that have been written on the topic so far. However, Hamman only devotes less than two pages to the topic of prayer and evangelization.[13] The specific focus of prayer and church planting is not even discussed. This subject is also neglected in subsequent seminal studies on New Testament prayer.[14]

Even as a New Testament scholar, it was impossible for me to check the extent to which the practical-theological church planting literature refers to the New Testament with regard to the influence of prayer. However, I did find one academic article in which the practical theologian Stephan Schweyer also examines the New Testament regarding the role of prayer in church planting.[15]

By studying the New Testament through the lens of the influence of prayer in the ministry and life of a church planter, this study attempts to make a contribution to both New Testament studies and

---

13. Hamman, *La prière*, 300–302.

14. Cf. e.g., Gebauer, *Das Gebet bei Paulus*; Cullmann, *Prayer in the New Testament*; and Ostmeyer, *Kommunikation mit Gott und Christus*.

15. Schweyer, "Sie hielten alle einmütig fest am Gebet. "

practical-theological scholarship on this important topic. In the following three sections, the New Testament's intercessory, communal, and personal prayers regarding church planting will be studied by focusing on the church planters Peter and Paul. The latter carried out his church planting ministry with the help of various co-workers, and their names will be mentioned in the respective sections.

The Influence of Prayer for the Church Planter (Intercessory Prayer)

Prayers for Peter

The first prayer to be investigated is special because it is uttered by Jesus himself who prays for Peter. During the last supper, Jesus not only predicts Peter's denial, but he also tells Peter, "Simon, Simon, Satan has asked to sift all of you as wheat. But I have prayed for you, Simon that your faith may not fail. And when you have turned back, strengthen your brothers" (Luke 22:31–32).

The "sifting" Jesus talks about refers to a satanic attack on Jesus's disciples. The metaphor comes from agriculture and "the picture is of grain in a sieve, where the head of grain is taken apart." Darrell Bock compares the meaning of the saying with that of the English idioms "picking someone to pieces" and "taking someone apart."[16]

However, by seriously but tenderly addressing Peter with the double, "Simon, Simon," Jesus encourages Peter by telling him that he has prayed for him. The verb *deomai* here clearly has the meaning "to pray." Bock aptly comments, "Satan fails to destroy Peter because Jesus intercedes for him. Jesus is stronger."[17] Similarly, I. Howard Marshall writes, "But the power of Satan . . . is limited; over against him stands Jesus with the power of his intercession."[18]

The prayer of Jesus for Peter comes with an obligation for Peter. After his denial of Jesus and his repentance later, Peter is to strengthen his brothers, i.e., his fellow Christian believers. This remorse after his denial is referred to by the phrase "when once you have turned back."[19]

---

16. Bock, *Luke*, 1742.

17. Ibid., 1743.

18. Marshall, *The Gospel of Luke*, 821.

19. Hengel, *Peter*, 44.

Luke then narrates the positive outcome and influence of Jesus's intercessory prayer for Peter (Luke 22:32) in the first part of the second volume of *Luke-Acts*, i.e., in Acts 1–15. Here, Peter's blessed ministry as leader of the Jerusalem church and as courageous preacher of the gospel is recounted. The reader of *Luke-Acts* will undoubtedly see a relation between Peter's ministry in the book of Acts and Jesus's prayer for Peter in the Gospel of Luke. The positive outcome and influence of Jesus's prayer for Peter is also testified to in 1 and 2 Peter.

It is therefore reasonable that, according to Martin Hengel, Jesus's intercession for Peter has in view the *entire* ministry of Peter up to his martyrdom.

> The word about the rock in Matt. 16:17–19, the reference to the faith of Peter, which will not waver because of Jesus's prayer on his behalf and through which he is to strengthen his brothers (Luke 22:32), as well as the threefold charge from the Resurrected One to feed his flock (John 21:15–17), are not to be minimized by applying them only to the earliest period; *they apply to the entire activity of Peter right to the point of his martyrdom.*[20]

Besides Luke 22:32, the New Testament contains another encouraging prayer of Jesus that is not only for his disciples but also all those who believe as a result of their ministry. According to John 17:20–21, Jesus prays, "My prayer is not for them alone. I pray also for those who will believe in me through their message, that all of them may be one."

While the Gospel of Luke narrates a prayer of Jesus for Peter, the book of Acts relates, in a quite amusing manner, a prayer of the Jerusalem church for Peter. While Peter is in prison, the church prays for him (Acts 12:5), either for his release/escape *from* prison, or for his protection *in* prison. God answers the prayers of the church for Peter in a tremendous manner (Acts 12:6–10). An angel comes to meet Peter in prison; the chains fall off Peter's wrists; together with the angel, Peter not only passes the prison guards, but also passes through the iron prison gate that is opened miraculously. After the angel has left him, the liberated Peter then goes to the house where the church is still praying for him (Acts 12:12). However, even though Peter knocks at the door and talks to someone from the church, they do not welcome him in initially because they do not believe it is really Peter standing in front of the door (Acts 12:13–15). They faithfully prayed for Peter, but they did not really believe

---

20. Ibid., 96–97; italics in the original.

that God would answer their prayers. Consequently, while the prison gate had been opened for Peter, the door of the church remained closed. It is only eventually that the church opens the door for Peter and learns that God has answered their prayers in a mighty way (Acts 12:16–17).

Prayers for Paul

In Paul's church planting ministry, his prayers for the churches go hand in hand with the church's prayers for him. Oscar Cullmann comments that his prayers for the churches are accompanied by the prayers of the churches for him.[21] In several of his letters to churches, Paul directly requests intercessory prayer for his church planting ministry (e.g., Rom 15:30–32; Eph 6:19–20; Col 4:3-4; 2 Thess 3:1-2). In Ephesians 6:19–20, for instance, Paul writes,

> Pray also for me, that whenever I speak, words may be given me so that I will fearlessly make known the mystery of the gospel, for which I am an ambassador in chains. Pray that I may declare it fearlessly, as I should.

With regard to this subject matter, it is particularly interesting to see that in 2 Corinthians, Paul informs the church in Corinth about the expected outcome of their (future) intercessory prayers for him. After telling the Corinthians about the affliction he and Timothy had experienced in Asia (2 Cor 1:1), Paul states with regard to God,

> He has delivered us from such a deadly peril, and he will deliver us again. On him we have set our hope that he will continue to deliver us, as you help us by your prayers. Then many will give thanks on our behalf for the gracious favor granted us in answer to the prayers of many (2 Cor 1:10–11).

The basic line of thought is clear: according to Paul, the affliction experienced in Asia was not the last one in his ministry. With regard to afflictions lying ahead of him, Paul expects divine deliverance through the (future) intercessory prayer (*deēsis*) of the Corinthian church. This prayer and its outcome, i.e., Paul's deliverance, will, in turn, motivate others to give thanks (*eucharisteō*) to God in prayer.

---

21. Cullmann, "La prière selon les Epîtres pauliniennes," 92.

The Influence of Prayer with the Church Planter
(Communal Prayer)

Prayers with Peter

The New Testament not only contains prayers *for* the church planter (above) and prayers *of* the church planter (below), but also communal prayers that are spoken by a group of believers *with* the church planter. One example for such a communal prayer is found in Acts 4:24–30.

The prayer's narrative context (Acts 4) presents Peter and John as preaching. The Jewish religious authorities, however, prohibit them to do so. Even though they threaten Peter and John, they eventually let them go (Acts 4:21). Peter and John then go to their fellow Christian believers and tell them everything the Jewish religious authorities had said to them and how they had been threatened.

In reaction to this alarming news, the community addresses God (Acts 4:24a) with a beautiful prayer (Acts 4:24b–30), calling him "Sovereign Lord," who "made the heavens and the earth and the sea, and everything in them" (Acts 4:24b). After a longer introduction that also includes a quotation from the Old Testament (Ps 2:1–2), the actual prayer request is expressed in Acts 4:29–30.

> Now, Lord, consider their threats and enable your servants to speak your word with great boldness. Stretch out your hand to heal and perform signs and wonders through the name of your holy servant Jesus.

The outcome of the prayer is then set forth in Acts 4:31.

> After they prayed, the place where they were meeting was shaken. And they were all filled with the Holy Spirit and spoke the word of God boldly.

The prayer of the church is answered in an exact and (on the level of the Lucan narrative) literal manner, as the following two observations demonstrate. First, the earthquake-like shaking of the place might be a direct response to the "signs and wonders" (Acts 4:30) requested in the church's prayer. So the prayer of the community is confirmed by a miraculous event, as Schweyer aptly comments.[22]

Second, the request in Acts 4:29 for the capacity to speak (*laleō*) the word (*logos*) with boldness (*parrēsia*) is answered literally because

22. Schweyer, "Gebet," 49.

Luke, in Acts 4:31, employs the same three Greek words to narrate that, through the filling with the Holy Spirit, they spoke (*laleō*) the word (*logos*) with boldness (*parrēsia*).

Prayers with Paul

It is not only Peter, but also Paul who is pictured in the New Testament as praying with church communities for his church planting ministry. Before the first missionary journey (in 48 CE), the church in Antioch (in Syria) prayed for the missionaries Paul and Barnabas. "So after they had fasted and prayed, they placed their hands on them and sent them off" (Acts 13:3). The narrative on the first missionary journey (Acts 13:1—14:28) demonstrates that these prayers for Paul and Barnabas were answered; people believe in Jesus Christ (Acts 13:48; 14:1, 21) and churches are planted in Lystra, Iconium, and Antioch (Acts 14:21–22). It is even recorded that Paul and Barnabas installed elders (*presbyteroi*) in and prayed (*proseuchomai*) for (and with) all these churches (*ekklēsiai*). "Paul and Barnabas appointed elders for them in each church and, with prayer and fasting, committed them to the Lord, in whom they had put their trust" (Acts 14:23). Bock remarks, "This is the first mention that Paul and Barnabas appoint such leaders as they establish new believing communities."[23]

That the prayers of Paul and Barnabas for (and with) the churches are answered can be seen in the further course of the account of Acts. About two years later, during the second missionary journey (in 50-52 CE), Paul visits Lystra again (Acts 16:1) and learns that not only this church and the one in Iconium still exist, but that there is a faithful Christian brother and co-worker there, namely Timothy (Acts 16:1).

The Influence of Prayer of the Church Planter
(Personal Prayer)

Prayers of Peter

With regard to the influence and efficiency of the personal prayers of Peter, Acts 8:24 is very interesting. The meaning of this verse, however,

---

23. Bock, *Acts*, 483.

is much disputed in New Testament scholarship. In order to understand this text, it is necessary to sketch briefly its narrative framework.

The local setting of the passage in Acts 8:4–25 is Samaria, where the evangelist Philippus is preaching the Gospel (see also Acts 6:5; 21:8). Among others, the magician Simon (*Simon Magus*) believes and is baptized. When Peter and John come from Jerusalem to Samaria to visit the new believers there, they pray for them so that they might receive the Holy Spirit (Acts 8:15). When Peter and John lay their hands on them, the new believers receive the Holy Spirit (Acts 8:17). Simon, after seeing the apostles' power to transmit the Holy Spirit by the laying on of hands, offers them money in order to receive the same power (Acts 8:18–19). However, Peter responds by telling him that it is wicked to think that God's gift might be obtained with money (Acts 8:20–21).

Peter then addresses Simon with the command to pray (*deomai*), "Repent of this wickedness and pray to the Lord in the hope that he may forgive you for having such a thought in your heart" (Acts 8:22). Simon, however, by employing the same verb (*deomai*) "to pray," responds by addressing Peter and John with the following request/command: "Pray to the Lord for me so that nothing you have said may happen to me" (Acts 8:24).

Some scholars interpret Simon's request in terms of his sincere belief that the prayers of Peter and John are more powerful than his own. Jacob Jervell, for instance, states that Simon has accepted the word of the apostles, because he is portrayed as a repentant sinner. He asks that the apostles pray for him because he considers their prayer more powerful than his own prayer. Still other exegetes understand Simon's request in terms of his disobedience and unbelief. Bock comments, "Peter can pray, but Simon will not."[24]

Unfortunately, the question as to whether Simon's request was sincere, and, accordingly, if Luke, as author of Acts, considers the prayer of Peter and John more powerful than that of Simon, must be left open. F.F. Bruce concludes, "Luke does not say if the apostles acceded to Simon's plea and prayed for him, nor yet (if they did pray) what the outcome was."[25] In spite of this open result, or perhaps because of it, the above discussion might motivate further reflection on the question as to what

---

24. Bock, *Acts*, 336.

25. Bruce, *The Acts of the Apostles*, 223.

extent the prayer of a church planter is more influential than that of other persons/believers.

The book of Acts does contain some prayers of Peter, the outcome of which are clearly recounted. In Acts 9:40, Peter raises Tabitha/Dorcas from the dead. Acts 10–11 tells how God, in perfect timing and fine tuning, answers the prayers (and vision) of Peter in Joppa by meticulously relating them to the vision of Cornelius in Caesarea.

Prayers of Paul

In the twelfth chapter of his second letter to the Corinthians, Paul refers to his "thorn in the flesh" (*King James Version*). According to commentators, this metaphor could, for example, refer to psychological anxiety, opposition to Paul, or a physical disease such as a malarial fever, defective vision, or migraine headaches.[26] By employing the verb *parakaleō*, Paul tells the Corinthians about his prayers with regard to this "thorn in the flesh." "Three times I pleaded with the Lord to take it away from me" (2 Cor 12:8). The context (2 Cor 12:9) suggests that "Lord" (*kurios*) here refers to the Lord Jesus Christ, and that Paul thus addressed his prayers to Jesus Christ.

While the outcome of Paul's prayers is usually not recorded in his letters, Paul here also tells the Corinthians how the Lord answered him. "But he said to me, 'My grace is sufficient for you, for my power is made perfect in weakness.'" (2 Cor 12:9) Murray J. Harris comments that, "Although Paul's request for the removal of his 'thorn' had been earnest . . . and repeated . . . it was denied."[27]

However, Paul receives the promise of Jesus Christ that Jesus's grace and power is sufficient for Paul. Cullmann's comment on this verse is worthwhile being quoted in full. In the English translation, it reads as follows,

> The threefold prayer in 2 Cor 12.8 was not heard. But a miracle took place at that moment. Paul evidently heard Christ's voice (as he did, according to Acts 9.3, at his conversion) giving an answer: "My grace is *sufficient* for you." "Sufficient", that means that no more is promised to him: "the miraculous power (*dynamis*)

26. For an instructive overview of the various scholarly interpretations, see Harris, *Second Corinthians*, 858–59.

27. Harris, *Second Corinthians*, 861.

of the Spirit is made perfect in weakness (in the illness)." That means that the illness remains, but the healing power of the Spirit has its effect despite and in the illness. While the prayer has not been heard, it has been listened to, and that hearing has taken place through the presence of Christ in the very fact that it has not been heard.[28]

Another reference to "unanswered" prayers of Paul is found in Romans 1:9–10, where Paul informs the Roman Christians, "I remember you in my prayers at all times; and I pray that now at last by God's will the way may be opened for me to come to you." However, the book of Acts narrates several prayers of Paul that are answered and/or have a positive influence on others. The prayers of Paul and Silas in the prison in Philippi are answered by an earthquake (Acts 16:25–26); while praying in the Temple in Jerusalem, Paul falls into a trance (Acts 22:17); through Paul's prayers in the middle of a storm, his fellow passengers on the ship to Rome are encouraged (Acts 27:35–36); Paul's prayer for healing for Publius' father on the island of Malta is answered (Acts 28:8).

Additional Insights

For the sake of completeness, some additional references to prayer in the letters of Paul should be mentioned, even though these texts do not contain any information concerning the outcome or influence of the respective prayers. The following five observations regarding the prayers of the church planter Paul might be an inspiration and motivation for Christian believers who minister as church planters in Europe or elsewhere.

- First, as the so-called "prayer reports" (*Gebetsberichte*) demonstrate, Paul continued to pray for the churches he had planted (1 Cor 1:4–5; Phil 1:3–11; 1 Thess 2:13; 2 Thess 1:3).

- Second, Paul also prayed for his co-workers Timothy and Titus (2 Tim 1:3; 2 Cor 8:16).

- Third, Paul requested in prayer that he might meet the Thessalonian church (that he planted) again (1 Thess 3:10–11).

- Fourth, in his prayers, Paul expressed thankfulness for his church planting ministry (1 Tim 1:12–13; 2 Cor 2:14).

28. Cullmann, *Prayer in the New Testament*, 85–86.

- Fifth, Paul not only prayed for churches and co-workers, but also for peoples, governments, and individuals in general (Rom 10:1; 1 Tim 2:1–2).

Summary and Conclusion

By studying intercessory, communal, and personal prayers related to the ministries of the church planters Peter and Paul, it becomes obvious that prayers for, with, and of the church planter have a whole variety of influences and outcomes.

While some prayers are and/or remain (seemingly) "unanswered" (2 Cor 12:8; Rom 1:10), other prayers are answered instantly in a mighty, miraculous, and powerful manner (e.g., Acts 4:23–31; 12:1–17). Some prayers lack an immediate answer, but in the course of time, it becomes obvious that God used them to plant and nurture the church (Acts 13:3; 14:23). Some intercessory prayers, because they are answered, result in prayers of thankfulness (2 Cor 1:10–11). Last but not least, Luke 22:32 confirms that Jesus himself prayed and interceded for the ministry of Peter, in the same way that John 17:20 presents Jesus as praying not only for his disciples, but also for all those Christian believers coming after them.

I would like to wrap up this chapter with a statement on prayer that is found in the Letter of James. It does not particularly refer to church planting, but rather to the harvest and fruit in the literal sense. Therefore, it is only indirectly relevant for the topic that has been studied above. The main reason for choosing this text as a closing passage is that it is a strong testimony for the great power and influence that prayer has. It should thus be an encouragement and motivation for our own prayer life, no matter if we are engaged in church planting or not. We recall here the words of James, who wrote,

> Therefore confess your sins to each other and pray for each other so that you may be healed. The prayer of a righteous person is powerful and effective. Elijah was a human being, even as we are. He prayed earnestly that it would not rain, and it did not rain on the land for three and a half years. Again he prayed, and the heavens gave rain, and the earth produced its crops (Jas 5:16–18).

4

HOW TO CREATE A JESUS MOVEMENT OF MULTIPLYING CHURCHES

Dietrich Schindler

MOST OF OUR LITERATURE on church planting is both theologically and methodologically keyed to the ministry of the apostles and of Paul. When reading the Gospels as church planters we discover Jesus as the first church planter. Jesus's lifestyle and message help us to understand how we can plant churches today in the way he did with his disciples who, with him, became the prototype of the church. Jesus gave us a model of how to plant multiplying churches. Practically, we learn how Jesus's model of planting churches helps us move from good to great church planting.[1]

Shifting the church planting focus from Paul to Jesus

Over the years I have thought much about church planting. I read about it, taught it, and experimented with many authors' innovations. I began to notice that the literature on church planting was weighted toward Paul and the apostles. Most, if not all, of the books I read described how Paul started new churches during his various missionary journeys, and how we can similarly follow in his steps. Without a doubt, we can and should learn much from Paul on the topic of church planting and church growth.

---

1. Schindler, *The Jesus-Model.*

However, was Paul truly the first missionary and church planter, or was there someone filling those roles before his time?

I began to reread the Gospels with a new question in mind: in what ways was Jesus modeling, teaching, and practicing church planting? I was astonished at the answers the Gospels delivered, and was surprised to see suddenly that all of the principles that Paul taught and lived out as a church planter were visible in the life and teaching of Jesus! Could it be that Jesus was the first missionary and the first "church planter," and that Paul and his co-workers, led by the Holy Spirit, looked to Jesus as their example?

Jesus, the first church planter (Matt 16:18)

Having expressly stated, "I will build my church," Jesus thereby makes himself the author and initiator of the church. Pentecost became necessary because Jesus was no longer bodily present with his disciples. Many look to Pentecost in terms of it being the birth of the church, but we can equally assert that Jesus began the prototype of the church when he called his disciples to follow him. The genesis and the destiny of the church is Jesus. She is both called into existence by him, and purposed to live her life with Jesus being the focus.

Jesus is, professionally speaking, a missionary sent by the Father, an apostle commissioned to carry out the work of the Father, and also a king. However, Jesus is also a church planter. How so? Jesus is a church planter because that is what he said he would do. "I will build my church" (Matt 16:18). By virtue of this one simple statement we draw two conclusions: starting the Church (and churches) is Jesus's main goal, and he himself intends to reach his goal. Even if we allow for the fact that Jesus was directing his words to Peter, and that Peter would start or build the church, it is in fact Jesus before and behind Peter who does the planting, starting, and building. Peter is the workman, but Jesus is the architect.

The Apostle Luke understood Jesus in this vein as well. He begins to chronicle the story of the early church by writing, "In my former book (i.e., the Gospel of Luke), Theophilus, I wrote about all that Jesus *began* to do and to teach until the day he was taken up to heaven, after giving instructions through the Holy Spirit to the apostles he had chosen" (Acts 1:1–2). The beginnings were the foundations that Jesus laid in the Gospels. After the *beginnings*, we read of the *progressions* in the life of the early church. We read of how the first disciples go out and preach the gospel, call their hearers to turn around (repent) and believe in King Jesus. We read that as people responded to the gospel and became followers of Jesus, new local churches were planted.

The growth of the body of Christ through the planting of new churches is so astounding that we read in the following summary statement: "So the churches were strengthened in the faith and grew daily in numbers" (Acts 16:5). Most readers entirely miss the startling significance of this verse. It is often understood that the number of disciples who came to faith and began to follow Jesus grew daily in numbers. The significance of this verse is not in the numbers of believers that increased, but in the *daily increase in the number of churches!*[2] During the era of the early church, new churches were being planted *daily*. And these new church plants were ultimately the work of the church planting architect, Jesus.

Jesus, the trainer of church planters (Matt 4:19; 28:18–20)

The Acts of the Apostles is a record of the extension of the works of Jesus on earth through the lives of his disciples. These followers were working hand in hand as partners of Jesus to see his vision of building his Church come into fulfillment. How was it possible that they knew what to do and how to do it, which thus resulted in the starting of many, many new churches? Simply put, they learned from Jesus and from those who actually walked with him for three years in apprenticeship. From Jesus they saw, heard, and participated in what it meant to minister to people in such a way that new churches could be started. In order to turn the world upside down, Jesus needed to invest three years of his life in the lives of twelve of his followers. In the Gospels we see how Jesus reveals to those around him that he is a church planter. If we pay attention, we will learn from Jesus the principles and practices needed in order for us to be partners with him in planting new churches in our space and time.

The Jesus model of church planting

The life and teachings of Jesus reveal to us specific ways in which we too can plant churches in our unique contexts today. Jesus's call to follow him

2. Schneider, *Theologischer Kommentar zum Neuen Testament*, 202.

is essentially an invitation to learn to live and work in the same way that he lived and worked. As we understand that we have been called into a learning community with Jesus, we will then be ready to learn the essentials of church planting from him. "Take my yoke upon you and learn from me . . ." (Matt 11:29) is the command to integrate Jesus's teaching (his yoke) and example in our lives today, thereby becoming what Jesus intended us to be. To emulate Jesus is to model Jesus.

The Kingdom and Church Planting

Archetypical for Jesus was his desire to build the kingdom of God through the proclamation and demonstration of the gospel. From start to finish Jesus spoke of the coming of the kingdom of God which came in his very presence. The kingdom of God begins to take root in the heart of an individual, expanding to his family, his church, and his environment. Especially in places where evil is overcome by good, the kingdom of God becomes evident. The kingdom of God is that realm of reality where what God wants happens. It breaks into the lives of Jesus's followers. They thereby become an object lesson, displaying the beauty of God by being influenced and empowered by him.

When a church is planted it becomes a visible sign of the presence of the kingdom of God, however weak and imperfect it might appear. What is significant in the church of Jesus Christ is not education, status, or wealth, but the evident influence of Jesus in the lives of his followers. Christians live and move differently from the rest of the pack because they are led by Christ. The church then becomes the anticipation of the new world order under Christ's lordship. In the life of the church we tend to find what we will one day certainly discover: the name of the Father is hallowed, his will is done, his influence is felt, and his joy is contagious.

> Church planting is thus the most urgent business of humankind. It is through the creation (or planting) of churches that God's kingdom is extended into communities which have not yet been touched by the precious surprise of the presence of the kingdom of God in their midst.[3]

The kingdom of God breaks through into society by means of the planting of new churches. That is where Jesus makes his kingship felt. Transformation of individual lives comes about in the church in a way

3. Shenk and Stutzman, *Creating Communities of the Kingdom*, 23.

that secular communities are not able to make happen. This is because Jesus Christ is the life, the DNA, the transforming power of the local church. In the same manner in which he built his church in the first century via the prototype of life lived with his disciples, he plants and builds his local church in our day and age.

The Jesus Model represents eight essential qualities, lived out and taught by Jesus, which we are called to emulate. These vital characteristics will be outlined here in a linear format, but are in reality overlapping, with some points being expanded, and others further complementary. These eight qualities orbit around a central point, like an atomic core that draws other subatomic particles to it and binds them together. Without the core, the surrounding characteristics would be lifeless and void. All eight facets extend from the central point and display in their out-working the essence of life that is mediated from the core.

The Jesus Model: Planting Churches like Jesus

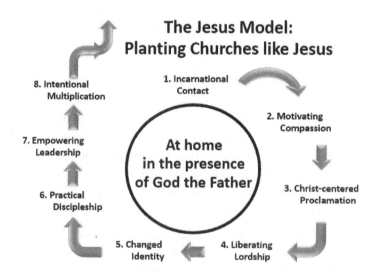

The Core: At home in the presence of God the Father

Those that swarmed around Jesus were often riveted in astonishment. He had something about him that was absolutely different and winsome. "The people were *amazed* at his teaching, because he taught them as one who had *authority*, not as the teachers of the law" (Mark 1:22, comp. Mark 1:27). The amazing thing about Jesus, the thing that was so fascinating for people, was his authority.

Authority is an expression of strength that results from having been in the presence of God. Authority cannot be earned, but it can be granted by God. "All *authority* in heaven and on earth *has been given to me*" (Matt 28:18). Despite the fact that no person can earn authority by himself, nearness to God the Father often results in authority being given to a person by God. When we look at the way Jesus behaved when he was not "working," we find him constantly searching for time alone with the Father. Jesus's nearness to the Father was the interface to authority, from which he taught and worked in amazing ways.

We find Jesus being at home in the presence of God his Father, and the Father being at home with Jesus. At the start of his ministry, people around Jesus at his baptism were able to visibly and audibly witness to the closeness of heart between Father and Son. "You are my Son, whom I love; with you I am well pleased" (Mark 1:11). During his ministry Jesus often sought out places in which he could enjoy undisturbed communion with the Father. "Very early in the morning, while it was still dark, Jesus got up, left the house and went off to a solitary place, where he prayed" (Mark 1:35). After long, exhausting days of meeting the needs of many people, Jesus sought the Father (Mark 6:46; 9:7). Just before the greatest trial of his life, his crucifixion, Jesus went off to an olive grove and prayed, "Abba, Father!" (Mark 14:36). "Abba" or "Daddy" is one of the first intimate words a child learns to say. Jesus's nearness to his Father/ Daddy was the oxygen of his soul, the joy of his heart, and the original power of his work.

Like the ravenous longing of a baby for its mother's milk, such is this longing after the Father's heart, which becomes the basic nutrition for the church planter. Jesus could not get enough of his Father. In this way the starting point for the church planter is a ravenous desire to be intimately near God the Father. Notwithstanding the failures and the successes in his life, the church planter will derive his greatest satisfaction, not in the ministry, but in the presence of God the Father.

Characteristic 1: Incarnational Contact

Jesus's nearness to the Father had a dramatic impact on the trajectory of his ministry. While spending time with his Father, Jesus longed to spend time with people. This is the first obvious indication of Jesus as a church planter; he was constantly seeking ways to connect with people. "Submerging to be with God, re-emerging to be with people," is the way Catholic theologian Paul Michael Zulehner puts it.[4]

We see Jesus walking along the shore of the Sea of Galilee, stopping to talk to fishermen at work (Mark 1:16), and he drops in to visit with some new friends (Mark 1:29; Luke 10:38–39). Even among the riffraff of Jewish society, among hated tax collectors and sinners, he finds time to linger gladly over a meal (Mark 2:15). He obviously wants to have people around him and even calls them to come to him (Mark 7:14). At one place we read, "Again crowds of people came to him, and as was his custom, he taught them" (Mark 10:1).

In some significant, and also in many seemingly insignificant, daily circumstances in the lives of myriads of people, we catch Jesus as "church planter" as he enters into their lives. We find him at a Jewish wedding celebration, even a week into the festivities, as if he had nothing else of importance to do (John 2:1–10). We find him sitting on the edge of a well having a conversation with a dubious woman (John 4), engaged in a conversation with a Roman centurion (Matt 8:5–13), or one night caught up in a deep talk on theology with a priest (John 3). He joyfully takes little children up into his arms (Mark 10:16), heals the sick (Luke 5:29–32), and mingles with those in a funeral procession (Luke 7:11–15). Why was Jesus constantly found traveling from one village to another, criss-crossing Israel in the process? Because he was seeking out people where they lived and worked, laughed and cried, hoped and despaired. They mattered to him.

Being near people, entering into their world and taking on their heart-issues is what incarnation is all about. "The Word became flesh and made his dwelling among us. We have seen his glory, the glory of the One and Only, who came from the Father, full of grace and truth" (John 1:14). God allowed himself to become a member of humanity so he can draw near to us. The incarnation of Jesus Christ is certainly unique, unrepeatable, and of the greatest salvation-historical significance. But it is also an example to us of how to extend God's love to people. It is a model for

---

4. Zulehner, *Mystik und Politik.*

church planters; for church planters will, like Jesus, seek to *dwell* among those far from God. Church planters will learn to be approachable and to approach in the hope that the living God will move through them to reach the lost.

Theologians of old used to write about such behaviour, labeling it the *condescension* of God.

> Despite His Unapproachableness and His Transcendance, God Himself goes down. In Jesus God condescends, leans forward and downward, for this is the only way to lift us up. Condescension means that God in His downward movement allows Himself to become involved in the circumstances of the lives of those He wants to reach.[5]

Church planting, as it takes its cue from Jesus, will thus be thoroughly people-oriented. As helpful as books, seminars, concepts, and plans pertaining to church planting are, it will always be real people in their real world of real need who will have utmost priority. This is why church planting does not come alive on the drawing table or on the computer screen, but through one person interacting with another. Church planters will behave the way Jesus behaved; in the name of God they will be among people. This is in essence incarnational contact.

Characteristic 2: Motivated by Compassion

On the surface, we observe Jesus as he travels around all the towns and villages in Galilee. However, when we look underneath the surface of things, we see what truly motivated Jesus to move among so many people. It was his compassion toward them in their great need, for they lacked direction, were living in fear, and were likened to sheep running madly in every direction because they had no shepherd. It broke Jesus's heart to look at them in this way, the way they really were in their hearts (Matt 9:35–38).

Compassion is the motivation behind all that Jesus did in ministry. Jesus was riveted by the widow who, having lost her husband, was now proceeding to bury her only child, a son. Mercy overcame him as his heart was broken because of her pain. "When the Lord saw her, his heart went out to her and he said, 'Don't cry.'" (Luke 7:13). Jesus had compassion on the crowds (Matt 9:36), and also toward lone sufferers (Matt

5. Herbst, *Und sie dreht sich doch*, 11.

20:34). He cried his eyes out over an entire city (Luke 19:41–44), and had a heart full of love for a man who loved his money more than God (Mark 10:21). If he taught his disciples anything, Jesus instructed them in word and by example to "Be merciful, just as your Father is merciful" (Luke 6:36). Moreover, Jesus made it extemely clear that mercy, or the lack of it, will be a deciding factor in the last judgement. Those that clothe the naked, feed the hungry, give the thirsty water to drink, visit inmates in prison—these are the merciful ones, and to them God will show mercy (Matt 25:34–40).

My collegue, Johannes Reimer, says it well when he writes about the important place of compassion in the life of the local church.

> The church is God's people for a needy world. Nothing disting- ishes the church more than mercy . . . Mercy is directed toward the sick and the sinner (Mt 9:12f) and does not judge the guilty (Mt 12:7). Mercy seeks out the needy person and tries to assuage his need (Mt 25:31f). Mercy directs the life of the church both to those inside the church, by honoring the lowly and by not overloading them (Mt 18:1–14), as well as toward outsiders (Mt 25:31f).[6]

Many ministries in our churches and church plants these days are being carried out very professionally. At no time in the history of the Church of Jesus Christ has there been a greater emphasis on excellence and quality as in our day. We take no fault in this—except when profes- sionalism interferes with matters of the heart. Professionalism in minis- try becomes idolatry when those in ministry no longer feel a pain in their hearts for the plight of the needy.

Characteristic 3: Christ-centered Proclamation

What purpose was there in the close contact that Jesus typically had with people and his compassion toward them in their need? Nearness and mercy did something to Jesus; they freed up his tongue. Over one hun- dred times in the Gospels we come across three significant words strung together so descriptive of Jesus: "and he spoke." And what Jesus said was sensational. "The people were amazed at his teaching" (Mark 1:22, 27). The disciples were commissioned to proclaim the gospel to all people

---

6. Reimer, *Die Welt umarmen*, 64.

everywhere (Mark 13:10; 16:15; Matt 28:19). Why? Because Jesus did it, and because Jesus was the content of this revolutionary gospel.

Healings, the casting out of demons, and the many signs and wonders that Jesus performed, were all most certainly astounding, but without an explanation as to what purpose these had, all we would be left with would be sensationalism. The truly good news is that behind the many signs and wonders is Jesus, the Son of Man, the Messiah, the Hope of the world, and that gives traction, fullfilling the purpose in pointing to new life in Christ.

The content of Jesus's gospel was the kingdom of God. He went into Galilee, proclaiming the good news of God. "'The time has come,' he said. 'The kingdom of God is near. Repent and believe the good news!'" (Mark 1:14-15). "But if I drive out demons by the Spirit of God, then the kingdom of God has come upon you" (Matt 12:28). Jesus preached the kingdom of God in order that his hearers would receive it and let themselves be influenced by it. In this kingdom it is Jesus who is clearly the king and who wills to be king in our lives today.

When we pray, "Thy kingdom come," we thus do not infer that it needs to become a reality, but that we want it to be the reality that is our daily living. As we allow God to reign in and over us, we thereby put ourselves on a path of change that will reorient not only our personal lives, but the trajectory of our society as well.

This leads us to consider an often widely held error among Christians. Christians sometimes succumb to the notion that God took the active part and came down to earth to die substititionarily for our sin, and to offer us forgiveness and a place in heaven with him forever. One becomes a Christian by accepting the person and the work of Christ for oneself. Jesus is active, we are passive; he offers us forgiveness and a place in his new world order. All we have to do is accept this. Many Christians allow this to take place for them and their future, but then commence to live lives under their own purpose and planning. They make the plans for their lives and ask Jesus to sign off on them.

Jesus's teaching concerning the kingdom of God comes into our lives as a new operating imperative and is diametrically opposed to the notion of so many Christians, as outlined above. The kingdom of God *comes* to us in Jesus Christ. Suddenly the king is here! He is active, working energetically in and through us. Only by this manner is freedom possible; freedom to live in the power of God today. Now Jesus is the unseen king in our lives, just as he was the seen king, the Lord, in the lives of his disciples. He teaches us how we can live his life in our contemporary lives. Becoming a Christian is becoming a disciple, a follower, an apprentice of Jesus.

Jesus placed himself front and center in his message. The gospel is all about Jesus because Jesus is the center of salvation.

Characteristic 4: Liberating Lordship

Characteristics of Jesus were the uniquenss of his identity, his teaching, and his demands on people. In many ways Jesus lived contrary to what Jewish religious folk thought was normal in his day. We see Jesus the contrarian in light of the selection of his disciples and the way he went about gathering and teaching them. We know much about Jewish education in first century Israel. In order to become well-versed in Jewish teaching, young men vied with one another to gain the attention of well-known Jewish rabbis in the hopes of being chosen as a student. The best rabbis took only the best of students who would live with and learn from them. It was not uncommon for young men to be rejected by religious scholars because they did not have the sought after qualifications.

Thus, contemporary Jewish scholars must have been more than a bit amazed at Jesus's selection of his students. The initial amazement was most certainly because of the manner of selection. Rather than wait for potential pupils to come to him, Jesus took action and chose who he wanted to be his students (Mark 1:17; 2:14; 3:13–14). Those whom Jesus proactively chose to follow him would not have had a chance under customary conditions. Jesus chose men to be his disciples who would have been scorned and rejected by society at large: fishermen, tax collectors, rebel soldiers, choleric personalities, the unwanted of society, and the uneducated. Simple background checks would have concluded that all of the disciples, perhaps with the exception of Judas Iscariot, were rejects. But to Jesus it was more important to have men around him who were willing to *follow him*, and not just to learn things from him.

In discussions that I have with people concerning the gospel I sometimes hear them retort, "But I believe in God." This is often a way of letting me know that they see themselves as being in the safe-zone. I congratulate them on their belief in God and then take them to a passage in James where I read, "You believe that there is one God. Good! Even the demons believe that—and shudder" (Jas 2:19). It doesn't take special ability or insight to believe in God because even devils believe in him. The difference between a devil and a Christian lies not in their belief system, but in their lifestyle. Devils bristle against Jesus; Christians submit themselves to him, and their submission is seen in their behavior. True belief will always influence behavior. We will therefore behave according to what we believe, whereas what we may profess might not be what we truly believe in our heart of hearts. It is behavior that will be the tell-tale sign of a person's real belief system.

The Lordship of Jesus Christ that is seen in the life of a follower of Jesus is simply the logical consequence of discipleship. Jesus calls people to follow him, thereby becoming his disciples, his students. It is in following Jesus that we are set free from following ourselves, and are placed on the path of living with God and for God. "Converts" and "believers," as *popularly conceived*, might "do their own thing," but disciples obviously must do the will of their Master.

Characteristic 5: Changed Identity

The man that Jesus healed of congenital blindness awakened to a double revelation; he came to realize who Jesus truly was, and he came to see who he had become through Jesus (John 9). With ever increasing progressive insight and understanding he comes to realize the identity of the one who healed him. Initially he refers to Jesus as, "The man they call Jesus . . . " (John 9:11). Afterward he says to the Pharisees, "He is a prophet" (John 9:17). His insight into who Jesus is reaches its high point when he says of Jesus that he is from God (John 9:33). Consequently, the unbelievable transpired; ". . . they threw him out" (John 9:34). This was the apprehension that his parents previously had when they were questioned by the religious leaders as to whether or not the man was their son, and they were at a loss to explain the origin of his healing. "His parents said this because they were afraid of the Jews, for already the Jews had decided that anyone who acknowledged that Jesus was the Christ would be put out of the synagogue" (John 9:22).

The dire straits of a person who, as a Jew, had been expelled from the synagogue is hardly fathomable for those of us living in the twenty-first century in the Western World. For a Jew in the first century, expulsion from the synagogue meant that he lost his place in society, both in the contemporary world and in the future kingdom of God. His moorings were gone. He was no longer a Jew but a foreigner, having lost the acceptance of his familial and religious community. Worst of all, he was thereby cut off from life in Yahweh. By being kicked out of the synagogue, this man effectively *lost his identity*. With the words, "and they threw him out," his world collapsed. Now he was worse off than when he was blind.

In this state of unconceivable deconstruction, Jesus finds him and asks, "Do you believe in the Son of Man?" At that the man answers, "Who is he, Sir? . . . Tell me so that I may believe in him" (John 9:35–36). At this point Jesus tells the man that the one speaking with him, Jesus himself, is the Messiah, the Son of Man. The formerly blind, now healed, expelled from the synagogue man turns to Jesus, and, looking him in the eyes, says, "'Lord, I believe,' and he worshiped him" (John 9:38). What had been a state of lost identity became a state of newly found identity in Jesus as the Christ (John 9:22).

I personally believe that the Apostle John recorded this incident in his Gospel because he was pointing to a greater reality than simply the healing of a man from congenital blindness. The fate of the man born blind, expelled from the synagogue, who found a new identity in Jesus Christ, is a parable for those of us who with this man have said, "Lord, I believe." Heredity, education, wealth, possesions, reputation, and achievement all fall away as markers of personal identity because Jesus has surplanted them. In Jesus Christ, the Christian knows who he is, to whom he belongs, where he belongs, and why he is alive. The context in which we lived until our entering into the Christ life may have remained the same; nevertheless, the basis for our self-identity changed. We have become Christians because we have been given life from Christ himself.

We find similar teaching on our new identity in Christ in the calling of the first apostles. "Jesus went up on a mountainside and called to him those he wanted, and they came to him. He appointed twelve—designating them apostles—*that they might be with him* and that he might send them out to preach and to have authority to drive out demons" (Mark 3:13–15). We notice here a calling and a commissioning that dare not be confused one with the other. The calling is to come and be with Jesus. The commision is to go out to preach and to do the works of God in the world. Our primary calling is to Jesus. Therefore we must be careful not to seek to fulfill the commission of Jesus without first living *in* the calling of Jesus.

The initial question that each person must ask and answer is that of identity: Who am I? Those outside the life of Jesus seek their identity in themselves, but come to the conclusion that they are unable to clarify the issue of self-identity by seeking it within themselves. This is because the answer to our identity always lies *outside* of the person himself. Everyone who becomes a Christian, by virtue of his friendship with Jesus, enters into a new identity. In finding Jesus, he finds his identity in Christ.

Why is it so important that church planters understand the reality of their new identity in Jesus? It is because our identity in Christ is also the identity of the Church and thus of the churches we seek to plant. Should we not understand and appropriate the reality of our new identity in Christ, then church planting is reduced to a mere founding of a club, a new organization, or a group of people united around a creed. But the Church is radically different. The Church is the miracle of God, wherein we belong to God as children belong to their parents, and wherein we are participants in the new workings of God in this world. The Church of Jesus is a new spiritual fellowship in which we have received a new identity in him.

Characteristic 6: Practical Discipleship

Viewed sociologically, the first disciples became a prototype of the Church. Jesus hand-picked twelve men with whom he intended to turn the world upside down. What kind of men were they? Thomas was a meloncholic skeptic. Judas was a money-hungry traitor. Peter was the impulsive bull-in-a-china-shop kind of a guy. Brothers James and John were hot-headed, narcisstic cholerics. Simon the idealist was a politically active underground guerilla warrior who hated the oppressive Roman authorities. Matthew, on the other hand, was the Matthew Arnold of the twelve, wanting to cooperate with the Romans in order to line his own pockets. All together, the twelve were an explosive Molotov cocktail that could go off at any moment. It is amazing indeed to realize that Jesus chose these contrary disciples to model to the world what unity and love should look like.

Jesus chose such men to be his apprentices. They were the ones he determined would do his works his way. The commission that Jesus gave these men was to make people into his disciples. One way to translate the Great Commission is this: "While going about your everyday activities, lead people in every culture to be my apprentices, submerge them into the reality of the triune God, and coach them to apply all that I have taught you. And be assured of this—I will be very present with you as you make these apprentices of mine" (see Matt 28:19-20). A disciple of Jesus makes disciples (apprentices) of Jesus. That is easy to understand. The manner of making disciples will, however, challenge us to the utmost.

Disciples that make disciples is the goal of church planting. People who have submitted themselves to the Lordship of Christ, having found their true identity in him, begin to learn to live the way he lived. This is why calling people to simply believe in Jesus will not suffice. They need to be led to learn of Jesus as his apprentices, "until Christ is formed in you" (Gal 4:19).

What was paramount in the mind of Jesus when he called people to follow him? He sought to transform them, not just inform them. This is what he meant by saying, ". . . teaching them *to obey* everything that I have commanded you" (Matt 28:20). To obey is to learn to apply the teachings of Jesus and the Bible in the everyday circumstances of life. Simply being aware of biblical truth will not translate into life transformation.

As a young teenager, Elvis Presley attended a summer camp facilitated by his Baptist church for five years in a row. He was raised in a family that lived on a very low income and therefore didn't have the financial means to pay the camp fees. The leadership of the church found a way to help such families. One day they announced that whoever could memorize three hundred and fifty Bible verses could participate in the summer camp for free! Elvis Presely was able to attend the camp at no cost to him or his family because for five years in a row he learned three hundred and fifty Bible verses each year by heart. In five years Elvis Presely had managed to memorize 1,750 Bible verses![7] Despite this vast expanse of Bible knowledge, it did not amount to a life lived that was pleasing to God. Bible knowledge without life application is merely a hobby.

For Jesus, making apprentices was never a theoretical endeavor, it was conducted under real life circumstances. His plan of making apprentices was both easy to understand and very effective. He began by giving his followers orientation, then he sent them out to minister, and afterwards he taught them. We often do the opposite. In our discipleship training we orient, teach, and then send people out to do ministry. We tend to train people "just in case" they might need the information conveyed to them. Jesus trained his followers "just in time." What they had experienced in everday living became the context for his instruction. Jesus trained his disciples to be church planters while on-the-job.

7. Ogden, *Transforming Discipleship*, 43–44.

Characteristic 7: Empowering Leadership

After making disciples, Jesus made leaders out of them. In many places in the Gospels we see Jesus taking charge as he set people in motion to influence and serve others. At the wedding celebration in Cana, he directs the servants to fill large water jars normally used for purification rituals, and to draw water to serve to the guests. Without their help, Jesus would not have been able to turn water into wine (John 2:1–11). The Roman centurion, himself a military leader, recognized the leadership ability of Jesus by saying, "Lord, don't trouble yourself, for I do not deserve to have you come under my roof. That is why I did not even consider myself worthy to come to you. But say the word, and my servant will be healed. For I myself am a man under authority, with soldiers under me. I tell this one, 'Go,' and he goes; and that one, 'Come,' and he comes. I say to my servant, 'Do this,' and he does it" (Luke 7:6–8). In another place Jesus compared himself with a shepherd herding his flock, which hears and follows him (John 10:27).

Had Jesus remained alone in his leadership role without making leaders out of his disciples, his ministry would have come to an abrupt end at his ascension. Because Jesus knew that the churches could not be started and grown without gifted leadership, he empowered his disciples to become leaders, and thereby trained them to do what he himself did right before their eyes—to preach, heal, serve, and cast out demons. To the twelve apostles Jesus gave authority and power to accomplish these deeds, and he sent them out (Luke 9:1–6). Following on the heels of sending out the twelve, Jesus sent out the seventy-two to do similar deeds in the name of God (Luke 10:1–11). After his resurrection Jesus gave his followers authority to make disciples of all nations (Matt 28:19–20). To the defeated and down-cast Peter, Jesus gave the commission to feed his sheep (John 21:15).

Robert Logan writes of a four-stage process of leadership training that is reflective of how Jesus made leaders out of disciples. Initially, Jesus invited his disciples to watch him do ministry, and afterwards to debrief ("I do, you watch"). Following this, Jesus gave them some responsibility in carrying out ministry, while he retained the lion's share of the work ("I do, you help"). In a third step, Jesus gave them the greater responsibility while helping them ("You do, I help"). The last phase of leadership training had Jesus transfering all ministry responsibility to his disciples while he observed them in action ("You do, I watch"). After every phase of training, Jesus took time with his disciples to examine their ministry, thus increasing their learning curve.[8]

Good leaders invest in the empowerment of other leaders in such a way that the new leaders learn to accomplish what their mentors did— and more. Only in this way can there be foundation enough for the expansion and the multiplication of churches planted.

Characteristic 8: Intentional Multiplication

Jesus's beginnings as a church planter were modest, and he concentrated on the *one* person who was willing to deny himself, take up his cross and follow him (Luke 9:23). He began small in order to win big. Despite humble beginnings, Jesus focused from the start on reaching multiplication growth.

In many of his parables Jesus lets us understand that he was concentrating on expanding the kingdom of God, and thereby church planting. The result of one life given over to the life-giving power of the gospel could be thirty, sixty, or even one hundred times more effective than what that one person alone could have accomplished (Mark 4:20). The follower of Jesus is likened to a farmer who sows seed, which, while becoming fruitful stalks of wheat, provides a vast harvest (Mark 4:26–29). Jesus speaks of multiplication growth so amazing that out of a single seed a tree could grow whose branches become so expansive that all birds might find refuge in them (Mark 4:30–32). In all of these parables Jesus clearly underscores the correlation between modest beginnings and bountiful results. Despite the relatively unspectacular entrance of the kingdom of God, it will nevertheless grow to global proportions that will usher in the eschatalogical reign of Jesus Christ. This was indeed Jesus's intention when he gave his followers the commission to "go into all the world and preach the good news to all creation" (Mark 16:15)

Shortly before he was to leave this world, Jesus spoke to his disciples concerning the blessing that he intended for them to leave behind. "This is to my Father's glory, that you bear much fruit, showing yourselves to be my disciples" (John 15:8). He prophesied that they would accomplish *greater works* than he himself had (John 14:12). What did Jesus mean by the blessing of greater works? In the Acts of the Apostles, Luke records four times in which the Lord *added to* or *brought to* the church on

8. Logan, *Be Fruitful and Multiply*, 95.

account of the testimony of the first disciples (Acts 2:41–47; 5:14; 11:24). Luke shifts into overdrive recounting a growth that takes on the status of multiplication (Acts 6:1–7; 9:31; 12:34; 16:5). The number of disciples, as well as the number of churches, grows exponentially. These are the greater works to which Jesus referred in John's Gospel. This is conversion growth that becomes the basis for church planting multiplication.

Sometimes followers of Jesus can be more modest than he ever intended them to be. Instead of believing God for great and bountiful fruit, we become satisfied with what has christianly become the expected, the status quo. Robert Logan has a habit of saying, "The fruit of an apple tree is not an apple, but another apple tree."[9] In this regard, the fruit of a church is not a church that gets larger and larger, but a church that can reproduce itself.

Conclusion

Jesus is the superlative example of how he, in his own life and works, has given us a model to follow of how we can plant churches today. Jesus planted the first church, and at the same time trained his initial church planters. As we aspire to plant dynamic and stable churches, we will learn to learn from Jesus. Those of us who risk by faith the challenge of starting new churches according to Jesus will most certainly experience the greatest joys and some of the deepest pain that we have ever known. Nevertheless, it will be worth it all because Jesus, and the people around us that he has come to seek and to save, are worth the risk.

Today, as in the first century, Jesus is looking for that one person who loves the lost people around him, who puts God above all things in his life, and who would together with others of like-heartedness go forth to plant new churches.

Discussion highlights

Schindler's presentation outlined a very practical model for planting churches that multiply. But as with any model, there may be perceived gaps, some of which were highlighted during the discussion time.

9. Ibid., 24.

One participant reflected that many people on her team were introverts. As incarnational living seems to be a predominately extrovert activity, what does being missional and involved in people's lives look like for an introvert?

"The whole area of personality types and giftedness can be a hindrance to what God wants to do through us," answered Schindler. "You do not have to be captive to your personality. I am an introvert, but my calling is to be a church planter. I have learned to behave in a way that undergirds this commission. It drains me a lot, but I have ways of recovering.

"But another aspect is that we all have different gifts and need to use them to complement each other. Most evangelical churches do not know the gift mix of the church. For instance, around ten percent of the members will have the gift of an evangelist. They are amongst non-Christians, sharing the Gospel and seeing people come to Christ, yet their church may not have identified them as evangelists. They may not have the gift of putting together food and drinks and a party atmosphere as an outreach event. Other people in the church can do that, and invite the evangelists who can evangelize. We need to find ways to work as teams."

The issue of theological formation was also raised. Many denominations require people to have formal training before they can lead a church or church planting team. But this takes time, resulting in church planting activity looking more like addition than multiplication of churches. Where does theological formation fit in Schindler's model?

"I would rather have people who are doing it than only thinking about it," said Schindler. "Sometimes great theologically trained pastors have never actually led someone to Christ. If we solely emphasize formal theological education, we will never get to a movement, so we need a more comprehensive approach.

"My successor in a church I began is a trained classical musician. I discovered him as one of my small group leaders. He was unemployed, so I said, 'Great, let's use this time for you to do a six-month internship with me and then I will tell you if you have the gifts to be a pastor.' Six months later I was convinced he was capable, and the church called him to work alongside with me for two years and then be my successor. While he is not formally theologically trained, he is doing distance learning. He is a very gifted speaker and leader, and the church is growing."

One church planter in Southern Europe shared his experience of working with a denomination that "was very much about kingdom multiplication," and wary of formal theological education. He further explained that "this created a dichotomy which should not be there. True theological education is a form of discipleship and you can be very spiritual and academic at the same time. Our experience was that the second generation of leaders had gained a lot of information from the first pastor, but not all, and they had less biblical discernment. The third generation had half the biblical discernment of the first, and by the time you got to the fifth generation, you got sects."

"We do need good education," agreed Schindler, "but we also need the ability to do it on the ground—can the leader really make disciples and generate new churches? We need a healthy balance and to be experimental with many different models of theological education, both formal and informal."

And how big should the church planting team be?

"The size is not that important," Schindler answered, "but you need at least six to ten people to begin the journey. The most important thing, however, is not to confuse starting a worship service with starting a church.

"Michael Frost identified four main functions of the church—worship, discipleship, fellowship, and mission. In most evangelical circles, the worship service has the greatest influence on the other three areas. So if you have a problem with mission and reaching people for Christ, you hold seeker-friendly services. If your people do not feel connected, you try to solve it through fellowship times after the service. But if you are a church of less than forty people and you start a service, your goal will become surviving from one Sunday to the next. You will put eighty percent of your energy into the service and have no energy for mission left.

"But if you look at the Bible and the nature of God, it is the opposite. Mission is paramount, and begins to influence disciple-making, worship, and fellowship. In Acts 13, God interrupted the worship service to call for Paul and Barnabas to be set apart for mission. What is more important on the heart of God than worship? It is mission. Why? Because mission exists for the lone fact that worship does not yet exist. But if your team is centered on worship from the start, you will not get this kind of behavior, and you will struggle to make an impact on the people of your town."

II

CHURCH IN EUROPE

5

CULTURAL RELEVANCE

Johannes Reimer

EFFECTIVE CHURCH PLANTING IS rooted in both a biblical theology of the church and of the culture in which planting is expected. *The Willowbank Report* declares, ". . . no Christian witness can hope to communicate the gospel if he or she ignores the cultural factor."[1] George G. Hunter III calls the cultural barrier "the largest and most widespread barrier that keeps people from faith . . ."[2] And Martin Robinson, analyzing the decay of Christian churches in Great Britain, concludes that, "cultural blindness" of the Christian church "is responsible for a great deal of the failure of the church to make a significant impact on the society of which we are a part."[3]

All relevant empirical studies analyzing the success of church planting in Europe prove how important and central the correlation between cultural relevance and a solid theological foundation is to church planting. At the same time only a few of them define a theological framework.[4] Even fewer theologians discuss the cultural and societal relevance of content and form for the established church. The Bible and theology are used eclectically, and culture becomes an issue only for cross-cultural church planting. It is widely avoided as soon as church planting is done at home. As we will see, this is a fundamental mistake. Most of the church-planting

---

1. Lausanne Committee, *The Willowbank Consultation on The Gospel and Culture,* 13.

2. Hunter III, *Church for the Unchurched,* 59.

3. Robinson, *A World Apart,* 37.

4. Murray, *Church Planting,* 39; Reimer, *Die Welt umarmen,* 23.

efforts in Europe fail because of their cultural irrelevancy. Let us discuss this issue in detail.

What in the world is the church?

We begin with a question of theology, or more specifically ecclesiology. To my surprise, most church planting manuals describe at length the practice of church planting, the how-to of planting, but never really say what the church that they suggest to plant *is*. Some even reject discussing the issue of ecclesiology because their aim is not church planting but gospel planting, as David Watson claims.[5] The church will supposedly be developed by the culture itself as long as the gospel is properly preached. But did Jesus not say, "I will build my church . . ." (Matt 16:18)? And did he not commission his disciples, "As the father has sent me, I am sending you" (John 20:21)? Why then is it wrong to plant churches? And who says you can plant without really accounting for what you plant?

The fact is, avoiding answering the question of a proper theology of the church is responsible for much of the misery that Western churches go through. Dean M. Kelley already pointed to this fact in the seventies in his book, *Why Conservative Churches are Growing*. Studying churches in America from a sociological perspective, he envisions the main role of religion as giving meaning to life in society.[6] Meaning is understood only as an "embodied meaning." Churches are by definition such bodies, giving meaning to life through their existence. When the church loses sight of being a meaning-giving body, she sooner or later loses her vital role in society. George Barna is right when he states, "The downfall of the church has not been the content of its message, but its failure to practice those truths."[7] Disembodied meaning has no attraction.[8]

Churches are institutes of society. They are bodies in a cultural setting. But what for? Do they view themselves as meaning-giving institutes in the culture in which they exist? Does the surrounding culture understand what they present? Around the world, the absence of a defined theology of the church, a theological *Handlungstheorie*, at the beginning of a church planting project has led to copying what has been known at home.

5. Watson, *Gemeindegründungsbewegungen*, 30–31.

6. Kelley, *Why Conservative Churches are Growing*, 36–38.

7. Barna, *The Second Coming of the Church*, 5.

8. Kelley, *Why Conservative Churches*, 44–46.

Just look around you. Do Baptist churches in Africa planted by Southern Baptists from the USA not remind you of similar ecclesial set-ups in Texas? Does an Evangelical Free Church in Brazil planted by a missionary from Germany not seem to copy the German sending church? And what about the Koreans, or the Dutch, or the British? We could go on here forever. But the copies prove to be inadequate. They seldom carry a clearly defined mission that is set in terms understood by the people around them. Proper church planting needs solid theological foundations. And any sound theology is a reflected reality. Where theology is left to personal emotion or to a self-regulating process, a copy of what is already known will follow. This un-reflected approach is widely responsible for the limited success of church planting everywhere in world.

A responsible biblical theology of the church will soon discover the fact that the Bible knows nothing about one model, one structure, or one form of church. Eduard Schweizer's analysis of church models and forms in the New Testament leads him to conclude exactly this—there is no unified church model in the New Testament.[9] In my own study of the New Testament, I arrive at the same conclusion.[10] The Bible story presents to us a contextually adapted church reality, rather than a unified construct. No wonder we witness all these different ecclesiologies through the history of the church, developed around formal issues rather than gospel-centered content. An appropriate biblical ecclesiology will point us towards a vital correlation of church and culture. Biblical ecclesiology is *per se* contextual.

The praxis of growing churches around the world pragmatically supports my argument. David Watson rightly observes growing Church Planting Movements as being highly culturally adequate.[11] Ed Stetzer's study of Transformational churches in the US, examining two hundred-fifty churches and interviewing more than seven thousand pastors and fifteen thousand church members, concludes that the successful among them all show their deep cultural and societal involvement. Fifty-eight percent of their leadership subscribed to the following statement: "Everything we do is in the language and the culture of the people we are trying to reach."[12] Successful church plants seem to find ways to relate to their

9. Schweizer, *Gemeinde und Gemeindeordnung im Neuen Testament*, 7.

10. Reimer, *Die Welt umarmen*, 92.

11. Watson, *Gemeindegründungsbewegungen*, 30–31.

12. Stetzer and Reiner, *Transformational Church*, 59ff.

respective culture and context. Against this background, a strong call for contextual church planting and church growth is rising.[13] A contextual theology of church planting is needed; a theology which is both biblically firm and culturally adapted, at home with people we seek to reach with the Gospel of Christ.

It is easy to see where the tensions of such a contextual theory of church planting may occur. First, the biblical foundations of the church have been discussed throughout centuries of mission history. What church *is* theologically has always been subject to debate and discussion. Even more so, the clarification of the correlation between the gospel and culture has also been discussed. A culturally relevant, and at the same time biblically based theory of church planting has to find a way to correlate gospel and culture.

What in the world is culture?

But what is culture? Tim Chester and Steve Timmis rightly observe that, "Recognizing our missionary context means we can no longer assume that the church understands the culture."[14] But a proper understanding of culture is essential to a sound theory of church planting. More and more writers and practitioners of church planting stress this. So what is culture?

No other term has consumed so much energy as the term "culture." Scientists from a plethora of disciplines seek to define the concept. There are hundreds of definitions standing side by side and very often contradicting each other today. So what is culture?

The Latin term *cultura* suggested that culture is the outward expression of people in a given social space. Modern day ethnology or cultural anthropology, however, uses the term to describe the totality of existence of a given group of people in time and space.

In his book, *Primitive Culture*, published in 1871, the father of modern cultural anthropology, Edward B. Tylor, included knowledge, beliefs, arts, morals, rules, customs, moral behavior, and traditions of humans belonging to a certain society in his definition of culture.[15] Tylor's ideas form the basis for our current understanding of culture.

---

13. Reimer, *Die Welt umarmen*, 220ff; Stetzer, *Transformational Church*, 59ff.

14. Chester and Timmis, *Everyday Church*, 43.

15. Tylor, *Primitive Culture*.

The German evangelical anthropologist Lothar Käser defines culture as "strategies to form human existence."[16] Such a strategy will include norms of right and wrong, good and bad, and customs and behavior, as well as religious convictions dominating the daily life of the people. In other words, culture is "a way of life of a people," a "design for living,"[17] and a complex reality determining the life of an individual in the context of the society he or she belongs to. There can be no human life without culture. This means that an accepted culture covers everything in human life. Therefore, there is no un-cultural Christianity. Wherever humans try to express their ideas on life, they will do so in cultural terms.

There is another crucial aspect of culture. Anthropologists describe culture as a "multifaceted reality," and identify four levels: material, social, cognitive, and religious.[18]

Religious culture informs the cognitive, forming what we know as worldview; the cognitive defines the social culture, with her norms and rituals of social behavior; the social level is responsible for material objectification, forming what we see and materially have around us. The power distribution in a given culture runs from the religious to the material. To access a given culture you will, however, take the exact opposite route. You start on the material level, then you enter the social. Through long conversations you access the cognitive culture, and may then arrive in the religious world of the people. So, to understand a culture properly, we need time.

Communication between humans requires cultural clarity. Language itself is a cultural phenomenon. To preach the gospel and miss culture is equal to failure. Church planting must therefore address the question of culture. *The Willowbank Report* stated,

> Sensitive cross-cultural witnesses will not arrive at their sphere of service with a pre-packaged gospel. They must have a clear grasp of the "given" truth of the gospel. But they will fail to communicate successfully if they try to impose this on people without reference to their own cultural situation and that of the people to whom they go. It is only by active, loving engagement with the local people, thinking in their thought patterns, understanding their world-view, listening to their questions, and feeling their burdens, that the whole believing community (of

16. Käser, *Fremde Kulturen*, 37.

17. Lutzebak, *The Church and Cultures*, 59–60.

18. Ferraro, *Cultural Anthropology*, 18.

which the missionary is a part) will be able to respond to their need.[19]

This simple truth is easily pronounced; the praxis of mission in general, and of church planting in particular, proves how complicated the matter is. How do we relate the gospel to culture? What is the correlation between culture and gospel? How does the church relate, or even correlate, to culture? These are questions not easy to answer. Missiology, especially European missiology, might be reminded of the words of Lesslie Newbigin, who appeals to us with these words,

> It would seem, therefore, that there is no higher priority for the research work of missiologists than to ask the question of what would be involved in a genuinely missionary encounter between the gospel and this modern Western culture.[20]

Church planting, as well as all proclamation of the gospel, will require a working relation between the gospel and cultures, i.e. the church we plant and the context in which we work. A theologically and culturally adequate theory of church planting will, by definition, have to be contextual.

Gospel and culture—tension and chances

But what does this imply? Contextual theology correlates text and context, theology, and culture. This proves enormously difficult, and different churches at different times have proposed different views. In 1951, in his famous book, *Christ and Cultures*, H. Richard Niebuhr (1894-1962) classified different approaches into five paradigms. He defines culture as an "artificial, secondary environment" which man superimposes on the natural. It comprises language, habits, ideas, beliefs, customs, social organization, inherited artifacts, technical processes, and values.[21] Culture, says Niebuhr, is what the New Testament calls "the world." Niebuhr's book has been widely read and is still one of the basic books on the correlation of Christianity and culture. He wrote his book in difficult times, right

---

19. Lausanne Committee, *The Willowbank Consultation on The Gospel and Culture*, par. 3.

20. Newbigin, *Foolishness to the Greeks*, 3.

21. Niebuhr, *Christ and Culture*, 32.

after World War II, with a growing skeptical attitude towards Christian values, and it must be interpreted against this background.

Niebuhr's classification has been revisited by a number of scholars. John Howard Yoder,[22] as well as D. A. Carson, corrected a number of presumptions and conclusions of Niebuhr, especially challenging Niebuhr's identification of culture with the world as it is defined in the New Testament, and a number of incorrect assignments of historical developments to some of his paradigms.[23] Others have questioned the ecclesiology behind Niebuhr's types.[24] The author does not address the church as such, rather, individual Christians seem to be the target of his deliberations; after all, he speaks about *Christ and Culture* and not *church and Culture*. But the relationship of the church to culture is rather at stake. Still others criticized the inadequate Christology in Niebuhr's book.[25] And I would take issues with Niebuhr's taxonomy.

Despite all the critique, Niebuhr's paradigms are helpful to mark church planting theories and concepts when discussing the potential relevance for culture. This is even if the types may at times overlap, as the author himself pointed out, or if some might prove less adequate. The taxonomy of Niebuhr offers a framework in which church planting praxis may be screened for its cultural adequacy. Let us quickly screen the five types presented by the author and apply them to church planting practice.

Christ against Culture

We start with the first type in the taxonomy of Niebuhr, which he calls "Christ against Culture." The adherents of this position radically separate the kingdom of God and the kingdom of the world, based on passages like 1 John 2:15, which reads, "Do not love the world or anything in the world. If anyone loves the world, the love of the Father is not in him."

You may find supporters of this position among certain nonconformist Free Church traditions, such as the Mennonites, Baptists, and Pentecostals. Niebuhr rightly points to a number of theological issues with this position, the most critical of which is a potential tendency to

22. Yoder, "How H. Richard Niebuhr," 54–55.

23. Carson, *Christ & Culture*.

24. Guder, ed., *Missional Church*, 115; Clapp, *A Peculiar People*, 64–65.

25. Carter, "The Legacy of an Inadequate Christology."

spiritualize Christ, neglecting his role in creation and incarnation.[26] Similarly, there will be a high view of the church as an alternative community.

Church planting in the "Christ against Culture" paradigm comes with an anti-cultural spirit, introducing not only a new relationship between people and God, but also a complete new culture. The Christian church is taken out of its natural cultural environment, which is classified as the evil world and therefore the demonic realm. The church they build is clearly defined as a sanctified alternative community with a tendency towards a *societas perfecta*—a "perfect society." The result is an internally focused church investing most of her energy on her *missia interna*. Issues of sanctification dominate the day, with ethics and morals being much more important than mission and evangelization.

Most of the modern missionary movement in the colonial era followed this paradigm in so-called pagan countries. In Christendom, the concept was practiced by Free Church traditions who followed their Anabaptist forefathers. You find them today in exclusivist circles—in Roman Catholic and Orthodox, as well as Protestant denominations. In Germany, for instance, the so-called *Umsiedler*, the migrant churches from the former USSR, and certain Brethren and Pietistic traditions, will be easily identified as such.

The disinterest in culture of these churches leads to a complete detachment of the church from society. Evangelism is predominantly done among their own natural families, and church planting, wherever it is attempted, will be more interested in gathering the faithful, with most growth as transfer growth. I cannot perceive any effective impact on the growth of the global church coming out of this type of new churches in Europe today.

Christ of Culture

The opposite of rejection of culture as the evil world is a wide acceptance of the world. Niebuhr describes this position as follows,

> On the one hand they interpret culture through Christ, regarding those elements in it as most important which are most accordant with his work and person; on the other hand they understand Christ through culture, selecting from the Christian

26. Ibid., 81.

doctrine about him such points as seem to agree with what is best in civilization.[27]

Reading Christ as the ultimate fulfillment of culture tends to lead the adherents of this position to accommodation, inviting culture into their system of belief. Pluralistic theologies can develop, and the danger of syncretism is obvious. Culture, as Newbigin rightly reminds us, is never neutral.[28]

You will find church planting theories following such a path in all nominally Christian countries with their concepts of State Church and *Volkskirche*, or nowadays in the theories of the so-called "Common Ground" theologies. This approach corresponds with the purported anthropological model of contextual theology as described by Steven Bevans.

What are the effects of applying this model? Identifying Culture and Gospel leads to a low theology of the church and an underestimation of ecclesiological issues. Salvation in Christ is put ahead of becoming a member of the Body of Christ, and belonging to a certain culture is viewed as a substitute for active membership in the church. Consequently, the idea of the church will be radically simplified, and its structures will be, in principle, culturalized. In Common Ground theologies, for instance, a mosque may then become a substitute for what we call Church, and the need of an extra church plant is dropped altogether.

Christ above Culture

The third paradigm suggested by Niebuhr puts Christ above culture. This view promotes a synthesis of Christ and culture. God has created the world as good, and although nature and culture are fallen, they are still subject to God. Niebuhr states, "We cannot say 'either Christ or culture,' because we are dealing with God in both cases, yet we must not say 'both Christ and culture,' as though there were no great distinction between, them."[29] Christ goes beyond culture. The kingdom of God is not from this world. But in his commands he directs us to act in culture. The church will, therefore, always be a part of the world and at the same time will stay above the world.

27. Ibid., 83.
28. Newbigin, *The Open Secret*, 161–62.
29. Reimer, *Die Welt umarmen*, 122.

The potential for danger is at hand. The church may in such a view soon claim authority over and above the culture; a view prominent in Roman Catholic as well as Orthodox lands. In Roman Catholicism, before the Vatican Council II, the Church was viewed as a *societa perfecta,* a mystery of the incarnation of Christ in the world. Consequently, church planting, the *plantatio ecclesiae,* became an instrument of political control as the territory evangelized was claimed for the church. All missionary activity on such territory is then declared as proselytism, and thus heretical.

Church planting in this paradigm means denominational political expansion. While it seldom happens today, you can observe examples, for instance, in the Ukraine, in Orthodox attempts to establish their own canonical territories and claim national Orthodox and political identity free from the external dominance of the Moscow Patriarchate, and thus of the Russian government.

Christ and Culture in Paradox

In his fourth paradigm, Niebuhr sets Christ and culture in paradox. The paradox view differs from the preceding one by maintaining that while both Christ and culture claim our loyalty, the tension between them cannot be reconciled by any lasting synthesis. Martin Luther's doctrine of the two kingdoms or realms subscribes to such a view. According to Luther, Christians live in two realms: the left-hand realm of the world—the state—is governed by law, and the right-hand realm of God—the church—is governed by grace. These two realms exist side by side in paradox, never to be resolved in this life. Christians will, as long as they live on Earth, be both sinners and saints, *simul justus et peccator,* and therefore subject to both kingdoms.

The paradigm is widely shared by Lutheran churches. As logical and helpful as the distinction between the two realms of life might be, it becomes problematic in practical church life. By assigning the societal involvement of Christians to the state, the church is left with the private spirituality of its members, and soon loses societal relevance. Today, most of those churches following the paradox paradigm seem to be outside the public discourse on faith and religion.

The adherents of this paradigm plant churches for the spiritual formation of their members. The church creates the space in which the individual Christian's relationship to God is shaped. It is personal, individual, and a matter of heart and soul. Day-to-day life, however, takes place in society. The church may inform her members about life in society, but she will not interfere. The responsibility to form a meaningful society is not hers, but rather a commission of God to the state.

It is easy to see that the idea behind the construct is a Christian society. But in post-Christianity this is becoming, of course, less and less our reality. The secular state is no longer willing to subscribe to Christian values, and secularized post-Christians will not see much sense in a religion outside of their day-to-day life. Therefore, church planting in a paradox paradigm is stuck. Very few projects develop in a promising way, and where they do, de-churched people are re-won.

Christ the Transformer of Culture

Niebuhr's last option affirms the universality of sin, but at the same time maintains that cultures can be changed and transformed. He does not suggest that humanity can be totally restored into God's image on Earth, but the Church can become an agent of transformation leading to a better society.

A number of today's approaches to church planting and church growth follow the pattern of such a paradigm. Ed Stetzer and Thom S. Rainer, for instance, strongly believe that "transformation is at the heart of God's mission to humanity."[30] As a result, they call their ideal church "transformational church," because it "focuses on the Gospel's ability to change people."[31] By people they mean "individuals, churches, and societies." The authors claim,

> In TC (transformational church) we found principles that transform people to look like Christ, congregations to act like the body of Christ and communities to reflect the kingdom of God.[32]

Chester and Timmis plead for an "Everyday Church" transforming neighborhoods.[33] And society-relevant church planting developed in

30. Stetzer and Reiner, *Transformational Church*, 3.

31. Ibid., 10.

32. Ibid., 33.

33. Chester and Timmis, *Everyday Church*.

the Philippines[34] or Germany follows a similar pattern.[35] In fact, most of the so-called *missional churches* tend to accept the transformational paradigm of Niebuhr.

The development of such churches is promising, but is this paradigm thus an ultimate solution to the tension between Church and cultures?

Towards a comprehensive relationship of church and culture

Critical voices of Niebuhr's taxonomy point to his undifferentiated definition of culture. Culture is never just good or bad. And culture is neither totally determined, nor neutral. Yoder writes,

> Some elements of culture the Church categorically rejects (pornography, tyranny, cultic idolatry). Other dimensions of culture it accepts within limits (economic production, commerce, the graphic arts, paying taxes for peaceful civil government). To still other dimensions of culture Christian faith gives a new motivation and coherence (agriculture, family life, literacy, conflict resolution, empowerment). Still others it strips of their claims to pose autonomous truth and value, and uses them as vehicles of communication (philosophy, language, Old Testament ritual, music). Still other forms are created by the Christian churches (hospitals, service to the poor, generalized education).[36]

Culture here is obviously never just the bad world Christians have to flee from. Yoder's critique on Niebuhr's typology seems, however, to read into his systematization of sharply defined definitions of culture. Niebuhr himself radically relativizes such a view by believing that all five options may exist in parallel and serve different contexts well.[37] Such contexts may even exist in one and the same social space. Still, Yoder's critique helps to clarify issues. Cultures are never monolithic, so the churches' attitude towards culture can also never be set in stone. The world around us is both corrupted by sin and yet in some instances shaping life in a positive way. The church will, as Os Guinness rightly suggests, do both:

---

34. See for instance: Maggay, *Transforming Society.*
35. See for instance: Reimer, *Die Welt umarmen.*
36. Yoder, "How H.Richard Niebuhr reasoned," 69.
37. Ibid., 231.

affirm culture where the culture is serving life, and reject and transform culture where culture is corrupted.[38]

If a church radically subscribes to the one and only paradigm, she will soon be endangered to develop a potentially problematic model of church life, which again endangers growth and mission. Niebuhr's taxonomy helps point to possible extremes which need to be carefully calculated before being put into practice. But it also opens perspectives for certain emphases in a given context. The church of Christ will stand against a corrupted and sinful culture and yet accept and even affirm those aspects of culture which are in symphony with God's word. While she rejects, for instance, any occult praxis in Islam, she will embrace hospitality in Muslim societies. While she might decide to establish a church in an Indian context in the form of an ashram, she will reject certain meditation practices, or the devastating attitude of the Hindu culture towards women. Not all culture is transformable, as well as not all culture is in need of transformation. Christian mission derives its strength through the fact that God's eternal word may become flesh (John 1:1–14) and live among people without being corrupted by sin (Heb 4:15). Incarnation into human culture is possible. Jesus is the best evidence for this. Contextualization is not only possible—it is needed in order to win people for Christ, as the apostle Paul says in 1 Corinthians 9:19–22.

Incarnational ecclesiology

Let us summarize. Church planting following the path of cultural relevance will by definition be guided by an incarnational ecclesiology that is a church theory responsibly addressing issues of theology of the church and issues of cultural adaption. Not surprisingly, the call for such a theory has become a critical issue for those interested in mission and church planting. A healthy church will not automatically grow out of a culture confronted with the gospel, as David Watson proposes.[39] Yes, David J. Bosch's famous affirmation that "the Christian faith is intrinsically incarnational" stands on its own.[40] The Church of Christ has proved to have an enormous ability to adapt to different cultural settings in time and space.

---

38. Guinness and Wells, "Global Gospel, Global Era; Christian Discipleship and Mission in the Age of Globalization."

39. Watson, *Gemeindegründungsbewegungen*, 31.

40. Bosch, *Transforming Mission*, 190–91.

But church history also witnesses that many such movements were led astray by the naïve belief that conversion alone is enough.

Leading people to Jesus and leaving them alone with their culture, is potentially dangerous. Jesus wants to shape his *church*—not culture. He says, "I will build my church, and the gates of hell will not overcome it" (Matt 16:18). The Church is sent to fulfill the great missionary commission (Matt 28:18–20). Cultural adaptation must follow a conscious decision and an informed way of incarnation in order to be adequate. Incarnation is in many ways a dangerous journey, as Michael Frost rightly reminds us.[41] You do not want to leave the issue to chance. But incarnation is unavoidable. There will never be a church without cultural appearance. So we do well by accepting the fact and working on models of incarnational ecclesiology for those who are ready to go and plant churches in the world around us. It is a needed theoretical foundation for successful church planting.

In their analysis of more than 50,000 US churches, the researchers of the Rainer Group underline the fact that churches and their leaders need an outwardly "focused vision" in order to grow.[42] The community's needs define the vision and the programs of the church.[43] Thus a differentiated, but yet in principle positive relationship between church and culture is required.

Church planters seeking ways to establish a church which is relevant to society, with an aim to transform society, will follow a missional methodology whereby "missional" stands for "holistic" in the true sense of the word. They will serve people in their material and social need, and by doing so will establish a relationship of growing trust. As Stetzer's study on transformational churches shows, social engagement leads to relational engagement, which in turn may open opportunities to share the gospel.[44] The key concept here is relationship. According to Marvin Mayers, mission requires basic trust between those doing mission and those who are being reached.[45] Viggo Søgaard puts the question of trust before all other questions to be asked in missionary communication.[46]

---

41. Frost, *Exiles*, 11–15.

42. Rainer, *Breakout Churches*, 64.

43. Ibid., 120–22.

44. Stetzer, *Transformational*, 69f.

45. Mayers, *Christianity Confronts Culture*.

46. Søgaard, *Media in Church and Mission*, 45.

Trust between people will only be established in relationships which are defined by the cultural norm and social organization of a given cultural context. You cannot avoid the question of adaption by intentionally establishing trust, because trust does not just happen. Stetzer summarizes his observations on growing transformational churches by declaring "relational intentionality" as a major issue in church growth.[47] The church which is transforming society in the power of the gospel will intentionally work towards establishing relationships and creating space in which such relationships develop and grow. She will, as Chester and Timmis say in their well-written book on what they call "Everyday Church," "eat with the non-Christians, hobby with the non-Christians, volunteer with the non-profits, participate in city events and serve neighbors."[48] In other words, the mission of the church is determined by loving Jesus, the people, and life in their everyday situations.

47. Stetzer, *Transformational*, 102ff.
48. Chester and Timmis, *Everyday Church*, 106-7.

6

CHURCH PLANTING CONNECTED TO SOCIETY

Johannes Reimer

OUR DELIBERATIONS IN THE preceding chapter lead us to propose an adapted variation of the so-called Missional Praxis Cycle developed by the faculty of missiology at the University of South Africa.[1] According to the cycle, the mission of the church always starts with involvement, meaning *an intentional decision of the missionary to enter a given context and accept missionary responsibility for the people living here.* Simply living with the people defines a platform to plant a church among the people. Here is the basic structure of the Missional Cycle:

Missional Cycle (Basic structure)

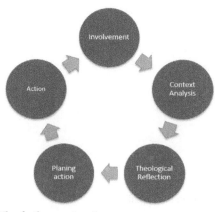

1. Kritzinger, *Who do they say I am?*, 149.

Involvement is followed by context analysis. Coexistence requires knowledge of those living in a given social space, effective mission is an informed action, and serving the need of a community requires knowledge of the felt needs. We propose that the context analysis must cover all levels of culture—the material, social, cognitive, and religious—so that we know what the people have, what they do, how they think, and what they believe. In other words, we learn to understand their culture, the bad and the good, and the corrupted and life-giving aspects of it.

Now knowing the context, we turn to God's revelation in Scripture and think about the context. We will not subscribe to culture that is foreign to God's will, but at the same time we embrace every aspect of the culture which is in accordance with God's will. We see the challenges and we see the chances of the context for the proclamation of the gospel in deed and word.

Only after a sound theological reflection are practical steps of action considered. This is best done in a framework of community development. We will intentionally seek to establish trust and relationships with the people we target. In practice, this means that we start by serving them and alongside them, seeking a meaningful dialog and conversation on issues of the context. In serving the context together, we enter a relationship, a life dialog. People around us will open up their lives and begin to participate in our lives, and an everyday community in which Christians participate develops. And the most powerful tool of mission will be used—witness. Observing our lives, people will start to ask questions and this leads to a conversation about values and beliefs starts, or maybe even a debate, a discourse. Such a conversation will potentially lead to direct evangelism. Our neighbors may decide to follow Jesus and join the church.

Process of society-relevant evangelism

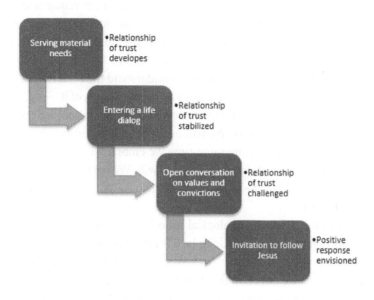

A church plant following such a pattern understands the context, joins the community in solving the felt needs of the community, and enters a creative dialog on values, convictions, and beliefs by offering a daily alternative in life; thus it earns the right to invite people to follow Jesus and join the church. Is this church against culture? Well, in part she is. Does she see Christ in culture? Yes, in part she does. But instead of overstressing the one or the other, she actively gets involved in a process of change and transformation, guided by her Lord and the gospel principles revealed to her in scripture. Is she culturally relevant and theologically sound? I tend to believe she is!

Planting a transformational church in a context

How do we apply this in practice? What steps will a missionary team take to plant a theologically sound and culturally relevant church?

Know your territory

Following the cycle, the planting team first asks, "Where does the Lord want us to start a church?" Ecclesia is a local agent of God, so planting will be done locally. A locality is clearly marked by a social space, a culturally and geographically defined territory called *ethnos* in Matthew 28:19–20. The church is called to disciple a social space and people living in a clearly defined locality, be it a village, town, or a part of the city. The disciples of Christ are the light of the world, clearly marked by Jesus as "city" (Matt 5:13–15). And this light is set on the highest place in order that it might shine for everyone. All the people living in this territory are subject to evangelization. The church is not allowed to pick and choose the more receptive and leave the others out. Ecclesia can never be guided by a homogeneous unit principle (HUP) as it was proposed by Donald McGavran and his school of church growth.[2] Such a principle may help to sharpen our missionary communication, but never determine our task. It is, as critics of McGavran pointed out, biblically unjustifiable and theologically problematic.[3]

HUP oriented approaches to church planting and church growth ask for a specific category of people they plan to reach with the Gospel, and tend to foster transfer growth rather than reach those who have never known Christ. Concentrating one's efforts on the like-minded will automatically attract Christians rather than non-Christians. Such approaches are to a large extent responsible for a middle class captivity of the evangelical churches in the Western world. Some speak of a "suburban captivity," referring to the fact that most of the evangelical churches in the USA concentrate on middle class people living in the suburbs.[4] Ecclesia, as Jesus proposes, will in contrast serve all people in the territory. A proper, biblically based approach to building churches, therefore, must be territorial.

Involvement presupposes the knowledge of where you want to become involved. Such knowledge comes first and foremost from the Lord of mission himself. He calls us into his mission. We are his workmanship, prepared to do works he has predesigned for us to do (Eph 2:10). We are

2. McGavran, *Understanding Church Growth*, 199.

3. See Padilla, *Mission between time*, 168; Shenk. *Exploring Church Growth.* 1973; DuBose. *How Churches Grow in an Urban World*; Conn. *Planting and Growing Urban Churches*, 135ff.

4. Reimer, *Hereinspaziert. Willkommenskultur und Evangelisation*, 97ff.

determent in our mission. There is NO freedom of choice. Picking and choosing what *we* want normally leads nowhere. The second missionary journey of the apostle Paul is the best example of this (Acts 14–15). He decides to go on a mission trip, he does not want to take John Mark with him, he runs into a separating argument with Barnabas, and he experiences how the Holy Spirit closes one door after the other in front of his face. It is only in Troas that the Spirit of God grants Paul a vision of the Macedonian man inviting him to come and help. This calling became the turning point for the missionary journey. Church planters are such missionaries. They will have to follow God´s call into a certain social space. Knowing where the Lord wants us to plant a church is crucial! Church growth will always correlate to God´s call. It is Jesus, after all, who builds his church (Matt 18:18). We are just his workers.

Two years ago I was invited to a small church in Cologne, Germany as an adviser to help them sort out issues of future mission and evangelism. My first question was whether they had identified their territory. "Where do you think the Lord expects you to locate your church in Cologne?" I asked. The church had no answer. So we began to pray. The Lord revealed their calling to the congregation through words and images of knowledge. In our prayer time, one person saw a huge yellow wall, another saw a park full of huge Adidas shoes, someone else was thinking of blue doors in a big building, and still others heard the sound of a highway nearby while they prayed. There were other words, images, and impressions, and I wrote all those things on a board. After prayer, I invited the church to go into the city and find all this. And indeed, the brothers and sisters in Christ found the huge yellow wall painted by the German Post Office, opposite to a park in which Adidas was advertising their newest shoes, and there was a school building with dozens of blue doors near a highway. The church prayed again and again over the marked territory and then decided to move all their activity to this part of Cologne. Miracle after miracle happened, and today the church is greatly thankful for having been obedient to God´s call.

"I have never before been so excited about God´s work in growing his kingdom in the church he entrusted to me," says the pastor of this congregation. "We have always invited the Lord to come to us and bless us, but for the first time we went to him, and his blessing is continuing."

Involvement also requires knowing who your team members are. Before you start any missionary action, take your team through an analysis of their gifts. This follows the four levels of culture we have discussed earlier. So you ask, what does your team bring to the context in terms of material, social, cognitive, and spiritual resources, gifts, and competencies?[5]

Analyze the context

Knowing the territory where you are called to establish a church and what potential you bring to the task, you will undertake the next step—to analyze the context. In order to do so, you need to realize that social and cultural space is never neutral. The German missiologist Peter Beyerhaus suggested that we view the world in a tri-polar way.[6] According to Beyerhaus, the world is created and governed by God, managed and formed by humans, and corrupted by Satan and his demons. Contextual analysis will have to help the planting team (a) to see where God is among the people they plan to reach with Gospel, (b) where humans are in their attitudes, actions, and desires, and (c) where Satan is actively corrupting culture and destroying lives. This information is enormously helpful. By definition, as a church planting team you will want to cooperate with God, see where people need your assistance and service, and where they may even be of assistance to you, and you want to know where Satan is prepared to fight a spiritual battle.

Proper contextual analysis uses two perspectives. It looks at the context from a sociological perspective and applies social analysis through using the tools of participant observation and interviewing experts of the context. On the other hand, it asks for God´s perspective in prayer and prophetic vision. You will observe, describe, listen to men and God, and draw conclusions.[7]

Now knowing your territory, your potential, and the material, social, cognitive, and spiritual condition of the people, you turn to God and reflect theologically on what is there. Let the Lord show you where your limited potential might be of greatest help to the people. You are the light of the world; your light is good to enlighten the darkest spots of society. Where would be the best place to start? There might be some guidelines for a solid decision.

---

5. Reimer, *Hereinspaziert*, 80–96.

6. Beyerhaus, *Zur Theologie der Religionen im Protestantismus*, 100–104.

7. Faix, *Kontextanalyse*, chapters 2–5.

First, look for the best possible spot in the city, "the highest place" where your light will make the biggest impression on the people. Such a place is always the darkest point where people have no way out. They may be aware that this problem can only be solved by a miracle. Only God can do miracles, and even some of the most unbelieving will have questions, and a possible conversation about God and faith might start. The point of departure for evangelism that is relevant to society is never the biggest possible ministry. It is rather the most impossible for the locals, regardless of its size.

Second, start with the material need and invite others to work with you. Loving service to people in need provides a foundation for evangelism. Society relevant church planting will look for inclusive ways to work *with* the people rather than *for* the people.

To illustrate this principle, let me tell you the story of our current church planting project in Western Germany. We did an analysis of the context and found out that the biggest problem in our city is the unemployment of migrants. Families are not able to feed their children three times a day. Our potential analysis revealed excellent managerial skills and gifts of faith and leadership. Reflecting on the context and our abilities before God, we concluded that we would start a kitchen to provide food for the needy families. As soon as the decision was made, we invited all willing people in the city to participate. It did not take long as the need to organize food for more than one hundred families became obvious. We gathered for prayer, and a number of non-Christian and even Muslim friends were with us. They observed us praying. The same evening God reacted with a miracle. Unexpectedly, we were offered tons of food. Everybody was amazed. After the third and fourth time, some of our volunteers came to us and started to ask questions about the power of prayer. Others stopped teasing us and took our faith seriously. Working with people for the common good gives them a chance to see the potential of our faith in Jesus Christ, and this is a place where trust develops.

Third, starting with joint service for the community will naturally lead us to conversations and dialog on issues of life. Be prepared to answer questions. People volunteering to work for the community will soon communicate with one another and a life dialog will follow. In our case, non-Christian and Muslim volunteers lost their negative attitude towards evangelicals like us. Slowly we became friends. In order to foster the dialog we opened an international café where we meet and discuss issues of everyday life. Additional projects followed, and then the first friends started to visit us in our homes. We were finally asked the first questions about our faith, and thus a conversation on issues of faith began.

Starting with a community development project is very important. Community development is historically a Christian enterprise, started in the nineteenth century by active Christians in the needy quarters of Chicago, London, and Hamburg, and it now represents the basis of all social work.[8] Catalytic community development, where the agents of development inspire the people in the context to join hands in developing their community, has especially promising potential for church planting. Our example proves the case. As a small church plant we have started projects together with the people, and today the same people are starting to join the church. Our vision is simple: join the people in their need and they will potentially join you in your faith.

A process that takes time

Evangelism is a process, and the process, of course, takes time. It takes both the gospel proclamation in life and deed, and the gospel proclamation in words. It builds on basic trust and earns the right to confront people with the gospel in time and space. In Germany, you may wait for two to three years until the first people start to be interested in our faith. But then it is genuine. And your church is accepted as a change agent in the context. You have become light to the city, people started to trust you, and you have earned the right to call them to follow Jesus and invite them to join you in the church.

Discussion highlights

Reimer's presentation outlined the five paradigms of "Christ and Culture" and applied them to church planting. The discussion that followed explored several issues relating to these paradigms.

One participant wondered whether there was a "church culture" which we needed to be aware of. Reimer agreed that ecclesiology is cultural but that many churches do not recognize it as such. Instead they

8. Cf. Reimer, *Die Welt gewinnen*, 276–77; Lingenscheid & Wegner, *Aktivierende Gemeinwesenarbeit*, 271–73.

believe that "culture is the world out there and that is bad, and we are different." Christians can also talk about a "Christian culture" and relate it to their own context. They are surprised when Christians from the other parts of the world have a culture that is different from theirs: the African Christian culture is different from the German Christian culture, and so on. Christianity is cultural, and theology and ecclesiology is by definition cultural.

"Is the Gospel itself cultural?" In answer to this question, Reimer explained that he understood the Gospel as the *saving act* of Christ. "The very act is not cultural; it is a life event, a reality. It happens in time and space and leads to an experience [of salvation] which is above all culture. It is repeated in all cultural settings. But as soon as I talk about the Gospel, I use language and apply cultural terms. This is where the problem comes in, because we have to dress the Gospel in cultural terms to make it understandable to people around us. This is an issue of contextualization."

The issue of language was raised again with a question about how Reimer's model of church planting compared with emerging church. "I think the terminology has been used in many ways," he said. "In the best sense of the word, an emerging church is a church that is in the midst of a context, which emerges among the people. I go and discover a context that God sends me to. I find out what the context needs. I take theologically based action to solve issues of the context. I become part of the context. And the best way to do meaningful church planting in post-Christian Europe is through community development, because I emerge out of the context."

Many of the participants work in countries where the Protestant Church is in a minority and not necessarily accepted by the general population. While acknowledging the importance of community engagement, they thought it would be harder to put it into practice in their context—in particular by asking the town mayor or other officials to be involved in church meetings where a project is evaluated for its community impact. They wanted to know what it was like for Reimer when he made his first efforts.

"I expected a negative reaction because that was all I knew," he explained. "We had never tried going to the mayor or school director before and I thought they might even refuse to meet me. But this didn't happen. In the six years I have taken this kind of approach, neither I, nor the group of trainers I work with, have had a totally negative reaction from state officials. I have introduced the concept to other countries including Norway, Finland, and most of the Eastern European countries, and I am still waiting for a completely negative reaction."

7

UNDERSTANDING EUROPE TODAY, AND SIGNS OF HOPE

Jeff Fountain

How do we view the state of Europe today? As Evangelicals, we lack a tradition of viewing Europe as a whole. Often we have seen "Europe" as a threat, if not "the Beast" of Revelation. Today's debates about the political future of Europe have roots in the north/south, Protestant/Catholic historic division of the continent. The further north one travels the more negative about "Europe" one tends to become. Catholics by-and-large have tended to see the bigger picture, belonging to a global church. Protestants emerged as members of territorial churches (*Landeskirchen*) with national synods, and are focused nationally. Evangelicals tend to be members of local churches, affiliated or independent, but primarily with a local focus. Catholics see woods; Protestants see trees; Evangelicals often only see branches.

In our evangelical tradition, we basically train *local* church pastors. Hence the leadership of the evangelical movement is primarily *locally*-focused. Where then are we encouraged to see the big picture, or to engage with the mega-issues?

During the Second World War, Robert Schuman spent much time asking himself questions about the kind of Europe that would please God. After escaping from imprisonment in Germany, he went underground in France for the last two years of the occupation and prepared for the post-war era that he knew had to come. As a devout believer, he wanted to see Europe become a "community of peoples deeply rooted in Christian values."

His vision remains a challenge to us today. Do *we* have any vision for Europe? Jean Monnet, Schuman's close colleague in the formation of the European Coal and Steel Community, once declared, "I have always been a believer in Harry Truman's saying: *where there is no vision the people perish.*" Harry Truman?? Obviously, Monnet did not know his Bible. We who know our Bibles recognize this as Solomon's saying, right?

But Monnet at least had vision for Europe. What vision do we "Bible-students" have for Europe? If none, then what, according to Harry Truman, would result? Could this explain the state of the church in Europe today? Let me try to sketch the state of Europe today in terms of *one book, two splits, three images, four apps, five crises, six Europeans,* and *seven signs of hope.*

One book

The single greatest influence on the development of European culture and society has been *the Bible.* When Paul arrived in Greece, he started a revolution that was to transform the peninsula we now call Europe. Messengers bringing the story of this book about one God and his one Son Jesus Christ introduced a totally new worldview; of God and of man, of the spiritual realm and the physical realm, of the dignity and value of human life, of linear history and time as past, present, and future. This understanding transformed the lifestyles of people groups from Armenia to Ireland, and from Cyprus to Iceland. Jesus became worshipped in many different languages by Greeks, Romans, Gauls, Celts, Scots, Angles, Saxons, Franks, Friesians, Allemani, Suevi, Slavs, Rus, Balts, and, eventually, Vikings.

This book shaped our art and music, agriculture and gardening, architecture and design, language and literature, law and justice, politics and democracy, healthcare and hospitality, education and training, ethics and morality, marriage and family, science and technology, and business and economics far more than any other single influence. We do not have to be believers to recognize this fact. Even arch-atheist Richard Dawkins says we cannot understand European history without understanding Christianity and the Bible. At the recent Hay Literary Festival in Wales, atheist professor Steve Jones told his largely secular audience that, while it was easy to be sarcastic about religion, many thought that the New Testament was the finest political document ever written. Our entire society was based on tenets of the New Testament, he added.

In light of the above, if the Bible is not given its due place in our European school curricula, then this must be the result of either ignorance or prejudice. It cannot be professionalism!

Europe is the "continent" that has been most shaped by this book, and paradoxically also by the rejection of this book. For, from the time of the Enlightenment onwards, various "-isms" have attempted to replace the Bible as a source of worldview: rationalism, humanism, socialism, communism, fascism, and secularism, just to name a few. And yet unconsciously they have assumed presuppositions drawn from biblical revelation, such as a linear view of time, the dignity of man, and the purpose of life. Even in reacting to the Bible, these "-isms" still assume certain biblical insights, revealing their parasitical origins.

Two splits

In both the eleventh and sixteenth centuries major church splits occurred, which even to this day continue to shape our headlines. Western Europeans are far more familiar with the latter split, better known as *the Reformation*. Or, should we say "Reformations," as we need to also recognize the Catholic Reformation and the Radical Reformation, movements which similarly brought major upheavals in political, economic, social, and spiritual areas of life across Western Europe.

In 2017, the 500th anniversary of the Protestant Reformation will be commemorated in many places and ways—hopefully not as a triumphant Protestant event, but as a respectful occasion looking at the positive legacy of this period. We must emphasize that what we have in common is greater than what separates us, while recognizing the pain and suffering caused by this split in the Body of Christ, which resulted in decades of religious wars.

Much reconciliation has been effected in recent years, especially through the efforts of recent popes. This has included the signing of the Joint Declaration of the Doctrine of Justification (JDDJ) in 1999 between Catholic and Lutheran leaders, and the unprecedented declaration by Pope Benedict XVI in St Peter's Square that "Luther was right" about justification by faith.

The earlier split of 1054, called *the Great Schism*, is less known in the west. The profound influence of this family feud within the Body of Christ, occasioned by an argument over the Trinity (whether the Spirit proceeded from the Father or from the Father and the Son), has created a deep spiritual fault line across Europe from the Baltic states in the north to the Balkans in the south, with profound social, economic, and political consequences. Was it coincidental that the tragic flight MH17 ended right on this fault-line when it was shot down in August 2014? As another example, Vladimir Putin is deeply resentful of the role Pope John Paul II played in the demise of communism and thus the implosion of the Soviet Union. As we commemorate the centennial of the First World War, we recall how it was triggered right on this fault line in Sarajevo. The more recent Balkan wars were, of course, fought across this line as well. NATO, the UN, and the EU are powerless to heal this spiritual rift; it is a matter for spiritual leaders.

The story of Europe cannot be understood without recognition of the deep impact of both of these ruptures in church history and their ongoing influence on politics, economics, and society. As major failures on the part of the church to flesh out a witness of unity and love, these splits and their ensuing phases of violence have given many cause to reject the Christian message and to seek alternative worldviews.

Three images

Fast forward to 2014, and we will describe Europe in terms of three images. The first is *a vase of wilting tulips*, ready to be thrown out. When placed in the vase they would have been truly beautiful, but from the moment they were cut off from their roots they were doomed.

Roots nurture and stabilize. Yet European society cut off from its Judeo-Christian roots is a cut-flower civilization. Hence, instead of drawing life, it draws from a culture of death. Europeans have decided to die out. Abortion, euthanasia, suicide, and low birth-rates all contribute to a crisis of demography. No European country has the birth rate of 2.1 sufficient to sustain its own population. This fact carries serious consequences for Europe's future—economically, socially, and politically. Yet a neo-liberal, secular pursuit of constant economic growth and ever expanding GDP without regard to relational implications tends to undermine sustainability.

A second image of Europe is that of *a field full of rocks, old tree stumps, and junk.* No farmer would go out to sow seed in such a field without preparing the soil first by taking away the rocks, stumps, and junk, and then plow the ground. Yet some efforts of evangelism attempt to do just this. Methods that are fruitful elsewhere in the world are sometimes attempted in Europe without recognizing the different state of the soil.

Yet a third image is of *a squatted house.* Most Europeans today are like squatters living in a house without being prepared to pay the rent. They have no idea of the Judaic-Christian foundations of the European house, or they try to live in denial of them.

Four apps

How do we then approach such a continent in need with eyes of faith, hope, and vision? Let me suggest four "apps" to download into our hearts and minds.

The first is the *God's will* app. Perhaps I'm being very simplistic, but it seems logical to me that it is always God's will for his will to be done. In other words, it is never God's will for his will not to be done. So why do so many Christians seem to believe that it is God's will for his will not to be done in Europe? That Europe is doomed to become "the beast"? That things *have* to become worse and worse towards the end of times? When Jesus taught us to pray the Lord's Prayer, was he really serious? Did he really want to see the Father's Kingdom come, the Father's will being done on earth, in Europe, as it is in heaven? Or was he just teasing us?

When we believe the future has been predetermined in this way, we find ourselves caught like deer in the headlights of a car, paralyzed by fatalism and pessimism, believing we can do nothing to change the future. This can become a self-fulfilling prophecy in which things do get worse—not because God willed it, but because we failed in our role as salt and light in the world.

The second app is that of *the wheat and the tares.* Jesus told the parable of the man who sowed wheat in his field, but his enemy came at night and sowed weeds, or tares. The two grew up together and the man's servants asked if they should pull the tares out. No, the man said, wait until the harvest time. Good and bad things are happening all around us. The media tends to emphasize the negative. The paradox of the wheat and tares is that both grow together. Look at the twentieth century, surely the worst, and the century of Satan! Think of the two world wars, a devastating depression, a cold war, the holocaust, the invention of the atom bomb, and names like Lenin, Stalin, Hitler, Mao Tse Tung, and Pol Pot. What a terrible century! Yet at the same time, it surely was the best century ever for the spread of God's Kingdom! It began with revivals in Wales, Azusa Street in Los Angeles (the beginning the Pentecostal movement), in East Africa, Indonesia, and Argentina. It saw the world's largest churches emerging in countries like Korea, where the gospel had only come a century ago, or in Nigeria, Brazil, and other non-western nations. China surprised the world when it opened up to reveal a large, dynamic, growing church. More people came into the Kingdom than in all the other centuries put together! Surely this was the century of the Spirit! Wheat and tares; the good and the bad are growing up together. We need to learn to discern what God is doing in our world.

A third app is the *death and resurrection* app. Christianity is all about death and resurrection, and most centrally and supremely, of course, that of Jesus. His resurrection is the starting point of God making all things new. It is the reason for our hope as we look forward to the restoration of all things when creation will be liberated from the bondage to decay. Yet all through history there has been a death and resurrection pattern, similar to the apostasy and renewal pattern of the book of Judges. God's people have experienced times of falling away and then renewal as the Spirit of God rose up new movements within and outside of established Christianity. He is committed to the fulfillment of his own purposes in history. He is working towards his goal of "the knowledge of the glory of the Lord" covering the earth "as the waters cover the sea" (Hab 2:14).

Therefore, as people of hope, we can look beyond the negative circumstances of any given period in anticipation of what the Spirit will do next. We are expectant people, pregnant with the future, as we look forward in hope to God's ongoing work in human affairs. Our hope is not based on current headlines, trends, or events. It is based on God's character and purposes, the two "unchangeable things" talked about in Hebrews 6:18.

Fourth, there is the *faithful minorities* app. God has always chosen to work through obedient, available minorities. The Bible is full of stories about people and families, not economic and political theories. God's ways are relational, and he works by starting with an Abraham, a Moses,

a Daniel, an Esther, and so on. He uses the weak to confound the strong;
the foolish to confound the wise.

I have learned to view history through the "faithful minorities" lens,
tracing the stories of those who were obedient to Jesus's teachings and
example. Much of church history can be very discouraging, and many
books about this topic should come with a government health warning
on the cover: *Beware; this book could destroy your faith!* While studying
history at university, I struggled with my faith while reading the terrible
things done in the name of the church and of Christianity through the
ages. But when I began to focus on those movements and groups who
chose to live in radical obedience to Jesus, I found myself being greatly
encouraged and inspired to follow their example.

Five crises

At last year's State of Europe Forum in Dublin, Jim Memory of Redcliffe
College presented a talk entitled, *Storm Warnings: Five crises that threat-
en Europe today*. We were sailing on uncharted waters, he said, and we
needed help to orient ourselves. Sailors listen to the shipping forecast to
find out what is ahead. To be a Christian engaged in life in Europe today,
he said, we needed to understand what was happening in our societies, in
the economy, in politics, and in the environment.[1]

The Economic Storm. The consequences of the current economic
crisis are evident. In Italy, Spain, Portugal, Greece, and Ireland, there
are paralyzing levels of debt. Measures have saved the banks, but at the
price of capital control. These nations have experienced all the pain but
none of the gain of devaluation. Unemployment is at frightening levels.
In Greece, six out of ten young people have no job prospects. Many house
owners are unable to pay mortgages and face an uncertain future. Four
possible scenarios include:

1. *Maintaining the status quo*, ten to twenty years of low or even negative economic growth. The current crisis will be the new normal.

2. *Disorderly breakup of the Euro*, devastating countries such as the
   "club med" grouping.

---

1. Schuman Centre, www.schumancentre.eu/category/inspiring-talks/.

3. *Structured break up*, in which certain countries would be "invited to leave," and supported through the transition.

4. *Full fiscal union*, unlikely to be acceptable to the whole EU.

The Political Storm. A high pressure area hangs over the EU. The long period of political stability in Europe may be over. Popular levels of trust in the EU have reached record lows. There has been a rise in nationalist, populist, and xenophobic movements. Extreme right wing politicians tap into rising unrest.

The Social Storm. Migration is a major concern now. Experimentation with models of integration has not been greatly successful. Secular Europe simply does not know how to handle religions which refuse to bow at its altar. Migrants make up 6.7 percent of the population in the EU. Then there is the *demographic change*. All EU states have a fertility rate below the replacement level of 2.1. By 2060, 33 percent of Germans will be over sixty-five, and the average Italian will be over fifty. This will have a devastating impact on population figures, and an aging population will add major strain to systems such as social welfare.

The Environmental Storm. Because of the economic storm, this is being ignored. Yet the summer ice in the Antarctic is melting. The sea level has risen by eleven mm. Extreme weather is becoming more common. In the UK, four of the five wettest years in history have happened in the last twelve years. The weather is getting more and more unpredictable.

The Religious Storm. Faith refuses to leave the stage despite predictions of its demise. Europe is becoming both more secular and more religious. Younger generations are more open to religious identification (although not in traditional forms). We find so little practice of faith in Europe because people have put their faith elsewhere (e.g., "prosperity"). The message is, "If we can return to economic growth, we will return to security and prosperity." Jim Memory says, " . . . I think not." He further predicts,

> A long period of economic stagnation • a reduced Eurozone • the east and south to provide migrant workers for the prosperous north • EU expansion to continue but also to suffer some losses • the UK will either leave the EU or renegotiate its status • independence of new states will slow down EU decision-making • demographic changes will create inter-generational conflicts (younger generation railing against the old) • age-related migration • extreme weather will become the norm • higher CO_2

levels will boost food and forest growth in higher northern lati-
tudes • a resurgence of religiosity.[2]

These crises must shape our mission in Europe today. Economic
hardships are being felt by the most vulnerable in society. The church
is one of the few intergenerational communities where rich and poor
gather as one body. As such, it must rise to the challenge to offer hope in
the midst of crisis. In a Europe where many services originally provided
by the church have been taken over by the state, this is an hour where the
church can step back into a crucial role.

Six Europeans

Europeans come in many different shapes and sizes. Perhaps the following categories of Europeans can help us in our effort to understand
Europe today and to know how to communicate with them effectively.

Let us start with Karl from Frankfurt, Germany, who is a typical
post-Christian European. Karl now works for a major international bank
in the financial district of Frankfurt. Raised a Lutheran, he has doubts
about the authenticity of Christianity, and as a student he gave way to
outright skepticism. He set his goals on pursuing his bank career and
becoming a millionaire before he was 40. As far as Karl was concerned,
Christianity simply became irrelevant for life in the twenty-first century.
His current girlfriend, Porsche sports car, and yuppie apartment are the
realities that interest him the most. Karl is a practicing pagan, or atheist, without necessarily any particular zeal for paganism or atheism as
ideologies. Missiologist Lesslie Newbigin described the post-Christian
pagan as being as different from the pre-Christian pagan as a divorcée
is from a virgin. He proposed that the post-Christian is a much more
difficult prospect for evangelism, and post-Christian society has become
the greatest contemporary missiological challenge.

Olga, from Kiev in the Ukraine, represents our second major category, *the post-Communist European*. In Western Europe we may not rub
shoulders often with this sort of European, but in the former communist
countries, post-Communists are the daily reality. Olga lives in a typical
Stalinist-architecture apartment block in Kiev, capital of the Ukraine.
A young mother, abandoned by her alcoholic husband, she raised her
two children who now have grown to adulthood. Twenty years after the

2. Ibid.

demise of the Soviet Union, she finds herself sometimes wistfully longing for the "good old days," when the state claimed to care for citizens from the cradle to the grave. Somehow the hardships of those days have been forgotten. Millions of post-communists like Olga now live on both sides of the European Union border, from East Berlin to Moscow. While some quickly converted from *dialectical materialism* to *consumer materialism*, changing their political spots (perhaps even now serving in the European Parliament), the majority of older eastern Europeans still live in an ideological vacuum vaguely described as post-Communism. For some, part of that vacuum is being filled by a return to the Orthodox faith of past generations, never totally eradicated by atheistic Marxism. Others are discovering new western expressions of Christianity in American-style mega-churches, often preaching a form of prosperity gospel which ignores the deep need for social reformation. Christian witness in Eastern Europe demands engagement with issues of justice and compassion, and a demonstration that the true gospel message will overflow into social transformation and reformation.

Now let us go to Prague in the Czech Republic to meet Katrin, who is in our third category, *the Postmodern European*. Like Olga's children, Katrin is too young to remember life under communism. She has been far more influenced in her lifestyle by Michael Jackson, Madonna, and MTV than by Marxism. She also shares with her peers from Western Europe little faith in modernity's assumption that science, reason, and human goodness promise a better future. In her view, all "isms" are "wasms"; ideologies that belong to the past. Ultimate Truth is an illusion. What may be true for others, like her parents, teachers, priests, or pastors, is not necessarily true for her. What counts is now; having fun now; living for sensuous gratification now. Belonging and peer-acceptance are far more important to Katrin than material gain or career advancement. The borders between reality and fantasy are blurred in Katrin's perception; why not just "mix and match" ideas wherever they come from?

We then meet Mustapha, our *Post-Migrant European*, in Amsterdam. He was born in Holland to migrant workers from the Mediterranean, and he belongs to the majority of urban youth in Holland's capital whose parents are non-indigenous Dutch. Yet he does not feel he fully belongs to his parents' world of Islam in their homeland when the whole family goes there on holiday. Nor does he feel accepted in the white European world. Sometimes he feels blamed for everything going wrong in Dutch society. He has few white friends, if any. Mustapha lives in an identity crisis. He doesn't really know who he is or who he wants to be. Some of his friends have become radical Muslims. Others have become secularized and seem to be successful in their careers. A few have even risked everything to become followers of Isa, as Jesus is called in the Koran.

In Paris, we find Celeste, *a Post-Secular European*. Like many French, Celeste firmly believes in the reality of the spiritual world, and has dabbled in various forms of the occult. In France there are more spiritualist healers than doctors, lawyers, and priests combined. Even the Vatican has dubbed France a nation of "baptized pagans"! Sadly, the last place Celeste would expect to find spiritual reality is in the church. Her experience is that the church is a patriarchal institution with centuries of suppression of women undermining its moral authority. Yet she knows beyond a shadow of doubt that the spiritual world is real, and has had multiple personal encounters with spiritual beings. She's not concerned with issues of morality, sorting right from wrong, doctrinal disputes, and all the other things she sees Christians arguing about. She is happy to pursue her own brand of spirituality and let others pursue theirs. Across Europe today there are millions of "Celeste's," following pop-stars and films stars who also dabble in do-it-yourself spirituality. In government, business, and academic circles, spirituality is being taken seriously, influencing decision-making processes, stress-management, office architecture, and corporate philosophies. Far from being part of a lunatic-fringe, they are becoming main-stream in European society.

And the sixth European? This is the *average European Christian* (not that there is really any such thing) who we will call "Jenny." As a typical evangelical believer, Jenny would be locally-focused, for whom "Europe" is far beyond any personal consciousness. With little historical awareness of how God has been at work in Europe's past, Jenny would have little expectation of what God wants to do in the future. Short memories breed short-sightedness. As an active believer, she would be "church-centered" rather than "kingdom-centered," engaged in the weekly church activities, but with little concern for the implications of the Christian faith in the public square other than issues of personal morality. Most likely, she is intimidated, consciously or unconsciously, by a secularism that tells us to "go and play church over there in the corner," but not in the public square. We must help such sisters and brothers unmask the myth of the permanency of secularism. Here is the greatest challenge in Europe today, where 522 million are still nominally Christian,[3] and even active believers have little faith, hope, and vision for their continent. Yet there is hope!

Seven signs of hope

Let's now take a look at seven signs of hope that God is up to something new in Europe.

1. New shakings of God

We have seen the permanent things of this world shaken before our eyes in recent times; the Berlin Wall and the Twin Towers disappeared right before us, triggering the mixed emotions of awe, joy, fear, and uncertainty in varying quantities. Scripture warns us that everything not based on God's kingdom will be shaken. Our security is not to be found in wealth, armies, power, and nation-states, but in God himself. He has been shaking the Marxist world, the Muslim world, and now the world of Mammon. God is still active in the affairs of humanity, and that is a sign of hope. The Holy Spirit has been given as a guarantee, a down payment, a deposit of things to come, the fulfillment of God's purposes for human history.

2. New spiritual hunger

Spirituality is in again. Popular spirituality is flowering like shoots springing up through cracks in a dry wilderness impoverished by two centuries of secularization. Postmodern dissatisfaction with the failure of material progress and scientific achievement to answer the deepest questions about the meaning of life, and post-communist frustration with the bankruptcy of atheistic socialism, have created a generation of Europeans wide open to spiritual exploration—of all sorts.

Yet all too often the Christian God is seen as a captive of the traditional church. Still, like Vincent van Gogh, the Dutch artist who rejected the church but remained fascinated with Jesus all through his turbulent life right up to his tragic death, young Europeans are not anti-Jesus; they just do not recognize him dressed in his Sunday-best. We must view this

---

3. *Operation World,* 2010, 75.

spiritual hunger itself as a sign of hope—and learn new approaches to evangelism not geared to atheistic secularism, but to post-Christian spirituality. This is a ripe field waiting to be harvested through incarnational mission. Some of my colleagues see seekers waiting in line for an hour to be prayed for at their stands at Mind Body Soul fairs.

3. New prayer initiatives

The nineties saw many fresh expressions of prayer emerging among Christian believers, including prayer concerts, prayer triplets, prayer walking, prayer marches, forty day prayer and fasting seasons, 24/7 prayer chains, and prayer for the Muslim world during Ramadan.

As the twenty-first century began, young people took the lead in initiating twenty-four hour prayer chains for seven days a week in the so-called *24/7 Prayer* network spreading contagiously across national and denominational borders. Prayer for the Muslim world has grown to unprecedented levels globally, and millions of Christians join in prayer during the *Ramadan prayer season* for revelations of Isa (Jesus) to Muslims around the world.

Global Days of Prayer that have emerged out of Africa, calling Christians everywhere to pray together over Pentecost, have mobilized more Christians simultaneously than ever before in history! Such new and diverse prayer initiatives that are involving greater numbers than ever before surely must be seen as a prelude of things to come. When God stirs this level of prayer, he must have something in mind.

4. New expressions of church

A large willow tree used to droop over the stream running down the side of our property. A storm forced a great split between the two main branches and the tree lay broken and forlorn. Council men came and cut off the trunk, leaving an ugly stump. When I asked the men when they would return to pull the stump out, they simply told me to wait until spring. Sure enough, as spring approached, lots of new wispy branches began to appear carrying green shoots. While the shape of the tree had been altered forever, the spring green curly willow leaves were exactly like the leaves of the tree before the storm.

That tree became my backyard parable of hope concerning the twenty-first century church. While the church as we have known it in Europe for many centuries may well be in the throes of a long-drawn out terminal sickness, signs of new shoots are emerging.

The Fresh Expressions movement has emerged out of the Church of England "stump," encouraging all sorts of new expressions of "koinonia" initiatives, in pubs, schools, businesses, community centers, and so on, parallel to existing parish churches.[4] Many in other denominations are also working towards a "church beyond the congregation," a community framework for a lifestyle lived out seven days a week, twenty-four hours a day, a way of living rather than an event merely attended one day a week.

5. New Europeans: from Africa, Asia, and Latin America

Yet another indication that God is up to something new is that he is bringing to Europe people from Asia, Africa, and Latin America with gifts we have lost; gifts of faith for church planting; gifts of boldness in proclamation; gifts of discernment of the spirit of animism, with which they are so familiar. Like the proverbial frog that gets cooked alive in water slowly heated up, we Europeans are being gradually accommodated to the daily barrage of post-Christian "non-values." Brothers and sisters coming from the two-thirds world can all too clearly see that Europe is in "hot water."

In many European cities, migrant churches have reversed the fall in church attendance. In London, six out of every ten church goers are from migrant backgrounds. A city council survey of Rotterdam carried out by university researchers concluded that churches and Christian volunteers played a crucial role in creating social cohesion and integration in Rotterdam, and saved the city up to €130 million each year in social services. Migrant churches contributed as much as traditional Dutch churches to society, according to the survey. Two out of five church-goers were migrants or migrant children, while roughly half of all churches were migrant fellowships, using thirty-five different languages, in addition to Dutch.

In Spain, the evangelical population is mostly migrant, with Latin Americans, Africans, and Romanians boosting numbers ten-fold in recent years, and Argentineans and Brazilians have been arriving in groups

4. www.freshexpressions.org.uk.

to pray for Europe. Surely it is a sign of hope that God is laying Europe on the hearts of Koreans, Africans, and Latin Americans for prayer—and action.

6. New ecumenism of the heart

A further sign of encouragement is the growth of a climate of unity and cooperation. An ecumenism of the heart—if not of full doctrinal agreement—has emerged in recent years in many European countries. The Charismatic movement, interdenominational youth organizations, prayer movements, trans-denominational conferences, and the secularization of society has promoted awareness that our common beliefs are greater than our differences. This is true within the protestant world, between Protestants and Catholics, and even in relations with the Orthodox churches.

Christian leaders are coming together saying we need each other. There has never been a season of such convergence as there is today. As already stated, Pope Benedict XVI declared in St Peter's Square that "Luther was right" about the doctrine of justification by faith. Who ever thought a pope would say that?

Most recently, Pope Francis and Patriarch Bartholomew of the Eastern Orthodox Church have agreed to call a Council of Nicea in 2025, the 1700th anniversary of the original council which gave us the Apostles' Creed. Leaders of all backgrounds are realizing that we must work together. We must find each other across denominational boundaries. We need to pool each other's strengths. This surely is a sign of hope.

7. Newly recovered Good News of the Kingdom

Lastly (although this is far from an exhaustive list!), believers are waking up to the holistic nature of the gospel; that the good news of Jesus Christ begins with salvation but goes on to the culmination of God's purposes for his whole creation. Personal salvation is, of course, the starting point of our spiritual walk, as Jesus told Nicodemus—but it's not the end point! It comes as a great surprise for most of us when we discover that Jesus actually said very little about the church. There is one subject however on which he is certainly not silent, and that is the Kingdom. It is his opening message: Repent for the Kingdom of God (or heaven) is near. That is the gospel Matthew tells us Jesus began to proclaim three years before he went to the cross (see Matt 4:23). In the Sermon on the Mount, as recorded by Matthew in the following chapters, Jesus refers to the Kingdom in the Beatitudes and the Lord's Prayer, and then tells his listeners to seek God's Kingdom first. In parable after parable, Jesus painstakingly explains truths about the Kingdom. He is obviously trying to get his point across: "The kingdom of God (heaven) is like."

Still later he describes the fulfillment of the Great Commission as the preaching of the Kingdom to all nations, the prerequisite for the end to come (Matt 24:14). And lastly, after rising from the dead, he appears to the disciples on numerous occasions over a period of forty days, and speaks to them—surprise, surprise—about the Kingdom of God (Acts 1:3).

Jesus defines the Kingdom for us in the Lord's Prayer. "May your Kingdom come"; in other words, "may your will be done on earth as it is in heaven." God's Kingdom is where his will is being done. When God's will is being done in the family, or in the church, in schools, politics, business, or healthcare, and every other sphere of life, his Kingdom is advancing.

What this means is that we are all to be Kingdom agents in *every* area of life God as calls us to serve him. As Abraham Kuyper famously declared when he opened the Free University in Amsterdam in 1880, "There is not one square inch of human life where Christ, who is Lord of all, does not say, 'Mine, Mine, Mine!'" More and more believers are waking up to this truth, and that, too, is surely a sign of hope.

8

CROSS OVER EUROPE

Evert Van de Poll

Wherever you go in Europe, a multitude of crosses can be found. You cannot escape them. They are atop church buildings, bell towers, beside the road, on mountain tops, in schools and hospitals, in private homes, and on book covers and posters. Countless people wear them as ornaments or amulets, or both. Sport clubs have crosses in their emblems, and they are even carried in processions. Europe is literally packed with crosses. The cross, of course, symbolizes the Christian faith. It stands for the religion that has created a bond between the peoples of this continent, despite their different cultures, rival interests, and more.

The omnipresence of this symbol in an almost endless variety of forms and formats is not just a curiosity or play of traditions, but a clue to understanding Europe. *Christianity has played a key role, not only in the emergence of the cultural unity of Europe, but also in the development of its social, political, and cultural diversity.* If there is one symbol that captures both the cultural unity and the cultural diversity of Europe, it is the Christian cross.

Brought together by the story of the cross

Although every ethnic group and nation on the European continent has its own unique story, and while they have fought each other bitterly and continuously, their histories are marked by some common denominators. We can speak of a combined history in which the fate of these peoples has been closely intertwined.

The first point is the Roman Empire, which brought the southern regions together under the umbrella of an administrative system, and spread the Greco-Roman culture over the existing local cultures and religions. This gave cohesion to the heteroclite population within its borders. It was, however, a Mediterranean empire, even though it spread into the northwest as far as Britain. The Romans called the ethnic groups beyond their borders collectively "Barbarians." A larger part of today's Europe lies outside the former empire.

The second common denominator is Christianity. Having become the official religion of the Roman Empire, it gave a religious cohesion to the peoples within this territory. Following the downfall of the western part of the empire, the Church stood out as the sole force of cohesion among its multicultural population. Quite remarkably, the invading tribes did not cling to their various religious traditions but adopted the religion of the people they had conquered or driven away. This new religion provided them with a common frame of reference, despite their cultural differences.

Moreover, the Christian message was spread much further than the Roman armies had ever ventured, to the north and to the east. The same Gospel that had found acceptance among Greeks and Romans now also spread to Gauls and Celts, Scots and Picts, Angles and Saxons, Frisians and Franks, Germans and Goths, Slavs and Rus, and a host of other peoples. As they became Christianized, they were integrated into a common realm with the same Christian frame of reference and world-view. From the eighth century onwards, this Christian territory was called "Europe." Over the centuries, values and behaviors took root that became known as "European," and are now generally taken for granted by Europeans today as being self-evident.

So here we have "the two streams of history that have flowed into the life of Europe during the past two millennia," as Lesslie Newbigin has formulated so well.[1] On the one hand there is the stream flowing from classical learning and administrative structures, with its fountainhead in the history of the Roman Empire, and on the other hand "the stream that comes from the history of Israel mediated through the Bible and the living memory of this history in the life of the Christian Church."[2] Newbigin goes on to say,

1. Newbigin, *Proper Confidence*, 2.
2. Ibid., 3.

What has made Europe a distinct cultural and spiritual entity is the fact that, for a thousand years, the Barbarian tribes who had found their home there were schooled in both the Biblical story and the learning of classical antiquity, the legacy of Greece and Rome. Their intellectual leaders were taught in Greek and Latin, but the story that shaped their thinking was the Bible . . . The biblical story came to be the one story that shaped the understanding of who we are, where we come from, and where we are going . . . And because Europe later developed that way of thinking and organizing life which is now known throughout the world as "modernity", we cannot understand modernity without understanding this part of our history.[3]

From Mediterranean ports to the abodes of Danes and Normans ("people of the north"), from the Irish and Scottish shores into the vast plains of Russia, people were remembering the same story of creation and salvation through the liturgical year in popular drama and songs, and in sculptures and paintings. The story was everywhere, and in whatever language or custom it was couched, or in whatever theology it was expressed, it was basically the same. "This laid the foundations for what was to emerge as a self-conscious geographical unity calling itself Europe, distinct from its Asian background", historian Norman Davis puts it.[4] (He is referring to the fact the many tribes had originally migrated from Asia.)

Diversity

Viewed from the outside, Europe stands out as a group of nations particularly attached to democracy and human rights, and as a cultural zone with specific characteristics. Looking from the inside, "we Europeans" are much more aware of our diversity. We find ourselves amidst a mosaic of ethnic origins, languages, national and regional histories, political traditions, cultures, and lifestyles. And many of us are strongly attached to our particular cultural identity, feeling "European" only in a secondary or accessory way.

When it comes to ethnic origins, we are a mixed rabble indeed. Incessant people movements in the past and migration today complicate the picture. Tensions between the modern nation state and ethnic minorities

3. Ibid., 13.

4. Davies, *Europe*, 216.

are a recurrent phenomenon. But when it comes to our many languages, there is some kind of a pattern; they are Latin in the south-west, Germanic in the north-east, and Slavic in the east—with some exceptional cases here and there. In the south-east, however, there is a mosaic of very different languages. In order to capture this diversity, the same cross gives us the key of understanding.

North versus South

One factor that has determined the culture of European peoples is their geography—in other words, their climate, natural resources, arable land, commercial routes, and access to ports. For a start, there is a north and a south in Europe. The divide between the Mediterranean world and the regions beyond it has a lot to do with climate and vegetation, and therefore with culture. Nature and weather conditions influence agriculture, food patterns, lifestyle, and traditions of a given society. The colder the climate, the harder one must work to survive and make living conditions more pleasant. Another consequence of climate is that families in the north live more indoors while in the south more time is spent outdoors. People drink wine in the south and beer in the north.

At the time of the Roman Empire, the natural north-south division largely coincided with the border between the "civilized" peoples linked together by a Hellenistic-Roman culture, and the "uncivilized" world of the Barbarians. In due time the Roman Empire declined. At the same time, the Barbarians adopted the (Christian) religion of their former foes. Gradually, the north-south divide lost its great significance. But traces remained. Even today, the Latin and Greek zones around the Mediterranean have distinct characteristics when compared to the north. In the south, for example, extended family structures are more important than any other social structure. Parents help their children with financial aid much longer than they generally do in northern countries.

It is a matter of interpretation as to where the north ends and the south begins. Belgium, for instance, has been called the northernmost part of Latin Europe; while people in northern France point out that the Latin mentality is only found in the southern part of their country. But wherever you draw the line, there is a difference between north and south. The Mediterranean world has a "feel" of its own.

West versus East

There is also the divide between West and East, which goes back to the old division between the western and eastern Roman Empire. After the Empire was Christianized, the division continued between the Catholic Latin West and the Orthodox Greek East.

During the Middle-Ages, peoples to the north and east were evangelized by Catholics and Orthodox respectively, so the division line spread as well. Germanic, and a small amount of Slavic peoples, were incorporated into the catholic realm, with most Slavs dwelling in the Orthodox territory. As a result, the dividing line went right up to the northern outskirts of the continent, separating Scandinavia and the Baltic countries from Russia.

Throughout its history, Western Europe has been more prosperous than the East, as it developed global trade routes and colonial empires. As the East seemed to lag behind, it maintained a desire to catch up with the West; to belong to the rest of Europe and not be left out. For a long time, Eastern elites were culturally oriented towards France and Germany.

Different interactions with Christianity

Christianity is a major, if not the main common denominator in the history of European peoples, and more than any other factor has shaped the cultural diversity. Europeans are all marked by an interaction between Christianity and culture, but this has taken on different forms. Again, there is a pattern in all this diversity, and it is striking that it largely overlaps with the linguistic pattern. South-west (or "Latin") Europe has almost exclusively been dominated by Roman Catholicism. North-west Europe, with its Nordic and Germanic languages, came largely under the influence of Protestantism while maintaining important Roman Catholic minorities. Slavic Europe was dominated by Roman Catholicism in the western part and by Orthodoxy further to the east, with Protestantism remaining a marginal influence.

Finally, there is the south-eastern part of Europe that seems to belong neither to its east nor west. While it is situated in the southeast, it is difficult to mark its frontier, and even more difficult to give it a name. In the nineteenth century, the name "Balkan" came to be used, denoting a region of incessant strife. Indeed, this is an area of tension, because it represents a mosaic of different ethnic origins, language groups, and religions. This is the only part of Europe where Islam has maintained a continual presence up to the present day (Bosnia, Albania, and Kosovo). And we should not forget that Istanbul, ancient Constantinople, is a Muslim metropolis on European soil!

A socio-cultural cross

There are many connections amongst the peoples of Europe, which is important to keep in mind when trying to understand what is happening in any given country. More often than not there are factors coming into play that are characteristic not just of that country, but of the region of Europe to which it belongs. Here again, the cross provides us with a suitable symbol and a key. When we combine the geographical, linguistic, and religious zones, we can identify an imaginative cross over Europe, indicating the four major socio-cultural "quarters"; four kinds of Europe, if you like.

Nordic Germanic Europe	Slavic Europe
• Germanic peoples and languages • "Beer" culture • Climate less hospitable • Culture mainly determined by Protestantism • Mostly Protestant with Roman Catholic minorities. Some Roman Catholic countries • Industrious, enterprising, commercial development • Used to a plurality of religious expressions • Largely secularized today	• Slavic peoples and languages (some exceptions) • "Vodka" culture • Climate less hospitable • Cultures determined by Roman Catholicism (western part) or Orthodox (eastern part) • Less prosperous than the West • Some countries are very much secularized (e.g., Czech Republic), others marked by widespread religious practice (Poland)
Latin Europe	**Balkan Europe**
• Latin or "Roman" languages • "Wine" culture • Hospitable climate • Culture determined by Roman Catholicism • Industrious, enterprising • Less secularized than NW Europe. High percentage of nominal Roman Catholics	• Latin, Slavic, Greek, Turkish and other languages • "Wine" or "black coffee" culture • Hospitable climate • Cultural mosaic of "pieces" determined by Roman Catholicism, Orthodoxy and Islam • Less industrious and prosperous than the West • Less secularized, because of relation between religion and national/cultural identity

The lines between these zones do not coincide with clear geographical borders; they are rather fluid and abstractions of a more complex reality. When you cross over Europe, you only gradually move from one cultural region into another. Travelers will, at some point, realize that they have entered into another world and another kind of society, even though it is still part of Europe. For instance, when someone goes from Amsterdam to Moscow, they might already get a feeling of transition at the German-Polish border, or at some point east of Warsaw, but that does not change the principle of the cross over Europe. When travelers go from Copenhagen to Barcelona, somewhere along the way they will realize that they have moved from a northern to a Latin or Mediterranean atmosphere and way of life.

Of course, this "cross" is a gross generalization of a more complex reality. It does not visualize the religious and ethnic minorities spread all over Europe: Jews, Muslims, Buddhists, or adherents of new religious movements. Nor does it bring out the increasing percentage of *non-religious* people. Secularization is taking place all over Europe, but it takes different forms in different zones. First, it comes by way of people who are not affiliated with any religious institution. We see this notably in Protestant and ex-communist countries, with peaks in the Netherlands, eastern Germany, and the Czech Republic. Second, it can be found in the non-practicing, nominal members of Christian churches. This phenomenon is most widespread in traditionally Roman Catholic countries.

It seems that people in north-east Europe are quite receptive to work models coming from North America, whereas people in the south often take a reserved and critical stance due to a larger cultural distance. Those in the south generally have much more difficulty learning English—and hence in adopting Anglo-Saxon ideas—as people in the north.

As to the "line" between east and west, it seems to be moving eastward as the EU expands in that direction. Slovaks, Slovenes, Croats, Hungarians, Czechs, and Poles like to consider themselves as being part of West. In their mind, the "east" is Russia, Belarus, and the Ukraine. Russian leaders often oppose the "Eurasian" culture of these countries as the "American" influenced culture of "western" Europe. Ukrainians themselves are divided as to which side they belong, and this is the undercurrent of the troubles that are currently ripping their country. Some would even exclude the Russians from the European civilization altogether, although Orthodox Church leaders insist that Russia and its neighbors are the inheritors of Byzantine Europe, standing in continuity with the Christianized Roman Empire, and therefore part of the "house of Europe."

Understanding affinities and differences at a regional level

As was mentioned above, this socio-cultural cross is a generalization, and a tentative one. We do not pretend to have analyzed in depth the various aspects of these zones; further research would be necessary to check and modify it. We have used a number of variables, but to check our provisional conclusions and refine the picture, other variables should be added—such as individual versus state initiative, tolerance of religious diversity in general and of Islam in particular, and attitude towards authority or the receptiveness of the American way of life.

Differences and affinities

Interestingly, this way of "mapping Europe"—on the basis of socio-cultural variables—has also been adopted by *MoveHub*[5], a website which helps people move abroad, and offers advice to would-be ex-pats seeking somewhere new to live. In order to help travelers find their way and to recognize and understand the part of Europe where they are, a team of researchers compiled answers to the questions: how does the world's second smallest continent look when split up by all manner of factors and situations, such as politics, money, geography, language, and religion? And what is the picture when we divide it up by rather more intriguing issues such as, which regions prefer wine to vodka (and which parts are happy with a tankard of real ale), and which areas serve inspiring food rather than bland grub?

In so doing, they identified socio-cultural borders, which were then used by designer Yanko Tsvetkov to produce a series of satirical maps, in much the same way as we have drawn our "cross." These digital "maps" show Europe carved up by 20 differentials—some amusing, such as tea drinkers versus coffee aficionados, and some more serious, such as areas of wealth and poverty, and attitudes to gay rights. Some generalizations include bad cuisine in the north, good cuisine in the south; people in the north work harder for 21 days a month, while people in the south work

5. www.movehub.com.

less strenuously and live 21 days a month; the modern way of life in the north versus a more traditional, classical outlook in the south; people in the east can fix their sink, whereas people in the west need a plumber for that.[6]

Of course, these are over-simplifications allowing for many local exceptions, but when they are seen, they do ring a bell among people of various backgrounds, and a general picture emerges that confirms our "cross over Europe." Despite its provisional state, the latter clarifies why certain national and regional cultures have more in common with certain others. Germans, British, Dutch, Norwegians, and Swedes recognize much more of themselves in each other than they do when they compare themselves to Italians, Greeks, Bosnians, or Romanians. Russians feel very different from French, and at the same time closely akin to Byelorussians and Ukrainians, and so on. It also helps workers in intercultural mission to understand that cultural dividing lines do not always correspond to national borders.

How does Evangelical church planting fit in?

An interesting question with respect to mission and church planting in Europe is, "Where and how does evangelicalism fit into the picture?" How receptive is the population in each socio-cultural zone to the evangelical expression of Christian faith, with its emphasis on conversion, personal relation with God, and individual responsibility? How do they relate to evangelical forms of church life, with its "low liturgy" and emphasis on participating in and contributing to the witness of the Gospel? We would tentatively say that evangelicalism is strongest in the north-western zone, and weakest in the southern zones. It seems that a population with a protestant background is more receptive than a population with a traditional Roman Catholic or Eastern Orthodox background. Is there perhaps a distance between the church model generally used by evangelicals, and the socio-cultural context of these zones?

One could further specify the enquiry by making a distinction between traditional Evangelical Protestantism on the one hand and Pentecostalism (including Charismatic movements) on the other. Interestingly, Pentecostal movements have done relatively well in countries like France, Spain, and Italy, where other Evangelical denominations have been much

---

6. Daily Mail, "The-disunited-states-Europe."

slower to "catch on." Additionally, these "Latin" countries have sizeable charismatic streams within the Roman Catholic Church. Could it be that the Pentecostal/Charismatic expression of Christian faith finds more resonance with people in a Mediterranean culture than the more rational approaches of those who present the Christian faith as a plausible world view, as truth, and as something we have reason to believe?

We should not underestimate the prevailing effects of ages of Roman Catholic influence in the Latin countries and parts of Eastern Europe, of Orthodox Christianity in the rest of the east, or of traditional Calvinism, Lutheranism, and Anglicanism in northeastern and central European countries. There is a lasting cultural imprint, which has colored people's ideas about God, Jesus, church, religion, faith, prayer, heaven and hell, sin and justice, baptism, etc. We would do well to study that in order to become familiar with it. This is yet another reason it is useful for mission organizations, churches, and church planters in a particular "quarter" of Europe to meet and discuss. As they minister in a very similar socio-cultural context, they have much to share, and much to learn from each other.

Discussion highlights

While the cross over Europe is a generalized concept taking into account the differences in culture and behavior as you move from one quarter to another, Van de Poll states that, "viewed from the outside, Europe stands out as a group of nations particularly attached to democracy and human rights." Part of the discussion centred around the question of how much are democracy and human rights historic values that form a true part of the identity and values of individual Europeans?

A participant living in Eastern Europe observed that while there is enforced democracy from the European Union, most people do not understand it. Another who works with Eastern European migrants agreed, and wondered "what ideals of communism are they bringing with them?"

Van de Poll explained that the word "democracy" has been applied in different ways. "The basic foundation of democracy is how the will of the people is expressed, but for some countries, this means having one centralized party that channels the will of the people into policy," he said. "This is why China is called the Democratic People's Republic, but it is not a multi-party system. In Western Europe we think it should happen through a multi-party system and pluralism. Some European countries have a very short history of democracy, for example Spain or Germany. But it is precisely through these tremendously traumatic experiences of unilateral democracy that people are now so attached to pluralism." He added that he was talking about democracy as it is perceived today.

"Historians have differences of opinion, but most go back to the Middle-Ages and point to monasteries as a sort of counter-culture where democratic ideals grew up. Others add that the differentiation between the spiritual authority of the Church and the temporal power of the prince, which was characteristic of Western Christendom, has eventually created a space for democratic forms of government. But one hundred years ago, democracy was not yet something Europeans agreed on. It took time for this idea of government of the people, by the people, and for the people to take root. Some countries only have a very short democratic tradition, but by and large, it is there and nowadays Europeans all over the continent criticize governments for not being sufficiently democratic!

"It is because of our history of internal wars that finally there is a consensus that democracy is how we should solve our problems. However, the tension is that the United States has been more successful at realizing democratic ideals, which creates a new dividing line between the Europe which looks to the United States, and the part which does not buy into that."

But some participants disagreed that it was possible to define a set of common values, such as democracy, across all of what is defined as Europe. "Where do you go for your basic values in times of crisis?" asked one. "In different parts of Europe, if you look under the surface, the basic values are different. For example in Eastern countries, you cannot think God and not say society, or think church membership and not talk about a collective fellowship at the same time. But Westerners, especially protestants, have separated these two realities. They have different values and there is a different undercurrent which actually determines their way of living. There are two Europe's at least, but we idealize it by saying we are all European."

"Yes, there are several Europes," agreed Van de Poll. "In his books, former Pope Benedict writes about three Europes, for example. One is determined by a Latin tradition, the other, in the East, by Orthodox traditions, while there is also the Enlightenment Europe, marked by the idea of a secular state and human reason as the basis of the public sphere. But even though there are issues and tensions between various parts of the continent, there is much more that we have in common than all these conflicts, and that is precisely our European history."

9

TYPICAL BARRIERS AND BRIDGES FOR THE GOSPEL IN EUROPE

Evert Van de Poll

IT IS COMMONPLACE THESE days to include Europe in a larger socio-cultural and political context called "the West." Viewed from this perspective, there might not seem to be the need to single out Europe as a special subject of analysis or special context for the communication of the Gospel. One is tempted to apply the same approaches that are used in other western societies, and this is quite often what happens. Strategies to evangelize un-churched North Americans are too readily transferred to Germany, Austria, Greece, or Spain on the assumption that un-churched people are alike everywhere in the western world. The success of such ventures is limited to those places where people closely share a North American mindset. In other situations, however, such efforts bear no fruit. This alone is sufficient evidence that we are dealing with different contexts in Europe.

Communicating the Gospel in this part of the world is not just a matter of applying the general theology of Christian mission. We cannot satisfy ourselves with adopting approaches and methods that have proven to be successful in other countries with similar western cultures. Many who try to do this discover for some reason or another that things work differently here.

Paradox

Why do the peoples of this continent constitute a specific context for the communication of the Gospel? The clue to better understand this is the paradox of Europe and Christianity. One could speak of a love-hate relationship, or a kind of "living apart together."

Europe is *the most Christianized of all continents.* No other part of the world has been exposed to the message of the Bible for such a prolonged period of time and in such a consistent way as this continent. Nowhere else is there such a rich Christian heritage. Its cultures are still rooted in Christian values, and Christian institutions were at the basis of the current social benefit systems. Without the spread of the Gospel, the impact of the Bible, and the influence of institutional churches, Europe as we know it today might never have come about. A sweeping statement indeed! But a justified one, given the crucial role of Christianity in the political and cultural development of Europe as a whole, and of each European country in particular.

At the same time, Europe is *marked by the abandonment of Christianity, more than any other part of the world.* Nowhere is the abandonment of the Christian faith and the retreat from institutional churches as wide-spread as in Europe, and nowhere else has this gone on for such a prolonged period of time. It is here that a secularized worldview, atheism, secular lifestyles, and secular political ideologies have emerged—so much so that Europe is now called "post-Christian," although it is much more precise to say "post-Christianized."

This is the paradox of Europe; its societies are marked as much by the Christian faith as by its abandonment and rejection. Failing to take into account both sides of the coin leads to misrepresentations. Either we draw a picture that is too optimistic with respect to the influence of the Church, or we depict an image that is too much the opposite.

Barriers

Having noted the paradox, the questions are then: How can the message that was important in the making of Europe have a positive impact on the secularized and multicultural societies of today? What does it have to say about the foundational values, identity, and the future of Europe?

In order to answer these questions, we can use the paradox of Europe itself to identify typically European barriers and bridges for the communication of the Gospel. We shall begin with the barriers and save the good news of the bridges for later in the chapter. The first barrier flows out of the specific socio-religious context of Europe.

Why God, or why religion?

The widespread secularization of European societies partly explains why some evangelism models that have worked well in Latin America or in Africa do not yield much fruit in Europe. In those parts of the world, the gospel is communicated among people with some kind of religion: Roman Catholic, animistic, or others. As they accept the evangelical message, they *remain* religious. They already believed in God, or at least in a divine reality. For them, the cosmos is inhabited by spirits and supernatural beings, and they do not have to change this religious worldview in order to accept the Gospel and become a Christian. What changes for them is their image of God, their doctrinal convictions, religious practices, and spiritual experience. Perhaps they only change denominational attachment. At any rate, they do not change their worldview on a fundamental level; it remains religious.

For secularized people in Europe, the situation is radically difficult. Accepting the invitation of the Gospel implies that they *become* religious, that their secular worldview is *transformed* into a religious one. Obviously, this is an additional obstacle. Their questions are not, *which* God; what religion? Rather they ask,, *why* God; why religion in the first place? Does God exist? What does the word "God" mean, and to whom or what does it refer? Are you talking about a force, a person, an idea, a projection of a human father figure? Can we experience this God? And if so, why is this important? What is the relevance of religion anyway? When I am not poor, depressed, lonely, ill, or jobless, what would I need a religion for? What does this "God" add to my life? This set of questions constitutes the first evangelism frontier in Europe.

There is another aspect of secularization to take into account, and it has replaced the religious practice of Christianity. Secularization, to be precise, is the secularization of Christianity. That implies that some Christian elements are retained, such as the idea of the intrinsic value of man, ideas of individual responsibility, freedom, and social and cultural values. Secularization is "post-Christian," but only partially. It takes over the humanist values but detaches them from their original religious context. This results in secular humanism. Secularized people do not see the need to *return* to a religious worldview in order to work for a better world. The general feeling is that "we can manage without."

A striking example is the recent book by the French philosopher and former government minister of education, Luc Ferry, entitled, *The Revolution of Love.*[1] In it, Ferry develops what he calls a "secular spirituality" based on the biblical concept of love. He thinks highly of Jesus, qualifying him as "the supreme example of an altruistic lifestyle." He takes the teachings of the church seriously on how to live the commandment to love your neighbor, and summarizes it in the principles of solidarity, the primacy of the common interest, and the value of selfless service. But he confesses to be an agnostic, almost convinced that the God of the Bible is a human creation. In the past, people needed this imagined divine being, he argues, but "we have to do without, and we can do without." According to Ferry,

> We have to move on from the humanism of the Enlightenment and its critics, move on from the antireligious stance of thinkers like Nietzsche, and develop a new spirituality: the sacralization of humanity by practicing the originally Christian principle of love.[2]

Viewed from such a perspective, secularization is a stage that comes after Christianity. What is the next step? There is no next step, at least not a religious one, because secular humanism considers itself to have advanced beyond all religions. For a secularized European to become Christian really amounts to a conversion in the truest sense of the word; a complete turnaround in direction. From the point of view of secular humanism, it goes against the thrust of the historical intellectual development of a whole continent! Embracing a religion, even Christianity, is seen as a step backward. If this is how secularized people feel about "becoming religious" or "adopting a religion," then it constitutes a formidable barrier for the communication of the Gospel.

One might object that the picture is not as grim as this. Are there not growing churches everywhere in Europe? Indeed, there are. But a closer look reveals that they are not as successful in reaching secularized fellow citizens as one might think. Their message and mode of church life elicit more response among nominal Christians who occasionally

1. Ferry, *La révolution de l'amour.*
2. Ibid, 7.

attend church, and among members of mainline Protestant and Roman Catholic churches; in other words, people familiar with Christianity, who hold a religious worldview. This is the "pool" in which they "fish" most successfully. As far as we can see, the majority of people joining an Evangelical church already had some religious beliefs. We do not say this in order to criticize these churches, but only to indicate how difficult it is for the same message to find a hearing among really secularized people.

Why Jesus?

Contemporary Europeans are often described as postmodern. It would be more precise to say that a considerable portion of the population (e.g., the young, the cosmopolitan, and the affluent) has a more or less postmodern mindset. Postmodernism has been characterized as a turning away from objectivity to subjectivity, which gives everyone the right to live according to his or her own "truth." One of the fundamental claims of postmodernism is that no human system—not even rational science—can claim to present absolute truth. Therefore, no single worldview can pretend to be superior to all the others. While there might well be an absolute truth, a unique explanation of all that exists, it is impossible for us to know that fully. So every claim to that effect should be critically dismantled. All religions, all moral and philosophical systems, every grand story about the origin and destiny of mankind (called "meta-narratives") are related by particular historical circumstances. They are culturally determined, and they all have a relative value.

Postmodernism is a philosophical corollary of the multicultural society. Cultural and religious differences should be accepted. Diversity is inevitable. This position leads to a pluralist outlook; let there be room for different values, ethical norms, religious beliefs, etc. If there is any universal value, then it should be tolerance. In practice, the demand for tolerance is related to individual lifestyles. Postmodern Europeans are generally very intolerant of undemocratic ideas, which include the violation of human rights, child abuse, attempts to impose religious beliefs, and radical Islamic movements, just to mention a few. The pluralistic society is not as permissive as it is sometimes portrayed.

The postmodern, pluralist mindset confronts us with a second barrier: "why Jesus?" If someone is interested in Christian spirituality, he will find it fair enough that Jesus be placed in the center. But is this necessary for everybody who seeks God? Is it not sufficient that each one has his or her own experience of the divine reality? If someone finds Jewish tradition more attractive, why is that not an equally valid option?[3]

Evangelists from other continents will find that people in Europe are so critical, so suspicious. They are not quickly convinced by a miracle. While short summaries of the Gospel might work in other contexts, most Europeans are not ready to accept any clear cut message demanding a simple" yes or no" for an answer. They have learned through their education that religious matters are more complex than that. Multicultural society presents them with various religious experiences. According to their European value system, they should be tolerant rather than trying to impose one religious point of view. They might well be interested in spiritual questions about the meaning of life, and they might be willing to take into account religious answers, but they are hesitant to respond when Jesus is presented to them as the unique way to find the truth about our human existence.

To this we should add another factor. The question, "why Jesus?" is not the same when it is asked in Europe as opposed to other regions of the world where Christianity is a relatively young religion, or a new religion altogether. In Europe, the name of Jesus is associated with a long history of the church, including the negative aspects of Christianity's record. At secondary school, teenagers learn about the crusades, the wars between Catholics and Protestants, the persecution of the Jews, and the abuses of power in the name of Christianity. As messengers of the Gospel, we have a lot to explain—in Europe more than anywhere else!

Why the Bible?

Closely linked to the question, "why Jesus?" is the question, "why the Bible?" How can a book written so long ago tell us what to believe and what to do? How can this be the complete truth for all ages? Historical science has made us aware of the historical distance between us and the writers of the Bible. Social scientists teach us that religious doctrines and practices are largely determined by the cultural context in which people follow them. Postmodern philosophers maintain that hermeneutics, the way in which we understand and interpret a text, is always a two directional affair. One text can mean different things to different people depending

3. Müller, ed. *Mission im postmodernen Europa.*

on the way it interacts with particular readers in a particular situation. So where does that leave the authority of the Bible in matters of faith and life? And where does that leave the authority of the Church Fathers and the traditions of the Church, which are so important in catholic teaching?

In the postmodern mindset, there is a critical attitude towards all forms of dogmatic thinking, whether in politics, science, moral issues, or religion. Theories should be studied, verified in practice, and related to their context, but not be declared final. Astrophysicists still do not have a general theory that explains all the aspects of the way in which the universe functions, and it is very postmodern to add that maybe they never will.

When it comes to religion, there is suspicion towards doctrines, creeds, and rules that everyone should follow. Truth is subjective rather than objective. At the same time, there is an interest in religious experiences. But why should these experiences be judged on the basis of biblical criteria? Why should spiritual experiences be "Christian" in order to be valid?

This is a real challenge for us as believers as we bear testimony to what God has done in our life through Jesus Christ. Who has not heard the reaction, "That is fine for you, but why should I follow the same path?"

Why church?

And then a fourth barrier rises before our eyes: "why church?" Remember that Europe is post-Constantinian. In the past, church membership was self-evident and an obligation. People simply had no choice. There was no salvation outside the church, said the theologians. In addition, there was no acceptance, no marriage, no civil service, no school, and no Christian burial except within the church.

This has left deep traces in the minds of Europeans even today. Becoming a church member is associated with obligations; a service to go to every Sunday, money to give, doctrines to believe, rules to obey, and do not forget the things you should *not* do. People like to be allowed the freedom to choose their activities and decide for themselves.

Today, Europeans are free from such constraints. Church membership is no longer expected. While it is no longer a must or a matter of social respectability, it is an option. There are still many nominal church members. In some cases, they are under social pressure from family members to become active members, but strictly speaking, they are under no obligation to attend a service, or even to remain registered. So why should people join a church if they do not want to commit themselves to all the associated obligations? Why can we not pray to God at home, they say, and why can we not just follow the ethical principles of Jesus in daily life?

We should add one important point here. In non-European countries, churches have to attract members on a voluntary basis. Church there is something you decide to participate in. If you do not want to belong to a particular church any longer, you go to another one. This explains why Europeans relate differently to church commitment than Americans, for example. This also explains why in post-Constantinian Europe, free churches of the Pentecostal and Evangelical type are doing better than historic churches in attracting new members; they have always had to reach out to people in order to arouse their interest.

But these churches are also at a disadvantage because of their view of church life. Emphasizing that Christians should live as committed disciples of Jesus, they insist on the minimum requirement of attending the weekly Sunday service. Additionally, there are Bible studies, home groups, and prayer meetings to attend, evangelistic activities to participate in, and youth groups and worship teams to volunteer for. People are also strongly encouraged to pray and read the Bible every day if they want to grow in their faith. And, of course, there are the moral principles to live by. These expectations are quite demanding when one compares them to the freedom offered by a permissive society, especially in the areas of living as a common-law couple and sexuality.

Of course, evangelical churches will not present these "obligations" as a burden, but individual believers might experience them in that way. This is not very attractive for people who have bad memories of church in the past.

In a post-Constantinian society, church membership is no longer assumed. This fosters the privatization of religion. Faith in Jesus Christ is not necessarily linked to membership of a religious institution—the famous "believing without belonging."[4] It also fosters the "behaving without belonging" attitude; people who are willing to put Christian principles into practice, but not necessarily in the context of a faith community. Sometimes this is called "cultural Christianity." Biblical values

4. Davie, *Europe: the Exceptional Case*, chapter 6.

have become part of people's worldview, but they are detached from their original religious setting.[5]

Apparently, these attitudes are making inroads in Christian assemblies known for the level of commitment of their members: traditional Protestant, Pentecostal, Evangelical, Baptist, Adventist, and so on. There is a tendency towards what we could summarize as "behaving and believing without too much belonging." This shows that the "belonging" side of Christianity is no longer self-evident, even for people who believe in Jesus.

What is new?

Then there is a fifth barrier. Given the long history of Christianity in Europe, and given all the efforts of evangelization that have been going for ages, it is not easy to present the Gospel as good *news*. The Bible, the church, God, and the stories of Jesus and the apostles are part of our cultural heritage. When people hear about it, their first and automatic reaction is, "we know all that." The problem is that they think they do, while in fact their perceptions of the Christian faith are colored by ages of tradition. But that does not change their reaction. The Gospel has been around for ages, so how can it still surprise? How can it be heard as good *news*? People certainly need to hear it as something "new" in order to be willing to change their minds. When it comes to the message of the church, false presuppositions, preconceived ideas, and traditional misrepresentations abound. They are much harder to correct than ignorance. Many people associate the Gospel with not-so-attractive images of the Church and the Christian religion, so they are put off by it rather than attracted to it.

In fact, most people are only superficially familiar with the person of Jesus. From what they know, they generally have a positive impression of his ethical conduct, but Christian faith in Jesus the Savior of mankind is quickly associated with the institutional church in their country, which enjoys a far less positive reputation. This creates a huge barrier for presenting Jesus as the Bible presents him. Some associate Jesus with what they call "Calvinism"; strict Sunday observance, boring church services with long sermons, and a whole list of forbidden pleasures. Others see him as the little baby in the manger, the child in the arms of Mary, the

---

5. Billings, *Secular Lives, Sacred Hearts*, 13–19.

sculpted figure on a crucifix, and practicing the Christian religion by going through the motions of a dull mass. As people connect the Christian faith with such preconceived ideas, they are hindered from taking a fresh look at Jesus. How shall they discover Jesus in a fresh way such as they have never seen before? How can we correct false images and preconceived ideas? How can we arouse curiosity for something that will be "new" to many Europeans—namely a living faith relationship with God?

Some years ago, there were posters put up in Germany that captured this double perspective very well: *Jesus ja, Kirche nein!* (Jesus, yes, Church, no!) This creates an opening for communicating the message, inasmuch as we succeed in disassociating the "real" person of Jesus from the traditional images of him. This is a tremendous missionary challenge.

Bridges

With that last remark we move from barriers to bridges. As Christians in Europe, we are in a privileged situation. The message we wish to communicate has influenced our societies for many ages and left many traces. Elements of Christianity are present everywhere around us, and they become bridges for communicating biblical truth. Here are some venues of action and further reflection.

Explain Christian heritage

There is a rich Christian heritage in every European country. It is there for everyone to see and hear, read about, touch, and visit. But who will be a guide? Many people visit cathedrals without understanding their symbolism. They enjoy sacred music and admire famous paintings of biblical figures without understanding the real meaning. They use the benefits of hospitals and schools that were once Christian institutions, but they have no idea why and how they came about. They give their children names of Christian saints while ignoring their history.

Here we have a countless number of bridges for the Gospel message. We only have to simply explain. Because we are familiar with the Bible, we have the key to unlock the meaning of this rich cultural heritage to our contemporaries. As Christians, we are ideally equipped to explain European culture to our contemporaries who are ignorant of its background.

Christian heritage centers have been developed in several locations, and they organize lectures and heritage tours. This is not a difficult endeavor, and every church can try to see what Christian heritage there is in their city and in the region and make efforts to study it. Before long, they can offer city walks, guided tours, and heritage talks. Throughout Europe, people are generally fond of discovering culture, ranging from local music to local cuisine and local customs, and also natural sites with history, architecture, and so on. In most cases, there is a link with the history of the church. Find out about it, and transmit it to others. One just has to explain the meaning of this painting, that building, a popular custom, or tell the story of a famous person in the past, and there is a natural occasion to explain the Bible.

David Brown, former general secretary of the French Evangelical Student Movement, *Groupes Bibliques Universitaires,* and pastor of a new church in Paris, has set up a public exhibition to show the unfolding story of salvation by using Christian cultural heritage. He has selected sixteen paintings of well-known painters—from Leonardo da Vinci and Rembrandt, to Goya and Van Gogh. Each painting represents a biblical story. Placing them in a certain order tells the story of creation, the fall, and salvation, from Genesis to Revelation. In a very professional glossy brochure, he offers background information about the artists and the story of each particular painting. He also invites the visitor to try and place their personal history in this grand story. In doing so, he uses Christian cultural heritage as a bridge to communicate the Gospel, but is wise enough to do this in an implicit way! Give visitors the freedom to look for themselves and to ask further questions if they like.

Christian institutions—where the world meets the message

A second avenue to pursue is the presence of schools, universities, hospitals, nurseries, rehabilitation centers, libraries, holiday resorts, and many other similar institutions that were originally created by churches and concerned Christian individuals. They are still a major part of the fabric of society in some countries, although there is a tendency to dissociate them from their original roots. In other countries, this institutional heritage has suffered from communist rule, and much of it has been wiped out. Even so, many of the existing institutions still have a confessional base. Even sports clubs! Several European countries also have trade unions and political parties with a confessional base. While they were created to defend the position of Christians, they attract many people outside the visible church community. Christian views on social and political issues receive tremendous exposure through these organizations, which gives credibility to the message of the church—provided we do not let the Christian identity be further diluted in larger structures that have a neutral character.

There is a growing awareness among politicians today that the state cannot and should not attend to everything that needs to be taken care of. There is a tendency to limit the scope of the welfare state while keeping vital services intact. Politicians recognize the need for intermediate organizations to play a crucial role in providing education, welfare, and medical care. This leaves more room for institutions with a Christian identity to serve a wider public.

Here we have an important bridge for the Gospel between the Church and the world, where people without a Church connection can meet the message on which these organizations were based. Christians working in these institutions can simply explain the origin and the vision of the founder, and the message of the Bible will be communicated in a natural way.

Postmodernism

It might be surprising to mention postmodernism as a third bridge. The Christian community, particularly in Evangelical circles, often takes a suspicious, negative stance towards this mode of thought.

For a start, Christians can join postmodernism in its critique of totalitarian regimes such as Nazism. Reacting against social structures and ideologies that claimed to represent absolute truth, postmodern philosophers argue that such claims for absolute loyalty were instruments of power.

Philosophers like Jacques Derrida, Jean–François Lyotard and Jürgen Habermas set out to deconstruct these systems in order to bring to light the political and economic interests behind them. They serve to oppress people, exclude all rivals, and maintain the ruling elite. This leads to oppression of individual freedom. Nazism and Soviet communism are prime examples, as they perpetrated the worst horrors of the twentieth century

Christians can largely identify with postmodern authors when they criticize the absolutist claims of modern rational science. And the critique of the terrors of atheistic, totalitarian regimes reminds us of the biblical critique of any Tower of Babylon kind of system based on human pride.

Postmodernism is not only suspicious of religious claims to knowing "the only way" to salvation and happiness, but in a similar vein it also criticizes the dogmatic attitude of secular rationalism. It deconstructs the idea, based on the Enlightenment, that modern science leads humanity on a triumphant march towards a brave new world. In fact, what are the grounds of this "belief" in progress? What kind of knowledge do scientists have of reality? Are there not other things to know, and other ways of obtaining knowledge? Human beings are fundamentally a mystery even to themselves, so instead of relying on the limited power of reason, this mystery can often be better explored by means of music, aesthetics, intuition, religion, and other rich worlds of experience.

Christians can take up these kinds of "postmodern" questions and bring to light the pretentions of secular scientific rationalism as it tries to impose its worldview. This creates an opening for Christians to come up with plausible answers to the questions people are posing today. A religious answer is not by definition less valid than a secular one. On what grounds can secular rationalists exclude the existence of God, the validity of religious experiences, and the biblical story of the origin of mankind?

Moreover, postmodernism is not in opposition to religious experience and practice. The postmodern outlook is not an alternative to religion as such, but a reaction to the dominance of truth systems. People with a postmodern outlook are not closed off to religious belief and spiritual experience. Quite the contrary. One can be postmodern and practice a religion—as long as one remains tolerant of other forms of "truth." From the Christian standpoint, the great problem of postmodernism is its pluralism, which leads to relativism.

Return of religion in the public sphere

A fourth bridge is the so-called return of religion in the public sphere in the arts, popular music, and philosophical debates. There is a growing interest in spiritual matters among a wide range of people raised in a secular environment. So much is happening in the area of religion and society. Look at the new religiosity that has spread among Europeans who have not been brought up in a religious context. Often labeled as "New Age" or "New Religious" movements, this can take the form of Eastern meditation, esoteric speculation, an interest in heretical movements of the past (Catharism for example), neo-paganism (Celtic cults revisited), or an ethical form of Buddhism combined with a bit of "spirituality": seeking transcendental truth in the inner self.

There is also a new interest in Christianity. This includes a growing number of adult baptisms in the Roman Catholic Church, many people taking part in spiritual retreats in monasteries, and the development of the Evangelical and Charismatic movements. Observers see signs that the decline of Christianity is about to come to a stopping point. In his book on the future of religion in Europe, Philip Jenkins has devoted a whole chapter to these phenomena, which is aptly called *Faith among the ruins*.[6]

Many social scientists now reject the classic secularization theory, according to which religious practice will gradually vanish from the public sphere as our societies become more and more modernized, ruled by rational science and technology. Instead, they notice not so much a process of extinction, but rather a change of pattern. We can observe a gradual shift away from an understanding of religion as an obligation and towards an increasing emphasis on satisfying personal needs and desires. Grace Davie speaks of an "authentically European mutation."[7]

Instead of trying to survive in the private sphere, those who seriously opt for religion are making their views heard in public as well as private debate. French sociologist Jean-Paul Willaime notices the following paradox.

> It is precisely the secularization of society that reinforces forms of religion in which people are committed, outspoken, and actively spreading their faith to others. Even because the structures of society and the framework of daily life is no longer religious, religion is no longer something that can be taken for granted but something to choose for, something to actively develop, something to defend against detractors . . . This is the religion of the convert.[8]

6. Jenkins, *God's Continent*, chapter 3.

7. Davie, *Europe: the Exceptional Case*, 148.

8. Willaime, *Europe et religions*, 252.

According to Willaime, Evangelical Christianity is most in tune with the "postmodern recomposition of the religious landscape."

> In a secularized and pluralist society, the individual is faced with numerous options. In the context of Evangelical groups, individuals become responsible actors. They take their life in hands, as they deliberately follow the revealed will of God and become part of a community of believers.[9]

Fewer people are inclined to remain faithful to the tradition of former generations; hence the decline of historic churches. At the same time, more people are receptive to the Christian faith through a process of personal enquiry, leading to a spiritual experience and to some kind of conversion. New types of religious practice emerge, such as the "pilgrim" who keeps seeking with an open mind but is not ready to commit himself to a particular doctrine, and the "convert" who has a transformational religious experience and is prone to witness.[10] Meanwhile, migrant churches are thriving in all the larger cities in Western Europe, thus changing the perceptions of Christianity among the general population.

In his classic study of the history of secularization, Charles Taylor ends with a look at the future, and argues that Europe is becoming "postsecular," a term that has become a catchphrase.[11] German philosopher Jürgen Habermas has taken the same view. He was engaged in a series of dialogues with Joseph Ratzinger (when the latter was still Pope Benedict XVI), which have been published in several languages.[12] The theme was the place of religion in society. Both agreed that secular science should not simply take over the dominant role from the Church of the past. Instead, secular people should recognize that religious people have intelligent things to say, solutions to offer, and answers to give. These voices may be portending days in which the Gospel will gain a larger hearing still.

The need to reinforce foundational values in society

Religion is important in today's society. Traditional religious practices are not disappearing as secularist intellectuals have thought they would,

9. Ibid., 257.

10. Hervieu-Léger, Le pèlerin et le converti.

11. Taylor, A Secular Age.

12. Habermas and Ratzinger, The Dialectics of Secularisation.

but remain important for a considerable part of the population. This creates problems (should ritual slaughter by Jews and Muslims be allowed; should the state help migrant communities to build better places of worship; what kind of religious education should be taught in public schools?), but politicians are often ill-equipped to make decisions. We notice here the effects of secularization, one of which is the systematic loss of religious knowledge. It then follows that necessarily sensitive debates are very often engaged by people who literally do not know what they are talking about with respect to their own faith, never mind anyone else's.

So this is a fifth bridge for Christians to use. They can play a positive role in the discussion about the place of faith and religious practices in society. Their own faith represents the roots of European cultures, and they are able to understand the needs of religious people in a society with a secularized public sphere so as to inform politicians about religious matters, and help migrants find their place in society as well. The discussion that is now going on everywhere in Europe as to what values we should put forward as foundational for our multicultural society can also be entered into. It turns out that most of these values have a biblical origin, as philosopher Jean-Claude Guillebaud has convincingly shown—the notion of history going towards a destiny, the concept of the individual, the aspiration for equality, the universality of mankind, and the concept of justice. To that, the ancient Greeks only added rational enquiry, but even modern science owes so much to Christianity.[13]

Christians therefore play a crucial role as they teach, transmit, and put into practice such values that are so important for society at large, and politicians are increasingly realizing the value of churches in this respect.

Discussion highlights

The discussion at the end of this session centered on several of the bridges to sharing the Gospel in Europe—namely our Christian heritage, and postmodernism. One participant asked how the Gospel could be presented through Christian heritage when the guides in heritage centers or churches are non-Christians, or the artworks themselves are not truly

13. Guillebaud, *La refondation du monde*.

representative of the Gospel? "That is why we need Christians to do the job," Van de Poll answered. "In Korea, there is a huge interest in European Art History. So you have Korean Christians coming to Europe, studying art history, and working in libraries and museums. They are the guides and can explain the biblical story behind so many works of art to European spectators who do not know that story anymore."

Art is one of the ways those with a postmodern worldview can connect with the Christian message, often because it engages people on an emotional or spiritual level rather than solely intellectually. "I get the impression that evangelism is about communicating propositions and content rather than the person of Jesus Christ," observed one participant. "In postmodernism, it is more about meeting people and exposing them to Christ—so you need to meet rather than preach."

Van de Poll agreed, adding that this approach requires a deep faith in the leading of the Holy Spirit; that the Spirit will convince where we do not. "The problem with the postmodern outlook is that it ignores the fact that there is a truth to be convinced of, but my arguments will not be the way in which people come to that truth. An inner conviction that God exists and wants a relationship with you must be experienced. It is the Holy Spirit who brings that."

The need to consider the diversity of religious experience in Europe when communicating the Gospel was also highlighted. For some, Western European Protestantism appeared to be merely an individualized and intellectualized repackaging of the Gospel. When people disagreed with what the church believed, they left. This is in contrast to Roman Catholic and Orthodox countries where people retain a link with the church even when they disagreed. Van de Poll suggested this to be because "their access to the faith is not just through words but through symbols which stay with you, even if your cognitive way of thinking changes. When we come to establish churches in these areas that look like garages, are as cold as possible with no symbols, and representing everything anti-Catholic and anti-Orthodox, are we not missing something deeply important? Could this be why the Western Evangelical church can struggle to be established in other parts of Europe?"

As a related question, was attending church on a Sunday the best measure? One participant observed that within culturally Catholic Europe, even if people are non-practicing in terms of church attendance, prayer and serving others are still a large part of their life. While these are very individualized activities, they could also act as bridges to introducing a holistic Christianity where Jesus is Lord of all of life, and not just on Sundays.

10

WHAT KIND OF CHURCH FOR POSTMODERN EUROPEANS?

David Brown

Former Canadian ice-hockey player, Wayne Gretzky, used to explain his goal scoring ability by saying, "I skate to where the puck is going to, not where it has been." Steve Jobs loved this quotation as an explanation of the success of Apple. Does it have any relevance to us as Christians?

As a convinced conservative evangelical, I firmly hold to the fundamental doctrines of the authority of Scripture, God's grace to sinners, and salvation received through repentance and faith. But how should we live this out as churches today? In the course of my lifetime I have observed two styles of church life:

- First, a rather *formal* approach, with the men in suits and ties and the women in dresses, observing silence in the sanctuary before the service started. The hymn sandwich was the standard order of service, with the use of an organ (or harmonium) for the music. Most of the meetings were held on church premises and led by the minister. This lasted as the normal type of church life through to the early seventies.

- Then followed a more *informal,* Californian hippy inspired approach with "praise" as the main aspect of Sunday services (often led by a worship leader) with a guitar backing, although a wider range of instruments were included as the years went by. Casual clothing is the norm, group leadership is often the preferred style of church structure, and we have seen a considerable development of home groups led by lay people.

Today, this informal style is in turn being challenged by an approach which goes by several names, such as "emerging church," "fresh expressions of church," or "messy church." There has been some resistance to the ideas coming out of these movements; their theology is sometimes doubtful, their thinking too often focused on a style of meeting rather than on the whole life of a church, and their approach is often inspired by a reaction to the church situation in North America, which is not the same as in Europe.

So the question we are facing is: where do we go from here in considering what kind of church for postmodern Europeans? Most of the books I have written are regarding cultural trends in the particular French context. However, I believe that the thinking I have developed is applicable in a wider European perspective, because I am not talking about short-term tactics but rather longer-term strategy. I am trying to see the main thrust of the New Testament as compared to what seems normal just because it is in widespread usage.

I would like to suggest four areas which a church for postmodern Europeans must address—and as a bonus, we will find that each component doubles up as being relevant in evangelism. This means that we do not have to choose between edification and evangelism since each bridge to unbelievers is at the same time a basic part of Christian life! I have developed these ideas further in my book, *Passerelles* (*Bridges*).[1]

As a final word of introduction, this thinking can be applied more widely than solely church planting. I believe in church planting, and have been involved in that ministry for the last thirty-eight years, but it is my deep conviction that existing churches also need to think this through. There has been a tendency in Europe to write off existing churches because church planting has been so effective in evangelism. But if for every new church plant an older church dies, we have not really advanced. In the mission for which I work (*France Mission*), we have seen churches that were planted in the second half of the twentieth century lose their initial dynamic. So it is also important to renew existing churches. My hope is that the next wave of church planting will be along the lines I suggest in this chapter, and that this content will be adopted in older churches, too.

1. Brown, *Passerelles*.

Four bridges

1. The human condition

One obvious thing that Christians and non-Christians have in common is our humanity. Believers face the same questions and challenges as every human being on earth, albeit with a different perspective. So how does this become an important part of our church life? I would like to suggest it should occur in three ways.

- *Our human solidarity.* Jesus made it very clear that after our love for God, the greatest commandment is to love our neighbor as ourselves (Matt 22:39). This can be simply helping in our neighborhood or at work, or it may involve a more structured approach, when money is involved, to help the poor. In the case of our church in Paris, situated in a fairly affluent district of the city, we have opened a Fair Trade shop so that our fellow citizens can help developing countries by purchasing products—the food grown, or handicrafts made in these countries—in such a way that the producers receive a decent income for their work. And, of course, the shop brings us in contact with non-Christians as a bonus!

- *Our human identity.* In postmodern Europe, identity questions are everywhere. Christians can help people to see their value as we proclaim and live out the fundamental truth that we have been created in the image of God (Gen 1:27). Rather than being obliged to construct our own identity, which is quite unnerving once people start to really think about it, we can find our true identity and tell people that "you can become the sort of person you really want to be," confident that the image of God in them is really pulling them towards biblical truth.

   The core issue is this: is there such a thing as human nature? Christians are "essentialists" since we believe in the fundamental essence of human beings, but postmodern thinkers follow the classical statement of the existential philosopher, Jean-Paul Sartre: "Existence precedes essence." His partner, Simone de Beauvoir, affirmed in similar terms (back in 1949!): "On ne naît pas femme, on le deviant" ("You are not born as a woman, you become one.").[2] So postmodernists are trying to construct their own identity, since

2. de Beauvoir, *Le Deuxième Sexe.*

nothing is predetermined. That is what is at stake, and Christians can bring a real feeling of relief into this situation. We really do have value and values.

- *Our human conduct.* The New Testament makes it clear that our conversion means the restoration of our relationship with God (John 17:3). But that is only half the story since conversion starts a process of the restoration of God's image in us so that we become like His Son, Jesus, the perfect man (Rom 8:29; 2 Cor 3:18). In other words, Christians should become the most human of all humans, and avoid false triumphalism. I believe that non-Christians would rather hear how we cope with our problems and difficulties with God's help than listen to implausible testimonies of complete and instantaneous deliverance.

2. The church is the new humanity

This leads on from the previous point. Christians are to become like Christ in their humanity, but it does not stop there. Our Trinitarian God is a God of relationships. The two greatest commandments exhort us to love God and to love others—both Christians and non-Christians (1 Thess 3:12; 5:15). But the church is God's letter that anyone can read (2 Cor 3:3), and it is most visible when there is a genuine love between the members of a church fellowship. "By this all men will know that you are my disciples, if you love one another" (John 13:35). Two New Testament texts beginning with the same words, "No one has ever seen God," illustrate this well. John 1:18 says, "No one has ever seen God," but he is made visible by the incarnation of Jesus. In 1 John 4:12 we also read, "No one has ever seen God," but he is made visible when Christians have real love for each other. In other words, an unselfish interest in each other's good in a spirit of practical service. The incarnation in the strictest theological sense is that of Jesus, but there is an incarnation in a secondary sense since Christians are the body of Christ (1 Cor 12:12ff; Eph 4:15–16). We are members of that body, and the main visible revelation of God in the midst of unbelievers.

Ephesians 2 starts with salvation by grace (v 8–9) to affirm that we are God's workmanship (v 10) and the new humanity, (v 11–18) which is explicitly stated in verse 15. And yet the apostle has to exhort Christians to live out this fact. Just as Jewish and Gentile believers did not find it easy in the early church, Christians today also have to make the effort to really form this new humanity by accepting our differences (of temperament, age, gender, culture, and so on) on God's basis. "Accept one another, then, just as Christ accepted you, in order to bring praise to God." (Rom 15:7)

3. True spirituality

Surprisingly, in the postmodern world there has been a resurgence of spirituality, the need for something to re-enchant the world. Some twenty-first century atheist philosophers in France have even written about the way in which they are attracted to spirituality. However, this postmodern spirituality is more concerned with immediate feelings of individual well-being, and not with God or eternity. "Living fully in the here and now," is the most often quoted definition of this return to the "spiritual life." In this context it has even been suggested that a synonym for evangelism could be, "initiation into true biblical spirituality"! This spirituality puts God's eternal salvation at the center, which we have already seen as first and foremost relational (with God, within the church, and with non-Christians), refusing the sacred/secular divide (since we are Christians 24 hours a day, 7 days a week).

How can we live this out? One analysis of the chronology of culture goes as follows. Pre-modernity is turned towards the past (traditions), modernity is turned towards the future (the idea of progress), but post-modernity is focused on the present. However, this is not a problem for Christians because the Bible repeatedly uses the word "today" (well over two hundred times, in fact), and exhorts us to live in the present—albeit in the light of eternity, sub specie *aeternitatis* (Eccl 11:9–10). In other words, God wants us to live seamlessly, not with two or more different identities according to the group of people we are with, as many post-moderns do without even realizing it. I suggest that there are four main aspects of the life of a disciple and that each one can be summarized by the word "today."

- *Worship.* "The living, the living—they praise you, as I am doing *today*" (Isa 38:19, emphasis added). Our deepest desire is to worship and glorify God day by day. "Your name be hallowed." This is a choice that God should be recognized, respected, and worshipped by the whole world . . . starting with me. The expression, "living *coram Deo*" has even come into contemporary evangelical language—a sense of God's presence and a sense of wonder about life where God is never absent from anything we do. How else can postmodern men and women understand the importance of faith in God as compared to a "lifestyle choice," which is a purely personal decision, and only applies to our lives when we feel like it?

- *Trust.* "So that your trust may be in the LORD, I teach you *today*, even you" (Prov 22:19, emphasis added). A large part of our Christian walk is to learn to depend on God in all circumstances. "Give us *today* our daily bread" (Matt 6:11, emphasis added). Bread is a very real and concrete example, but as disciples of Jesus, trust is a characteristic attitude in every area of our life. A great many of the Psalms dwell on trust in God when everything seems hopeless. The New Testament teaching on prayer comes back repeatedly to the fact that Christians need not be anxious about anything but, "in everything, by prayer and petition, with thanksgiving, present your requests to God. And the peace of God, which transcends all understanding, will guard your hearts and your minds in Christ Jesus." (Phil 4:6–7)

- *Obedience, fighting the good fight, day by day.* This is the bravery of down to earth sanctification; this is our Christian "fight club." "But encourage one another daily, as long as it is called *Today*, so that none of you may be hardened by sin's deceitfulness" (Heb 3:13, emphasis added). The model of Alcoholics Anonymous (AA) is very useful here. A member of AA never promises that he will never again drink alcohol. His biggest problem is to abstain today—those 24 hours are the only ones when he can act. Yesterday has gone. Tomorrow never comes. But he can decide not to drink today. The same principle applies to the Christian in his daily fight to please God and resist temptation. It is heroic to live in the present since most people prefer to wallow in nostalgia (things were better in the past), or to live in a hypothetical future (everything will be fine when . . . I pass my exams, I get a job, I find a husband, I can buy a nice house, I am retired). I believe that this concept of heroism is a particularly good approach for men who are often in short numbers in our churches.

- *Loving people.* The Christian life is not only heroic; it's also a daily adventure. Each day we can ask God to put people on our path, and for him to help us to recognize them when they appear; people whom we can care for and love, and with whom we can share the Good News.

> *Devote yourselves* to prayer, being watchful and thankful. And pray for us, too, that God may open a door for our message, so that we may proclaim the mystery of Christ, for which I am in chains. Pray that I may proclaim it clearly, as I should. Be wise in the way you act toward outsiders; make the most of *every opportunity*. Let your conversation be always full of grace, seasoned with salt, so that you may know how to answer everyone (Col 4:2–6, emphasis added).

I love a sentence from a recent book that was explaining the situation of women in the early church:

> In a world where the majority of people were suffering poverty, illness or abuse, a woman would have countless opportunities to help where help was desperately needed. She would then naturally explain how she had learned this happy way of life from Jesus who had done so much for her.[3]

Yes, indeed! The best evangelism is each Christian's daily life, but too often churches feel the need for a "campaign" to mobilize the troops (in the same way we say that a trade union in France needs to organize the occasional strike to remain plausible for its members!). But compared to the proven way of spreading the Gospel—through relationships—I have the impression that these promotions can be counter-productive.

In my view, this was confirmed by the results of a questionnaire organized in France in 2013 by the Evangelism Commission of the *Conseil National des Évangéliques de France* (CNEF, the National Council of French Evangelicals). In answer to the question, "What is the best form of evangelism today?" a massive 87.6 percent of pastors chose: "Encouraging church members to build relationships with non-Christians." Unsurprisingly, the type of training most requested in the contemporary context was how to successfully build such relationships in order to share the Gospel (75.3 percent of respondents)!

4. The story line of human history.

For most postmodernists, history is going nowhere. There is no meaning, no direction, and no goal. Just a whole population that wants to make

---

3. Daniel, *Missionary Strategies Then and Now*. See also Orr, *Not So Secret*.

their own choices and feels in need of protection from society in order to keep this freedom. Thus, the only widely accepted value is the concept of tolerance. But the Bible does provide a story line for human history, which allows us to make sense of what is going on around us in the world. The outline the Bible presents is in five stages:

> creation > fall > redemption > the present age (already but not yet) > eternity

The very fact that Christians think history is neither circular nor meaningless, but is moving towards a goal (when God will be all in all), can be seen as a shocking claim in today's world—it seems arrogant and intolerant. But there is a French proverb: *chassez le naturel, il revient au galop* ("If you drive out what is natural, it will only come galloping back."). We believe that humans are made in the image of God and will respond to the truth. One of these truths is that we live in an abnormal world since the Fall. The seventeenth century French scientist and philosopher, Blaise Pascal, became a Christian at the age of thirty-one, and wrote in his *Pensées,* "No other religion has taught that man is born in sin. No philosophers have affirmed it, so none of them have spoken truly."

This means that we can call our contemporaries to repentance in the deepest sense of the word; to change their way of thinking and their mental constructions (their picture of reality, their vision of the world). This is so important today! And, in fact, the process of transformation continues as we grow in the faith. "Do not conform any longer to the pattern of this world, but be transformed by the renewing of your mind. Then you will be able to test and approve what God's will is—his good, pleasing and perfect will." (Rom 12:2)

As Christians, we have the privilege of taking our place in the unfolding of history, seeking to do God's will, and seeing his eternal plans come to fruition in Christ in our local churches, and worldwide as well. Since God is our Creator as well as our Redeemer, the story line of history helps us get the right balance in our life and witness—namely that the spiritual is not more important than the material, but that the eternal is more important than the temporal.

Practical ways towards the outworking of these four bridges

To conclude this chapter, I would like to suggest four ways in which all this can be worked out as we look at the form of church which will be plausible, relevant, and biblical in the twenty-first century.

1. As we meet together as churches, we must consciously aim at being the people of God who know each other and care for one another. Small groups are one way to do this, but I would also plead for the weekly service to be more like a "gathering" with (i) worship that is both festive and meditative (and adapted to each culture), (ii) teaching which engages with an intergenerational church, and (iii) space for fellowship (we have a meal together practically every week in our church in Paris). This enables us to encourage real face to face relationships—and to provide a useful counterbalance to the more impersonal side of social networks!

2. In the city, the best strategy could well be to multiply progressively the number of services and meetings at various times throughout the week to meet the diverse needs of people in this context. Hours of work can be very varied, but the cost of property might well make constant growth prohibitively expensive if the aim is to bring all the members of the church together at the same time. "Micro" churches help people to really get to know each other, but all these congregations make up just one church since they share the same premises, the same website, and the same overall leadership group.

3. We need to ensure that we give space for people to travel towards faith at their own speed within the Christian community. This does not mean that we will lose our Christian identity since baptism and church membership will continue to keep our churches functioning as "confessing churches." But people do need time in today's context to understand what it means to become a Christian. Society has moved so far from our European Christian roots that we must extend a welcome to people and let them see our day in/day out, week in/week out way of life, so that they can move beyond the two big barriers to faith, which are,

    •   Ignorance of what the Bible says

    •   Lack of plausibility of Christianity

The questions each Christian then has to ask is: Would I be happy to invite someone to my church who has not yet started on the journey to faith? Will they understand what is going on? Will they see that the Christians are really interested in the whole of life? That applies not just to the individual Christian; each church should also be looking at itself and asking the same questions.

4. But at the same time, it is not enough to be plausible within the four walls of our church building. Churches need to have visibility in the community. They need to be seen as partners (at least in some sense) with the local authorities, and to be present in the municipal magazine and on the town's website. A humanitarian project involving non-Christians may well be another bridge towards the community.

Conclusion

Coming back to my original question, "What type of church for postmodern Europeans?" I am aware that the cultural forms of the past also contain elements which are important to remember. In the first church style I mentioned, there is the notion of respect for the majesty of God ("you would put on your best clothes to meet the President of the Republic?"). In the second church style, there is the recognition that God is present and sees the heart, so the outer surface of our being is not so important ("Come as you are").

However, I contend that what we should be aiming for today is simple, no-frills Christianity, which in postmodern society is the new radical. Therefore, a church for postmodern Europeans will be integrated into culture (and therefore not become a sub-culture), and be vitally different, because the Christians will be living out *today* the basics of discipleship. And we will find that this is also the best form of evangelism.

Discussion highlights

Much of the discussion focused on two sections of the population: migrants and families. One participant wondered whether migrants in Paris fell into the postmodern category as described during the presentation.

Brown responded that in his experience there was a "double immigrant population." There were Christians who expected their church life to be the same as in their country of origin, and non-Christians who would be happier to be involved in the type of church outlined above. A distinction also needed to be made between first and second-generation immigrants, as those who are French-born are more similar to the indigenous population. The churches' identity was French, as Brown explained, "In one sense if we want to reach the majority population, we need to be as integrated into the majority population as possible. I have always said I want in my church to be Franco-plural—so we are plural but we are French as well."

Another participant noted that Brown had not mentioned working in and through families as a means of growing the church. Brown replied that they recognized the importance of being an intergenerational church, and people of all ages attended their church, from babies to octogenarians. However, the high cost of living in central Paris tended to mean families moved to the suburbs. In their present context, therefore, they do not work so much with families as previously.

Brown ended with three questions of his own about the church of the future. First, he was not completely convinced about the emphasis of structured programs for disciples making disciples, and put this forth as a question. He spoke to the topic, saying, "I much prefer to say I disciple someone when they have a question. That is the time when we go further with them. I do meet with some people to discuss all sorts of things, but I am concerned about the tendency in some quarters to more or less reduce discipleship to only being soul winners."

Second, he brought up the issue about the impact of the growth of social networks and new technology on relationship-building, commenting that there is a place for churches to help people have face-to-face relationships with others—which can be more difficult for people today than sending a message to someone who they do not see.

Third, he asked whether new and emerging churches were losing their vision for the world and missions. "There seems to be so much to do where you live, but I wonder how we can bring world mission into the forefront of the church's concern," he said.

Brown was certain about one thing, however. "We do need to say that we are entering a new phase. The paradigm of the church as we have known it over the last forty years cannot last any longer. We have to think of new ways of being church for today's world."

11

THE CHURCH IN A MULTICULTURAL SOCIETY

ANDREW POWNALL

I LIVE IN AN area called Ménilmontant, in the 20th arrondissement on the east side of Paris. It is situated at the boulevard on which the eighteenth century wall of Paris used to be found. My apartment is just opposite a Metro station, and sits on a busy cross-road. There are people around all the time—from five in the morning until the middle of the night. We even have the occasional brass band concert at one o'clock in the morning!

As long as the city wall survived, Ménilmontant was an area where Parisians came for leisure. There were bars and cabarets, and the wine was cheaper than in Paris. Then people flooded in from the countryside, and small industries set up business. Poor Germans and Belgians came looking for work, and Jews and Armenians sought refuge from persecution in Eastern Europe and Turkey, along with Spaniards from their Civil War, followed by Italians and Portuguese. France was an attractive destination, and in the 1950s/60s, North Africans flocked in as well. During the 1970s, Chinese Boat People came from Indochina, and in the 1980s and '90s economic refugees arrived from Africa. Today, there is a very mixed community, with a Jewish school on one side of the street and Islamic bookshops on the other. When we bought our apartment, our non-Christian friends said how lucky we were, and our Christian friends thought we were mad! Why choose to go and live in such a multicultural area? I would like to speak here about five challenges.

The Challenge of a Multicultural World

The world changed so fast in the second half of the twentieth century. Colonies became independent, the economy was globalized, and international transport was democratized. Major European cities witnessed an unprecedented influx of immigrants, the scale and complexity of which went far beyond any recent experience. This raised scores of questions and threw up enormous challenges. Assimilation into French society had always worked well with the immigrants from Eastern and Southern Europe. The children went through the State school system and adopted local culture. Our former president, Nicolas Sarkozy, is the son of a Hungarian immigrant, and our current Prime Minister is from a family of Spanish refugees. There was a broad social consensus in France around immigration policy until the middle of the twentieth century.

In the 1960s the government expected to assimilate the next wave of immigrants just as easily (North Africans, West Indians, and black Africans). However, as the economy slowed down in the 1970s, the government was proved wrong, and explosions of violence broke out in the suburbs of Lyons in 1981 and 1990, and in the suburbs of Paris in 2005 and 2007. Strong popular feeling against immigration began to find expression in votes for the National Front.

How is immigration viewed in other countries? In the United States and Britain, for example, "race" is an important issue. In France, however, race is not an official category (even if we acknowledge that we have a problem of racism). If you appreciate French cheese and wine, and French humor, you can be well accepted in French society, whatever your origins.

In France, culture is the principal stumbling-block for the integration of immigrants, and we live in a world which is increasingly multicultural, where new subcultures are constantly coming into existence! Culture is a very complex reality. The Report of *The Willowbank Consultation* defined it like this,

> Culture is an integrated system of beliefs (about God or reality or ultimate meaning), of values (about what is true, good, beautiful and normative), of customs (how to behave, relate to others, talk, pray, dress, work, play, trade, farm, eat, etc.), and of institutions which express these beliefs, values and customs (government, law courts, temples or churches, family, schools, hospitals, factories, shops, unions, clubs, etc.), which binds a

society together and gives it a sense of identity, dignity, security, and continuity.[1]

What is going to bind people together in a multicultural society and give them identity, dignity, security, and continuity? If culture were easy to define and live with, we would not have a problem with it. But it has been compared to icebergs, which provoke shipwrecks! Much of human culture is invisible to the naked eye and is assimilated unconsciously. It is composed of many implicit beliefs, mental constructions, and judgments, which influence every aspect of our behavior, and are very difficult to change.

For a time, a certain fascination with the "exotic" character of another culture may give wings to a relationship, but it will not last long. In our personal and collective relationships with people of other cultures, we do not always discern the potential traps. In intercultural relationships, conflicts are often provoked on an unconscious level, and this only serves to increase confusion, frustration, and all manner of misunderstandings. If culture is like icebergs, the avoiding of collisions will require an important measure of sensitivity—both to the other person's and to one's own culture.

Real or perceived inequalities, for example, have a major influence on the communications, relationships, and functioning of a group, because people habitually accord more or less value to other cultures. According to their cultural origins, people perceive themselves as equals, superiors, or subordinates to others, and this has quite an impact on group dynamics. In a group composed of equals, the leader can simply "direct the traffic" like a policeman in the middle of a busy cross-road. With people used to functioning as subordinates, the leader will have to be more directive or solicit participation more actively.

In multicultural groups, representatives of the dominant culture often fix the agenda, monopolize the conversation, and make most of the decisions. They can feel guilty at times when they see the representatives of other cultures taking a back seat, but they see no remedy to such a state of affairs. We have probably had some similar experiences, because failures in intercultural relationships are frequent. But patience in their construction can bring very great satisfaction.

---

1. Lausanne Committee, *The Willowbank Consultation on The Gospel and Culture.*

Healthy intercultural relationships are only possible, however, when the value of all cultures is recognized. Relationships can be in danger from certain ideas, even if these ideas are well-meaning and draped in a semblance of piety, humanism, or common sense. For example,

- In the name of shared humanity, some try to deny any differences, but they only succeed for a time.

- Others try to simplify matters by applying stereotypes corresponding to broad categories of culture (Western, African, or Asian), but these soon prove to be inadequate.

- Alternatively, others affirm common identity and look for points of resemblance while avoiding all expressions of difference, which are judged as potential sources of conflict, but the result of this the impoverishment of the relationship.

- Still others, feeling guilty about any differences, stigmatize them and complicate life for everybody. Alternatively they pride themselves in their success in accepting differences and then become intolerant of those who fail to do so, and reject them.

I grew up in a society where everybody shared the same national identity and the only problems of culture were related to social class. My children grew up in a very different world!

The Challenge of a Multicultural Church

At the same time as all these changes were happening in the world, secularization made an impact on Europe. Traditional churches emptied, and immigrants began to arrive in our local churches. The experience of French Protestant churches was similar to that of society. They were tempted to believe that the presence of ever-growing numbers of immigrants in their congregations was the proof of successful integration.

Of course, there were some false notes; misunderstandings between French and immigrant members; the sympathy for extreme right-wing views expressed by some members; the complaints of discrimination by some immigrant members; a few unexplained departures. These false notes hardly gave cause for concern, but were we really ready for the multicultural experience in our churches?

Are there any good biblical reasons for considering culture as important? Are we not "all one in Christ Jesus" (Gal 3:28)? True, there is no explicit or systematic treatment in the Bible of the question of cultural diversity, but attentive readers often see it hiding between the lines at every mention of languages, families, households, tribes, and nations. And migration has always been a part of human history, with the question of the respect due to immigrant workers already raised in Mosaic Law (Exodus 22:20, etc.).

The sanction against the builders of Babel (Gen 11), when God "confuse[s] their language so they will not understand each other" (v7), means that cultural diversity is often experienced as a curse! Or is it simply a return to positive normality? It all depends how you read your Bible! The articulation between the actions in Genesis 10–12 merits careful attention. In chapter 10, the author notes without the vaguest suggestion of disapproval, ". . . the maritime peoples spread out into their territories by their clans within their nations, each with its own language." (v5) The construction of the tower of Babel can thus be considered as a refusal of the diversity God put in his creation, and the divine call addressed to Abraham in chapter 12 as a remedy. God invites Abraham to travel in the direction of a new country, and to adopt a new identity in order to become a blessing for all the families of the earth (Gen 12:3).

At Pentecost (Acts 2), the sanction of Babel is overturned, because the Holy Spirit gives people of different cultures and languages the possibility of understanding each other. Have you noticed, however, how the cultural diversity of the church in Jerusalem soon provokes tensions? The Greek-speaking disciples complain of injustices by Hebrew-speaking disciples in the distribution of food to the poor. The apostles resolve the problem in a very culturally wise way; by allowing the church to elect a group of "deacons" from the minority group (they all have Greek names, Acts 6:5). I like to consider that the Church's welcome to people coming from other cultures is one of the central themes of the Acts of the Apostles, but it is not all plain sailing for them; the disciples continue to feel very Jewish, the Church takes a long time to mobilize in its mission to the ends of the earth, and passionate debates take place around the conversion of pagans (Acts 11:15).

At the "conference" of Jerusalem (Acts 15), the Church learns how to distinguish between what is essential and what is accessory, what belongs to human culture and what is part of the core of the Gospel, and to exchange unnecessary "either/or's" for "both/and's." In fact, the multicultural Church of the twenty-first century is just a dress rehearsal for the New Jerusalem! The last book of the New Testament presents the vision of an immense and colorful crowd in the heavens; ". . . a great multitude that no one could count, from every nation, tribe, people and language . . ." (Rev 7:9). It thus seems that culture will not be abolished in the afterlife, but it will no longer be a barrier to communion!

The multicultural nature of the early Church was a powerful witness to the world. The destruction of the "dividing walls of hostility" separating Jews and non-Jews (Eph 2:14), and reconciliation in Christ ("no Greek or Jew . . . barbarian, Scythian . . ." (Col 3:11)) were proof of the power of the Gospel. In the history of the Church, however, the culture of churches has very often been the dominant culture of the nation and of the church leadership, and church life has often been mono-cultural. In the Middle-Ages, each national church developed its own culture and was often very intolerant of the culture of religious minorities. During the colonial period, national churches exported their culture to their colonies, and it was not so much the missionaries who made an effort to adapt to local culture as it was the native Christians who adapted to Western culture. The Anglican Church of my youth had a single liturgy and a single style of music, which was played on the organ.

The experience of the Unites States can be instructive for us; they have had cultural and racial "segregation" of churches for over two centuries. African-Americans were traditionally relegated to church balconies and barred from all responsibility in church life, so they began to found independent churches at the end of the eighteenth century. There are several powerful African-American denominations today with their own seminaries, schools, and social institutions. Pentecostal revival at the beginning of the twentieth century had little impact on this situation, and more than a century later, in spite of all the progress made in civil rights, and the courageous experiments initiated in various denominations, it seems that Sunday morning is still the time of the week when racial segregation in the United States reaches its biggest proportions. Are integrated, multicultural churches to be considered as a missed opportunity in the USA?

The Challenge of Welcoming Immigrants

How should the churches in European cities in the twenty-first century react to cultural diversity? Where should we place the cursor on the continuum between emphasizing the importance of culture at one end, and attaching only relative importance to it at the other? Based on our understanding of the words of the apostle Paul, some will be tempted to consider that the question is of no importance because, "There is neither Jew nor Greek, slave nor free, male nor female, for you are all one in Christ Jesus" (Gal 3:28). At the other extreme, based on the work of certain missiologists, others will advocate the multiplication of evangelistic initiatives and the planting of churches in every culture.

I think we should note that the Son of God became flesh in a particular human culture, and every statement about God and all forms of Christian conduct are situated in the context of human culture. Far from looking down on culture, the Bible takes it very seriously, and surprisingly, our God chose to reveal himself in the context of different human cultures. This contrasts with Islam, for the Quran was written over a short period and exclusively in Arabic, while the Bible was written over a period of more than one thousand years, in widely varying contexts, and in three different languages. It is thus my belief that churches in a multicultural society should take culture seriously and each develop their own particular cultural policy.

At the same time, the Bible calls all cultures into question and invites people to transcend them by giving priority to the values of the Gospel. The apostle Paul writes, "Do not conform any longer to the pattern of this world, but be transformed by the renewing of your mind" (Rom 12:2). The Lausanne Covenant resumes the question this way:

> The development of strategies for world evangelization calls for imaginative pioneering methods. Under God, the result will be the rise of churches deeply rooted in Christ and closely related to their culture. Culture must always be tested and judged by Scripture. Because men and women are God's creatures, some of their culture is rich in beauty and goodness. Because they are fallen, all of it is tainted with sin and some of it is demonic. The gospel does not presuppose the superiority of any culture to another, but evaluates all cultures according to its own criteria of truth and righteousness, and insists on moral absolutes in every culture. Missions have all too frequently exported with the gospel an alien culture and churches have sometimes been

in bondage to culture rather than to Scripture. Christ's evangelists must humbly seek to empty themselves of all but their personal authenticity in order to become the servants of others, and churches must seek to transform and enrich culture, all for the glory of God.[2]

So what have secularization and immigration done for mission? How is mission in Europe different from mission in the time of our parents? There have always been foreign-language churches in our big cities, and every capital city has "expat" churches for embassy staff and business people. But in the 1980s, a new wave of immigrant church plants arrived in Europe bringing profound changes to the ecclesiastical landscape

The existence in the colonies of expatriate congregations alongside "native" ones seemed to be perfectly natural, but the recent multiplication of immigrant churches on the home turf of the former colonial powers is apparently more problematic! The arrival of Christians from other cultures generally makes churches in European cities more conscious of the challenge of coping with cultural diversity in the same way as the early church in Jerusalem; only when intercultural conflict breaks out (Acts 6)! Many urban churches now attract people from ten, twenty, or thirty different cultural origins. Creating relationships with these people, welcoming them into the church, and building up the church community with them represents so many new challenges for churches, and the culture shock is sometimes quite brutal.

The necessary effort of contextualization and of cultural adaptation means renouncing the security of well-established traditions and cherished habits of church life, and mustering the will to accept people from another culture as they are. This also means taking account of their culture in future developments, responding to the expectations of the immigrant community, and making room for them in church structures.

How can this be done while maintaining unity? This management of cultural diversity can take several major directions, and any number of intermediate paths.

1. When immigrants have few linguistic skills, there is the temporary solution of the bilingual or multilingual church, where the different congregations (or small groups during the week) allow each linguistic group to worship in its mother tongue, while benefitting from shared facilities under the direction of a united pastoral team.

2. Lausanne Committee for World Evangelization, *Lausanne Covenant*, par. 10.

2. Where different cultures claim a separate identity, but share a common language, it is generally sufficient for them to give expression to their culture in the context of church services and other activities, insofar as they show respect of the other cultures.

3. When immigrants choose to be assimilated into the culture of the host country, the church can actively help them to master the language, adopt local customs, and find their place in the local community.

Because they do not always receive the welcome they expect in European churches, Christian immigrants, like their African-American brothers in the USA, plant their own churches. Even if they faithfully follow the model of church life used by the historic Western mission agencies (Baptist, Methodist, Pentecostal, etc.), these immigrant churches, apart from rare exceptions, arouse suspicions in local pastors and are not welcomed into their respective denominations. A *de facto* segregation is thus created. Even when these churches join a local denomination, they do not always succeed in being fully integrated and able to take part in denominational life. This is often for very simple reasons, such as the difficulty for unpaid pastors to attend week-day pastors' fraternal business meetings. Typically, local churches under-estimate the phenomenon of immigrant church plants and initially tend to ignore them. They do not know how to handle the question, and hope it will soon go away!

It is only after several years, once the number of churches has multiplied and the first immigrant denominations come into existence, that local churches begin to take notice of what is happening and treat it seriously. In Germany in 1998, the United Evangelical Mission, conscious of the official church's need to reflect multicultural society, set up a "Program for Cooperation Between German and Immigrant Congregations," and organized a symposium, "From Reverse Mission to Common Mission," in May 2001. In a meeting some years ago with the general secretary of the Association for Missionary Services, an African pastor exclaimed, "Can't you see that we are like manna from heaven? God has sent us here to help you evangelize Germany. Why don't you make use of us?"[3]

The question, "sent by God, or a handicap?" calls for earnest self-examination by European leaders. Some German pastors react very negatively. Why should Germany be evangelized by Africans or Pentecostals? African pastors castigate German churches for their deadness because

3. Währisch-Oblau, "Mission in Reverse."

there are no extraordinary manifestations of the Spirit, and there is a fear of being controlled if they enter into partnerships. On the other side, German pastors fear emotion in worship, and have contempt for the lack of language skills and cultural awareness, instability, and rivalry among immigrant churches, and for the theological ignorance of their pastors.

In the 1990s, the Bible Institute of Nogent-sur-Marne (a suburb of Paris) set up a program for African pastors on Saturday mornings. The Protestant Federation of France admitted the *Communauté des Églises d'Expression Africaine* (CEAF), and the National Council of Evangelicals welcomed the *Entente des Communautés et Œuvres Chrétiennes* (ECOC), two Congolese denominations. In 2005, the Protestant Federation also established the "Mosaic Project" in order to build relationships with immigrant churches.

The Challenge of Cross-Cultural Evangelism

Cross-cultural evangelism is indeed a challenge, especially with unreached people groups. For a very long time our churches have traditionally preached the Gospel in their home region to people sharing the same culture as them, and sent missionaries abroad to evangelize people of other cultures. If churches in modern multicultural European cities are alert, they are discovering that they have a new mission—cross-cultural mission right on their doorstep! The tools which were once reserved for foreign missions are now indispensable for local evangelism, and new tools need to be developed for future generations.

Are our churches waking up to the possibilities? At a time when the church in Pakistan is a tiny minority, there are millions of descendants of Pakistani immigrants in Britain. But apparently only a few become converts to Christ. Why is this? Fear of Islam? Fear of Pakistani ghettoes? Lack of vision in churches?

There is a similar situation in France, with five or six million immigrants from North-Africa. The mission agencies of *Pioneers* and *Campus* have small teams of evangelists at work among them. There is revival in the midst of the non-Arab Berber population in the mountains of Algeria, but few local churches have seriously taken up the challenge of evangelizing their cousins in France. The situation is complicated by the colonial past, a dirty war of independence, racial prejudice, and cultural differences—and a host of opportunities have been lost. I wonder how my maternal grandfather would have reacted. A hundred years ago, he was a missionary to Muslims in the Middle East, and he was probably far from imagining that there would one day be a vast mission field among Muslims opening up in Europe!

In Montreuil-sous-Bois, in the eastern suburbs of Paris, we have the biggest concentration of Malians after Bamako, the capital of Mali. There are many among them who represent unreached people groups. In Mali, there are immense barriers to conversion, but in France, the churches have complete liberty to preach the Gospel to Malians. So far, sad to say, efforts have been very timid, and there is no permanent evangelistic personnel. My paternal grandfather was also a missionary, and he served in West Africa. He, too, probably could not even imagine that such a broad mission field would open up among West Africans in Europe!

Where is the vision in our churches for evangelizing the nations that have come to live on our doorstep? How much longer are we going to wait before we bring mission resources to European cities?

The Challenge of Partnering with Mission in Reverse

During the 1970s, it became common for citizens from the ex-colonies to minister to immigrants, and before the end of the twentieth century, the notion of "mission in reverse" came into being. According to Pentecostal bishop Bart Pierce of Baltimore (Maryland), "the African is the midwife for the next great move of God in America." Within two or three decades after the end of the colonial period, the balance of numbers in the worldwide Church (if not of power) had shifted. The number of Christians in Africa jumped from ten to 360 million in the twentieth century, and the number is set to double before 2025.[4]

The arrival of Christian immigrants and their church plants has slowed the process of secularization in Europe—and could even one day reverse it. In London, more than half of the people in churches on a Sunday morning are from immigrant families, and as of 2010, four of London's ten mega-churches are African. In Paris, immigrant churches represent half of the total number of protestant churches. In the Bible school where I taught, three-quarters of the students came from immigrant families, and many of these students will become leaders of the French churches of tomorrow.

4. *The New York Times*, April 12, 2009.

The Redeemed Church of God ("made in heaven, assembled in Nigeria, and exported to the world") already had 250 churches in Britain in 2007, and, according to its leader, Pastor Enoch Ajiboye, the plans are to plant a church "a five minute drive or walk from anywhere in the world."[5]

Many immigrant churches in Paris claim to be multicultural and that they evangelize the native French population, but in practice, "mission in reverse" is still in an embryonic state. Immigrant churches often keep traditions of church life imported from the homeland, and they have so far given very little thought to the contextualization of their message. In some churches the first generation of immigrants cling to their mother tongue, but the second generation is much less at ease and threatens to desert the immigrant churches.

I think of the example of one of my students. He has twenty years' experience in evangelism, church-planting, and church leadership in his home country, and came to France in 2013 on a student visa, with a call to evangelize France. He was impatient for action, and attended classes, but did none of the assignments. He was impatient with his local church, and his pastor had difficulty taking him seriously. Was there a whiff of contempt for our feeble efforts and a suspicion of over-optimism on his part? He made contact with one or two French denominations, but there was no structure prepared to take him on, no funding available for him and for his church-plant project, and he decided to go it alone. He will preach and take up an offering, and he will found another African church.

An African commentator writes the following on mission in reverse:

> African Churches in Europe are making many contributions and are bringing renewal to a continent that is fast losing its Christian roots and values. However they do have their shortcomings . . . lack of ecumenical partnerships, transplanting African Christianity to Europe without contextualizing, mono-ethnic mission strategies, abuse of prosperity theology, lack of involvement in global issues such as human trafficking and poverty. Nevertheless, it must be mentioned that these churches, compared to European missions in Africa, have only been in Europe for a relatively short period, and that they are still in the process of adapting and acclimatizing to their new environment. Let us give them a chance.[6]

5. *The Washington Post,* June 10, 2007.
6. Olofinjana, *Reverse in Ministry.*

Conclusion

The end of the twentieth century produced a cultural revolution whose consequences may only be revealed later in the twenty-first century. The cultural diversity of Europe is a continent-wide reality, with an increasing impact on church life. We live in an unexpectedly complicated situation, and our churches will have to give serious thought to culture, discern what God is saying in this situation, take account of it, and make some brave choices, or European churches will soon be as segregated as American churches. The *Manilla Manifesto* clearly lays down our responsibilities:

> City populations are extremely cosmopolitan, so that the nations come to our doorstep in the city. Can we develop global church-es in which the gospel abolishes the barriers of ethnicity?[7]

And the Cape Town Commitment adds:

> We long for the day when the Church will be the world's most visibly shining model of ethnic reconciliation and its most active advocate for conflict resolution.[8]

Discussion highlights

Many in the audience had experienced some of the challenges of being church in a multicultural society as outlined by Pownall. The discussion centered around practical examples and ideas as they shared both high-lights and discouragements.

A sense of distrust often exists between national and immigrant churches. Pastors feel threatened by the vision of immigrant pastors who want to "evangelize all of Europe," starting in their town. As one participant shared, "In Belgium we use a room in a public building. I was amazed to find a Nigerian church had a meeting in another room. I invited them to eat with us, but with no success. It seems that neither my

---

7. Lausanne Committee for World Evangeliziation, *Manilla Manifesto*, 1989, par. 10.

8. Lausanne Committee for World Evangeliziation, *Cape Town Commitment*, section II-B, par. 2-B.

church congregation nor the other church wanted to have meetings or contacts with one another."

"[Part] of the reason you struggle is because of the history between immigrant and national churches," said Pownall. "We look at their churches and say that we do not know what is happening, but they look at our churches and say the same thing about us. We need to break down the barriers, but at a deeper level than just pastor to pastor. How many immigrant Christians and church leaders do we have as personal friends?"

Pownall added a particular experience: "I was saddened by the comment about a West Indian evangelical leader in Paris. He told me that even after thirty years of integrated ministry working alongside French pastors to reach West Indians, he did not have a native French friend in the city. Friendship is a wonderful gift we can give to immigrant pastors, just as if we are missionaries; it is a wonderful gift for a local person to accept us as their friend. We can be doing that for Africans, Chinese, Koreans, and other colleagues. But to do that, we need to spend time with them, do things that we might not even like at first, and change our own thinking. Then when we approach them as a church we have a deeper understanding of where they are coming from. It is a challenge because it takes time, but this way you will probably have more success in the end."

The difference between cultures is identified as the biggest difficulty in building partnerships. Immigrant churches may do things that are not culturally acceptable, ranging from making everyone on the city Metro listen to a loud evangelistic conversation between a "non-Christian" and "Christian," to violently exorcizing "evil spirits" during their meetings. "How do we relate to the pastors when their theology is unclear and we have no idea whether they are orthodox in their beliefs?" a participant asked.

"Have some wise pastors from these countries give advice," Pownall suggested, "and, in addition, seek to build relationships. Rather than excluding new immigrant pastors from the pastors' fraternal because you are unsure of their theology, have an initial associate membership to help get to know them. A preaching workshop would give the opportunity to discuss theology together and see what their theology is like. And if they ask to use your church for meetings, why not attend one of their current services to see what happens there.

"These are our brothers and sisters and they are part of the body of Christ," he added. "We need to make room for them with us. We are

going to have to extend our training to them to help them become culturally aware in the new world they are living in.

"If you are like me, with the first few contacts you do not realize how
important this is going to be. When I saw the first African church arrive
in Paris, I didn't think it had a future. I was invited to preach to a Haitian
congregation, but I never imagined that forty years later there would be
seventy or eighty Haitian churches in Paris. We find it difficult to realize
the importance of what is happening around us. By building relationships and offering resources you will be giving input to churches who will
be major players in the future."

12

MUSLIMS IN EUROPE AND THE NEED FOR CHURCH PLANTING

Ishak Ghatas

Muslims come to Europe for various reasons; some as students, others as refugees, or some who are simply following influences of former colonialism. But the majority are those who come as "guest workers." Their presence in Europe is a reality that Christians should be concerned with. Christianity and Islam are two large faiths, and both involve a missionary mandate to be in witness and discussion with others. As Christians work to build the kingdom of God, they need to learn to relate their message in the context of all spiritual traditions, including that of Muslims. Christians should see Muslims as a part of local European communities. The struggles of Muslims deserve Christian involvement. Muslims, both the radicals and the moderates, have the right to hear and to experience the Christian message. There should not be any missing faces in the church of Christ. All are invited to become disciples and active members.

The Presence of Muslims in Europe

European Muslim communities are growing. Europe has about thirty-eight million Muslims constituting roughly 5 percent of the population. European Muslims make up slightly more than 2 percent of the world's Muslim population. About twenty to twenty-five million Muslims are living in the European Union, where they account for 4 to 5 percent of a total population of 505.7 million. Another sixteen million Muslims are living in Russia.[1] The Muslim population in the EU is expected to double by 2025. Khettani has noted that,

> The percentage of World Muslim population with respect to the total World population has increased steadily and will continue to increase, from 17% in 1950 to 26% estimated by 2020. While the total European population will increase from 548 million in 1950 to 744 million by 2020 the percentage of Muslims in Europe will increase from 2% in 1950 to 6% by 2020.[2]

These statistics also show that the growth in the Muslim population in Europe is higher than their worldwide growth, (2 percent in 1950 to 6 percent in 2020, versus 17 percent to 26 percent worldwide) and the growth is significantly higher when compared with other European citizens' growth.

Local history and development of European Muslim communities

After World War II, the major industrial nations of Western Europe introduced "guest-worker" systems through which large numbers of immigrants were received into the labor force during the post-war economic boom. They were considered migrant laborers recruited to work temporarily in a host state. Successive waves of guest laborers from Morocco, Algeria, Tunisia and Turkey came to Europe to compensate for shortages on the European national labor markets. Many came to former colonial countries. In the beginning these labor agreements sounded like invitations for temporary residence; "guest workers" came to meet the needs of the domestic labor market and were considered as short-term sojourners. However, the majority of these "guest workers" came from countries with Muslim majorities, and they stayed in Europe. The settlement of these labor immigrants in the receiving country was neither expected nor desired. Therefore, the future of immigrants was not clear. Hansen states, "The history of migration in Europe is one of unforeseen developments and unintended consequences."[3] It seems that Europe was not prepared

---

1. Eurostat, "News Release 173/2013."

2. Kettani, "Muslim Population in Europe: 1950–2020," 154.

3. Hansen, *Migration to Europe*, 25. See also Prugl and Thiel, *Diversity in the European Union*.

for long settlements, and immigrants themselves had no clear vision of their future.

A restriction of labor migration took place following the 1973 oil crisis and the subsequent economic decline. At that time, European countries tried to put a stop to labor migrations aiming at "zero immigration."[4] The proposed official large-scale labor migration stop spread from one country to another. Across Europe, all countries ended primary migration in the early seventies. The UK acted first in 1971, and France and Germany followed in 1972 and 1973 respectively. Everyone else did the same within a year or two. These restrictions may have ended the "legal entry" of labor migrants, nevertheless, the deed was done, and many migrants had become citizens, and as such claimed a right to family reunification.[5]

It is evident that in the last forty years, post zero immigration, the control of migration did not end the flow of immigrants and their family members. Muslims increased due to both external and internal reasons. Hansen observes,

> Family reunification and higher birth rates locked this population in and expanded upon it, and the result in Europe is a non-white . . . population.[6]

Consequently, Muslims became a permanent component of the European population. Their estimated population varied from one author to another, and that made it difficult to obtain accurate estimations. However, their permanent presence in Europe became a reality.

The arrival of immigrants could be divided into two main stages: their arrival as guest workers, and the arrival of their families. The taking of partners from home countries for marriage and the birth rate contribute to the immigrants' increase in number. From the European perspective, as immigration became permanent, it must then be managed. However, the community is far from being settled. The questions of assimilation, integration, or multiculturalism have been important topics in Europe in order to find ways of accommodating migrants. Recently, attention has been given within the EU to consider the development of what they call "transitional migrant communities," linking together

---

4. Triandafyllidou and Gropas, *European Immigration*, 3.

5. Hansen, *A Superabundance of Contradictions*, 22–25.

6. Hansen, *Migration to Europe*, 33.

their societies of origin and the societies of settlement.[7] The continued changes of strategies in managing the influx of immigrants show that the situation of migrants, from a European viewpoint, remains unsettled.

Diversity, living patterns, and new generations

It should be noted that European Muslims are not a unified community. Though they share common values, they should not to be considered as a monolithic whole. Their differences are related to ethnic, cultural, religious, and linguistic elements. Muslims have a tendency to live in big European cities and settle together in particular areas of the city.

The second and third generations do not appear to have changed into any kind of "trans-national Muslims" or "European Muslims." They are still shaped by their (grand)parents' culture, although at the same time they have non-Muslim friends, and might be formed by the positive or negative experiences in the host countries. Some suggest a possible, but unclear, shift.

> There is shift from an "Islam of parents" to an "Islam of children." But still not clear what forms this Islam will take.[8]

Will the children adopt a form of Islam that considers the European context, or simply depend on traditional institutions as in the countries of origin?

It is also important to consider that the European-born generations from Turkish or Moroccan background carry ethnic differences that might distinguish their identities. Anna Triandafyllidou reports that "different communities are allowed to maintain their own cultures and identities and live in parallel societies with a single state."[9]

Ethnic groups are a growing phenomenon, and Muslims particularly form significant clusters that have become part of the fabric of European life. Different forms of accommodation have been introduced to facilitate life in pluralistic Europe. Multiculturalism has been used as a policy label on how to deal with collective ethnic, cultural, and religious diversity in Europe. It is becoming more and more a pluralistic continent.

7. Triandafyllidou and Gropas, *Integration, Transnational Mobility and Human, Social and Economic Capital*.

8. Landman, "Islam in the Benelux Countries," 118.

9. Triandafyllidou, *Addressing Cultural, Ethnic, Religious Diversity Challenges in Europe*, 28.

All of this has a bearing on our mission to communicate the Gospel and plant churches in Europe. "Generally speaking," writes David Bosch, "we are dealing with three tensions: between 'danger and opportunity,' as mission grapples with the present crisis; between 'divine providence and human confusion,' as mission works out what is an 'ambivalent enterprise' between text and context; and between the two callings of the Church in its 'being called out of the world and sent into the world.'"[10]

We shall now see how this applies to church planting among Muslims in the European context.

The need for Church planting among Muslims in European contexts

What church planting models and strategies could serve the best? I will survey here the principles, methods, and strategies for church-planting among Muslims in European contexts. I also hope to draw the attention of theological schools in Europe to seriously consider relevant programs to train ethnic leaders for this great need.

The church has developed church planting strategies that consider this new reality in Europe. Muslims, the subject of concern, are not the people who live somewhere else, but are our neighbors in all European states. They are in Europe to live and stay, and they have the right to hear the good news. The universal church should include all without missing any people groups in its memberships. The redemptive plan of God (John 3:16) includes all people, and the image of the church in Revelation 7:9 portrays the church as including all nations. Peter Wagner defines church as,

> All that is involved in bringing men and women, who do not have a personal relationship with Jesus Christ, into fellowship with him and into *responsible church membership*.[11]

While it is true that the universal church is supra-culture and supra-national, the New Testament makes us aware of mono-ethnic/multi-ethnic questions in the portrayal of early local churches (for example, Acts 6,10,13,15, or Eph 2:14–22). Could this provide biblical grounds to guide any search for better church planting models and strategies? One

---

10. Bosch, *Transforming Mission*, 7–11.

11. Wagner, *Your Church Can Grow*, 12. (Emphasis added)

must examine the aim of the Church and how this may apply to a church in which Muslim converts would feel at home.

The generally hoped-for objectives in any church planting situation should aim to make mature, active, responsible, and reproducing members. Many individuals and churches in Europe have begun to face the challenge and have developed strategies in response to the Islamic presence. However, there remains a great need to plant more churches for those who may come out from Islam to Christ.

Church planting among Muslims in a European context

Doing church planting among Muslims in Europe could prove to be more difficult and complicated than doing the same in their homelands. The principles of tolerating the other, and the fear of racism in Europe are but some of the challenges for church planting. Furthermore, foreigners are often viewed as unwanted, and even as a source of trouble. Such attitudes may discourage European churches from engaging in church planting among Muslim people. The fear factor in dealing with Islam may discourage Christians who would otherwise consider working among Muslims.

As for the Muslim community itself that lives as a minority in countries with a non-Muslim majority, they may feel threatened by evangelistic efforts, and therefore turn inwards to become more protective.

Churches are expected to be caring communities including the true meaning of "*Koinonia*," fellowship. I consider the meaning of "fellowship" here to be deeper than just social functions. It involves working together, and responding to all felt needs of its members, not just the "spiritual" needs. These expectations demand consideration, and enforce the need to engage nationals in church planting. In church planting efforts among Muslims there is often too much theory and not enough practice. During early stages of evangelism experts put much emphasis on apologetically based questions such as: Is the God of Islam the same as the God of the Bible? Could there be other ways for salvation than through the cross of Jesus?

In my perspective, it is not an exaggeration to say that there is something unique about Islam, but we need to produce an effective contemporary biblical apologetic to emphasize the uniqueness of Christ and the importance of ethnic churches. Other questions should be sorted out after accepting the Lord.

In general, the average person who comes to faith is encouraged when attending a local church service in which he feels comfortable and understood. For the Muslim convert, the feeling of being at home includes the aspects of fellowship ("sharing things in common"), and growing into a sense of shared ownership as partners. This type of church is even more important to Muslims who are used to thinking of the mosque as not only the center of religious life and a meeting place for prayers, but also for public announcements, and for obtaining counsel and permission for major life decisions of all kind.

Given this context, Muslims in Europe are different than the average European, and therefore need a church model that is different from the typical European church. "Human beings exist not as discrete individuals but as interconnected members of some society," points out Donald McGavran.[12] Muslims living in Europe clearly demonstrate this principle and may extend it as a means for protecting their identity. Older generations often reject integrating into the new society, while many of the younger generations struggle between the two worlds. In many European countries Islamic organizations are created not only to protect their prospective communities, but also to influence the legislation of the host country so that it becomes more favorable towards Muslims.

In addition, elderly people have more difficulties understanding European languages and cultural issues. Very often they become proud of their "Muslim package" of culture and faith and see no need to add from or adapt to the new society. They desire to pass this package to the younger generations as well. The younger generations are more exposed to the "European package" of ethics and culture. Although they receive the "Muslim package" from their parents and religious leaders, they seem to be more aware of the need to learn the language of the host country and to adapt from "the European package" what suits them. However, in most cases Muslim families in Europe are protected by their communities and religious leaders.

All these factors, and the Muslims' confusion between religion as a personal faith and as a determinant in social and legal relationships, highlight the need for ethnic churches. At the secular level, the full integration of Muslims in Western societies still remains a complicated issue.

12. McGavran, *Understanding Church Growth*, 207.

Finding the right church for those who may accept Christ is critical. The question is: Which kind of church or fellowship would best fulfill the goal of bringing converts to the place of becoming vital, responsible members of a church? Which kind of church would be most able to help Muslim converts during this process? Here we should also consider the fact that for the Muslim converts, the commitment to become vital responsible members is made during a long process of several steps. Could the older generations feel more at home in ethnic churches? Would the younger generations in Europe see less need for ethnic churches or fellowships and prefer to integrate directly into existing churches? Will they prefer to continue the contact and activities with their own culture?

Different Church planting Models

To my knowledge the church planting models for Muslim converts in the European context could be summed up using the following four categories:

1. The autonomous ethnic church model

This model stands for ethnic churches that use ethnic languages. It works better if the selected ethnic group is big enough. Such ethnic churches may remove the feeling that Christianity is western and irrelevant, or that it may damage the ethnics' identity. Ethnic churches show the Christian faith as an applied dynamic for "life change," and may have a more direct impact on the community. Ethnic churches in Europe serve as living examples of expressing ethnic converts' new life in Christ without any fear of losing identity or feeling unbalanced due to major unnecessary changes. Through this model, Christian faith can be better translated into cultural forms, emotional factors can be adequately recognized, and the new converts can feel the side of Christianity where their emotional needs are met in a more family type atmosphere. Ethnic converts could be better trained and given leadership which would positively affect their growth and witness. They may easily develop culturally acceptable ways to reach their own people for Christ.

Ethnic churches in Europe may be less attractive to the younger generations due to their greater desire to be integrated into European life. They may see such a church as a cause for more isolation and foreignness in the host country. Christians from host countries may see a foreign element in ethnic churches as well, and feel foreign in its community, which would keep them from being helpful to such groups and even more sensitive towards them. However, strong ties within the ethnic families will make it possible for the younger generation to accept coming to such churches with their families. The ethnic churches should be part of the wider European church, and if languages of the host countries are used side by side with ethnic ones, it may encourage European attendants, especially of mixed marriages, to feel part of the ethnic church. The use of European languages is also important for younger generations who may speak the ethnic language but are unable to read or write it.

2. The European church with a sister ethnic church

According to this model, a European church will plant an ethnic sister church or fellowship that uses the building of the mother church. This model works for European churches who want to engage in Muslim work. When they have converts they encourage the forming of ethnic fellowships. The mother church and the ethnic groups may or may not have separate membership and leadership policies, so there are two types of this model.

Type 1

- Sunday worship together with weekly ethnic fellowships encouraged.
- The European and ethnic church form one membership and one leadership for all attendants.
- European language for church services and Sunday school.
- Ethnic and European languages are used for house groups/fellowships within the sister church.

Type 2

- European churches with sister ethnic church(es).
- Separate membership and leadership, but not totally independent from the mother church.
- Moral responsibility of mother church.
- Ethnic church uses the building/resources of mother church.

3. The model of a multi-ethnic or international urban church

The church in Antioch as described in Acts 11 and 13 could serve as a model for a multi-ethnic or international urban church. It works as a "melting pot" for people from different racial and religious backgrounds.

In some situations planting such a heterogeneous church is more in keeping with the demographic makeup of the local population. This model could work in urban areas where different but small ethnic groups live side by side. It demands more cooperation and equal involvement from its members. In such a church different languages, thought patterns, growth speeds, and value systems may co-exist, although it often chooses the language and leadership model of the host country. This church will encourage small ethnic Bible study groups, and youth and women meetings with their respective leaders. However, in order to enhance growth, the gatherings during the week should not merely be an "add-on" to the Sunday worship. The multi-ethnic church should adopt a holistic ministry strategy in order to meet spiritual as well as social and other felt needs of the community.

This model may give a positive image of the church in the multicultural society, as a community where people from different ethnic, social, and linguistic backgrounds are at home and care for each other. As such, it is an eloquent witness to the reconciling power of the Gospel.

4. The integration model

According to this model, Muslim converts integrate into existing local European churches. Integration is an option for a newcomer in a host church when he chooses it of his own free will. It implies that he or she agrees to respect the basic guidelines of the host church, while possibly retaining some of the original cultural identity. This model may appeal to second and third generations who prefer European culture. This model assumes that complete integration of Muslim converts into existing churches in Europe is possible, and that it is relatively easy for them to adapt to Western style church worship, evangelism, and fellowship.

However, it is important to consider that integration is a dynamic two-way process. It demands some efforts from the side of the receiving church as well. A key factor is that integration into existing European churches should be accepted by both parties. Otherwise, the process of belonging is hindered, and both groups are really united. Existing churches are not expected to become like ethnic churches, but they should develop an appreciation for other cultures. As long as Muslim converts feel foreign in the host church, they will be hindered from functioning effectively. Sooner or later, this may result in opting out or even falling away.

The starting point

The best starting point is an adequate understanding of our Muslims neighbors in their context, especially in the areas of family life, loyalty, and concept of community. We should not lump all Muslims together into one category. Muslims in Europe are not a single homogeneous group; there are differences in religious practice, language, ethnic background, and cultural traditions. Most Muslims in France have their origins in Algeria, while more German Muslims are of Turkish origin. Church planting for Muslims should therefore be selective. It is important to identify the community in which one wants to work, and to ascertain the perceived and "felt needs" of the people. Church planters must learn to look at the population from both an anthropological and a theological angle.

Culture shapes the human voice, and when people become Christians, they carry their culture with them. New Christians should only be required to refrain from aspects of their culture which are anti-biblical. Some cultural aspects can be retained. Some aspects may be transformed, while others need to be rejected.

It is a mistake to confuse the European culture with the biblical model. European churches ought to consider that their worship, music, and leadership patterns are to a large extent culturally determined. Converts should be encouraged to develop habits in conformity with biblical values, especially in areas where cultural habits are in conflict with contradictory biblical teaching.

Furthermore, whatever model we adopt as being the most adequate for our situation, we should always take care to equip and help the members of our community to face spiritual warfare and possible persecution. At the same time, converts may expect to experience the power of Christ demonstrated through visions, dreams, healings, or any other dramatic answer to prayer.

Conclusions

First of all, regardless of the church model, converts desire to be received for who they are as brothers and sisters in Christ, without having to jettison their whole past. They may have different patterns of worship and leadership from those adopted by Europeans.

Second, church planters should not focus on the religious side and limit interchange to this level. The lack of personal contact between Muslims and Christians is one of the obstacles in Muslim evangelism. Developing "interfaith dialogue" provides good relationship-building encounters.

Third, church planters should develop distinctive holistic ministries that may open new doors and increase ministry opportunities. Holistic ministries take the Gospel beyond being just a theological abstraction and intentionally demonstrate it as a dynamic reality for all aspects of life.

Fourth, it is difficult to plant churches as long as the people concerned are mostly in a transitory or unstable situation, such as refugees. It seems to me that in order to plant stable and reproductive churches, we should focus on permanent groups, and give priority to "families."

The choice of the right model is crucial. I am deeply convinced that all models are relevant in some situation or another, but from my perspective, the model that best fits the European context is that of an ethnic church in which the leadership is in the hands of the ethnic group. There can be elders from the host country and career missionaries integrated in the leadership, and this should be encouraged. Sunday services should be in the ethnic language, with simultaneous translation into the language of the host country to meet the needs of younger generations, mixed marriages, and members from outside the ethnic group. Separate house groups for discipleship in both ethnic language and host country language are to be considered. The ethnic church must put more emphasis on evangelism and developing ministries to meet the felt needs of the community. It must never consider separating itself from the wider European churches.

Discussion highlights

The discussion after Ghatas' presentation focused primarily around the importance of building relationships and maintaining open dialogue with Muslims and Muslim converts.

When asked why he did not include references to models of contextualization, such as the C1-C6 spectrum, which describes the different degrees in which believers with a Muslim background identify with the customs and traditions of their (former) Muslim environment, including Islamic religious practice, Ghatas stressed that while it is important to develop sound theology for working in Muslim contexts, traditional theological arguments do not work with Muslims.

"We have to develop a theology that speaks to them in their contexts and use vocabulary in the way they understand things. For example, when a Muslim says, 'we have a place for Jesus in our religion—do you have a place for Mohammed?,' I ask, 'well what do you mean by believe?' If you just limit your belief to a historical belief that Jesus existed as a prophet with a message from God, but you don't practice the teaching of Jesus—well I do the same thing. I believe that Mohammed was a man who had a message for his people and did something good, but I don't pray five times a day." This approach, said Ghatas, creates the opportunity for dialogue.

Understanding the Muslim context also means understanding the value of community. When someone converts, the family feels ashamed. The issue is not leaving Islam per se, rather it is the sense of what the community will say about the family. Ghatas explained that "the individual is surrounded first by the family, second by their community, and third by the religious leaders. We try to be a new family for them and encourage them as much as possible to not have any confrontation. We do not want them to lose contact, because we want to be the means to introduce change to the family."

Part of being family means creating genuine fellowship within the church context. Converts expect that the Christian leaders, church, and community will give them at least what the mosque and Muslim community gave.

"Fellowship is really important," said Ghatas. "We eat together, go outside together, and enjoy events together. When there is an Islamic feast, we do it in a new contextualized way. We do not want them to lose their social life as long as it doesn't affect their Christian life negatively.

But when I defend Muslim culture, I do not accept the whole package—some parts should be rejected and some should be contextualized. For example, there is a biblical principle in the role of men and women. In our church, women can lead the worship service, pray publically in the church, and choose to sit separately or next to their husband. We give freedom. Our basic principle in the church is that everyone is equal in Christ. However, for practical reasons there are some limits and we should respect the culture. I don't send my wife to follow up with a Muslim man—even if he is a Christian. It is not culturally acceptable, so we have to respect the culture."

Alongside questions of contextualization, the issue of identity was raised. Were second and third generation Muslims more or less Islamic than their parents and grandparents?

Ghatas commented that if the second and third generations in Europe are determined to become more Islamic, it is because they feel frustrated. "They look for identity. They are not well accepted as European, nor well accepted as Muslims. There is an identity crisis. They are more open to look to Islam as the solution to give them this kind of missing identity, but this is also an opportunity for the church."

III

CHURCH PLANTERS

13

MISSIONAL SPIRITUALITY AND TAKING NEW INITIATIVES IN CHURCH DEVELOPMENT

Joanne Appleton

Who (not "what") is the Missional Church? The "missional" conversation has existed for almost two decades, although its roots go much deeper into the writings of Lesslie Newbigin and other mission theologians. It has spawned a host of books, blogs, and more, to the point where the word has almost become meaningless. No less than seven of the books currently on my desk have "missional" in the title, and they represent only a tiny cross section of the available literature.

Van Gelder and Zschiele identify four commonalities across the range of missional writing:

- God is a missionary God who sends the church into the world.

- God's mission in the world is related to the reign (Kingdom) of God.

- The missional church is an incarnational (versus an attractional) ministry sent to engage a postmodern, post-Christendom, globalized context.

- The internal life of the missional church focuses on every believer living as a disciple engaging in mission.[1]

While we can argue that a missional identity is not only for churches wishing to engage a "postmodern, post-Christendom" context, these

1. Van Gelder and Zschiele, *The Missional Church in Perspective*, 4.

statements helpfully emphasize the ideas that mission begins and ends with God, and he sends us into the world to join him where he is already at work.

The book credited with bringing missional concepts to a wider audience is called *Missional Church*.[2] One of the most prolific "missional" authors, Alan Hirsch, states that

> . . . missional church is one that allows the mission of God to determine how it is the church . . . missiology determines ecclesiology.[3]

In other words, the outward focus of mission drives how the church behaves. The question, "how does this happen?" can lead to the temptation to prescribe what a missional church should look like and reduce it to lists of external behaviors. Van Gelder and Zscheile explain how,

> It is important to resist the common tendency to reduce missional church to a set of rules to follow, discrete characteristics or summary principles. There is no model for what a missional church looks like. Rather, a missional church needs to be defined by the church's dynamic participation in the Triune God's movement in the world.[4]

But who is the missional church? We need to re-write the final sentence above to read: A missional church needs to be defined by *our* dynamic participation in the Triune God's movement in the world. Brings it a bit closer home, doesn't it? *We* are the missional church.

So how then do we live?

How we perceive and thus relate to God greatly influences our lifestyle. If we only know God as a judge who is angry at our sin, our faith will be expressed through rules and behaviors aimed at helping us avoid sin, in case we make God even angrier.

From a missional perspective, our spirituality and lifestyle are equally intertwined, and this is recognized to varying degrees in missional literature. Some encourage us to view practices such as prayer and reading Scripture through a missional lens rather than a private

2. Guder, *Missional Church*.

3. Hirsch, "What Is a Missional Church?."

4. Van Gelder and Zscheile, *Missional Church*, 149.

devotional activity. Chester and Timms explore how groups of Christians or "gospel communities" can be missional in everyday life, through being good neighbors. They emphasize the need for prayer as one of the resources for missional living, asking,

> Why do we not make prayer more central? Perhaps because we think mission depends on us . . . if we think we are central to gospel growth then our activity will always seem more urgent than prayer.[5]

This includes prayer when you are together, impromptu prayer when the needs arise, and offering to pray for not-yet-Christians, which creates opportunities for God's power to break into a situation in visible ways.[6]

In *Missional, Joining God in the Neighbourhood,* Roxburgh encourages us to dwell within the Scriptural story, rather than "abstracting principles that are then applied, in some claimed objective form, to our current situation."[7] Instead, we are invited into a drama where God is at work. While he focuses on Luke 10:1–12 as a new paradigm for viewing mission in the church, the final chapter outlines practical steps to help us discern what God is doing in our communities and how we can get involved, which includes meditating on scripture in the community. For example, he suggests that groups use the parable of the Good Samaritan to pose new questions about who is our neighbor.

Others identify theological perspectives that have consequences for how we live. For example, a missional spirituality is lived out in community with others. Zschiele gives a theological rational for this through an emphasis on "participation."

> God's mutual participatory life in the Trinity; Christ's participation in human life and suffering in the incarnation and passion; our participation through Christ and the power of the Spirit in the lives of our neighbors; and our promised participation in Christ's resurrection and eternal communion with the Trinity.[8]

Missional spirituality requires sacrifice—laying down our own agenda and taking up Christ's. Frost advocates the adoption of a "cruciform

---

5. Chester and Timmis, *Everyday Church,* 173.

6. Ibid., 174.

7. Roxburgh, *Missional,* 80.

8. Zscheile, *Cultivating Sent Communities,* 10.

spirituality." The cross "is God's way of entering into the sin and broken-ness of this world to redeem it and make friends with sinful people."[9] It is also the example that Christ gives us for how we relate to the world—he emptied himself and made himself nothing, taking on the nature of a servant. Our attitude should be the same (Phil 2:5–8).

In addition, a missional spirituality is one that is rooted in love for God and our neighbor. Both Helland and Hjalmarson, and Hirsch and Hirsch base their exposition on missional spirituality on the verses so well known to the Jewish audience in Jesus's day—to "love the Lord your God with all your heart, mind, soul and strength, and love your neighbor as yourself" (Mark 12:30–34).[10]

Our love is not only expressed upwards through our devotion to God, but outwards towards our neighbor. And as we reach out to our neighbor and experience God at work in their lives, we are brought closer to God, and our desire to make him Lord of our lives grows even greater. And this is no more or less than many Christians have experienced since the birth of the Church—it is the experience of true discipleship.

Missional discipleship in practice

As mentioned at the beginning of this chapter, Van Gelder and Zscheile identify that "the internal life of the missional church focuses on every believer living as a disciple engaging in mission."[11] However, with the need to re-orientate the life of the congregation beyond the building's walls, we are in danger of over-emphasizing the final phrase, "engaging in mission," and forgetting the idea of "living as a disciple."

As disciples, we learn from Christ. We go into the world because that is what he did, and in response to his command to "go and make disciples of all nations" (Matt 28:19). The Christian message spread from Jerusalem to the ends of the earth because disciples went and made dis-ciples—who themselves have gone out and made disciples.

Breen describes the missional church movement as a shiny new car which won't go anywhere without the engine of discipleship, stating,

---

9. Frost, *Road to Missional*, 88.

10. Helland and Hjalmarson, *Missional Spirituality,* 31; Hirsch and Hirsch, *Un-tamed,* 27.

11. Van Gelder and Zschiele, *Missional Church,* 4.

The reason the missional movement may fail is because most people/communities in the Western Church are pretty bad at making disciples. Without a plan for making disciples (and a plan that works) any missional thing you launch will be completely unsustainable.[12]

Why is this so important? Because true discipleship is about imitating what Jesus did, and, in the process, becoming more like him. If this happens, we cannot help but focus beyond ourselves and want to share God's love and redemption with the world.

The following research and case studies give three perspectives of what missional discipleship can look like in practice. The first explores the needs of young people; the second encourages everyone to get involved; the third describes the joy and challenges which can occur when you take the Gospel to people in a particular context, rather than expecting them to come to you. Remember that missional discipleship is not a set of rules or principles, and these examples are just snapshots of what God is doing in these particular contexts. There are questions at the end of each point to help you identify some principles and apply them to your context.

Encouraging young people

The 2008 European Values survey included questions about belief and church attendance across seventeen European countries. Sixty-eight percent of people said they believed in God (although they did not define who "God" was). Amongst 20-29 year-olds, this figure dropped to 63 percent, a difference of 5 percent overall. In some individual countries, however, there were much bigger differences between the percentage of young people believing in God and the average. For example, in Spain there was an 18 percent difference, in Finland 16 percent, and in Belgium it was 13 percent. Analysis of the statistics also showed that while 15 percent of respondents overall attended a religious service at least once a week, this figure dropped to 10 percent amongst 20-29 year-olds. Poland was the only country where more than 20 percent of this age group attended a weekly service.[13]

12. Breen, "Why the Missional Movement Will Fail."
13. Memory, "Spiritual Values," 3–4.

It is clear from these statistics that there are fewer young people in the church today than in previous generations. If we are to empower young people to reach their generation, helping to disciple them to live missionally is key.

For my master's dissertation at Redcliffe College,[14] I researched the perceptions of a missional lifestyle amongst young people attending the 2011 Mission-Net Congress in Erfurt, Germany. The theme of the conference was *Transforming Your World*. I chose this gathering because these young people are most likely to be part of a church and to want to live out their faith in society.

Despite representing a range of Western European countries, the young people surveyed there had surprisingly similar perceptions of a missional lifestyle. In summary:

- A missional lifestyle happens anywhere—it is an everyday activity which could be here (at home) as much as doing "mission" overseas.
- A missional lifestyle involves loving and serving others.
- Living missionally requires a strong relationship with God.
- Jesus is the example of a missional lifestyle.
- Living missionally means sharing the Gospel.

Surprisingly, social action and justice issues were not a high priority amongst the young people surveyed, and they considered a missional lifestyle as something "more" than the lifestyle of a practicing Christian. As a 21 year-old German girl said,

> I believe the essential elements of a missional lifestyle include the essential elements of an authentic Christian lifestyle, but a missional lifestyle includes more obedience and trust.

The young people reflected the missional thinking that living for Christ is as much about serving others in the everyday as living and working in another country. They are also clear that living missionally requires God at the center, as a nineteen year-old from Finland and a twenty-seven year-old from the UK explain,

> First of all, a relationship with the Father is a priority. From that "flows" the rest — relationship with God by prayer and Bible and relationship with other people, loving and serving them.

14. Appleton, "Missional Lifestyle."

> Being in a living relationship with God and being able to give to others from this place of receiving his grace/strength.

From other questions in the survey it became clear that a missional lifestyle was an aspiration for many, rather than something they felt they already lived. They identified that reasons such as pride, self-centeredness, distractions, fear of what others would think, and lack of time stopped them from living the way they wanted to.

So what is the answer? How can we promote a missional spirituality among young people? My research suggests that church services alone are not the answer. Only two of the over thirty respondents thought that church or sermons influenced them missionally. One of them said:

> Sermons help me live a missional lifestyle, but only in a small way. Other organizations help me much more.

These results are similar to a survey by Faix amongst German young people.[15] Respondents ranked church ninth in answer to the question, "what helps you grow in your faith?"

But there is hope. Young people today are incredibly relationship orientated, with friends and family playing a significant role in their lives. Corvi *et al* found that 90 percent of 18–30 year-olds felt that family was "a particularly fundamental element of their growth."[16] And a 2001 European Commission poll stated that young people considered family and friends the biggest influence in encouraging them to be actively involved in society: 27 percent in Germany, 22 percent in Italy, and 37 percent in Austria.[17]

The example of other people wa the biggest inspiration for a missional lifestyle for Mission-Net attendees and most often the "other person" was someone they knew personally.

> My friends who use to lead a home for young people—who live in community, working in their everyday job, but who show love to those who usually wouldn't receive it, who invest in people's lives even though it costs them a lot.

> My sister, some friends of mine [who are] on fire for Jesus can't stop talking about him.

15. Faix, "Unsicher Zwischen Tradition & Aufbruch."

16. Corvi, et al., *The European Millennials Versus the Us Millennials,* 9.

17. European Commission, "The Young Europeans in 2001."

When asked how the church does help them live missionally, the answers also highlighted the importance of relationship.

> The pastor is living a missional lifestyle himself. He doesn't only do the "talk" but lives according to what he preaches. This life-style, including everything in life, not just Sunday mornings, is a great example to me.

> [Church] offers a community of brothers and sisters that can help each other living the same way.

Young people are crying out for mentoring, where they can be challenged to live for Jesus and learn from example. They are growing up in a secular society with few Christian friends their own age. Rather than being encouraged to withdraw from "the world," a mentoring relationship with older, more experienced Christians could give them the confidence they need to reach out to their non-Christian friends.

Research carried out by the Barna group in the US explored the difference between young people who left the church and those who remained.[18] Those who remained are more likely to have a mentoring relationship with an older adult, be taught how Christians can be meaningfully involved in society, see their vocational gifting as part of God's calling, and are actively encouraged to contribute to the life of the church. They are also encouraged to have a meaningful personal relationship with Christ that is integrated into the whole of life, and not just something that happens in isolation.

Living a missional lifestyle does not happen in isolation. If we want to encourage young people, we need to create community where they can be taught, supported and challenged to live for God, even as they reach their friends outside the church.

Questions for discussion/reflection:

1. Who in your church could draw alongside young people to encourage them in the way of Christ?

2. What opportunities can you give your young people to be involved in the missional vision of the church?

---

18. Barna Org., "Five Reasons Millennials Stay Connected to Church."

Empowering congregations

Within some churches there is a tendency for the minister or church leader, or even the leadership team, to be responsible for spiritual direction, pastoral care, and mission to the community. The church member's responsibility is solely to behave, give financially and turn up for services at the appointed time. In September 2013, I attended my church's annual vision evening. A long strip of thin white card lay on every chair, and at the appointed time we were told to pick it up and write on it where we felt called to be part of what God was doing—be it with international students, the homeless, single mothers, the elderly, or in our everyday jobs. Then we had to put the card around our necks, like a vicar's dog collar. "You are all ministers now," we were told. The expectation and culture of the church is that we all have somewhere outside church meetings where we can be active for God and reach others.

This is a great example of the priesthood of all believers. Helland and Hjalmarson state that:

> Missional spirituality is practiced by the priesthood of all believers at work, in the neighborhood, in the community and in the wider culture . . . leaders practice the priesthood of all believers when they equip, release and trust the laity to serve vocationally in ministry wherever they are.[19]

The key to this is helping congregations move away from the sacred/secular divide that so permeates Christian thinking. There is the church, and there is the world. We go to church on Sundays and worship God, and then we go to work on Mondays and serve our company. And churches can unwittingly promote this thinking.

In the UK, the London Institute of Contemporary Christianity aims to equip Christians to be salt and light at work. LICC's Director, Mark Greene writes,

> The vast majority of Christians feel that they do not get any significant support for their daily work from the teaching, preaching, prayer, worship, pastoral, group aspect of local church life. No support for how they spend 50 percent of their waking lives. As one teacher put it: "I spend an hour a week teaching Sunday school and they haul me up to the front of the church to pray for

---

19. Helland and Hjalmarson, *Missional Spirituality*, 68.

me. The rest of the week I'm a full-time teacher and the church has never prayed for me. That says it all."[20]

Living for God in our everyday world needs to become part of the culture of the church. It must be modeled by the leadership and talked about when you meet together. Are you as a congregation learning to see the signs of the Kingdom where you live and work, to listen to God's voice prompting you to share your faith, to pray for a colleague, to speak up against injustice? And then to act on it?

When people are encouraged to put their faith into action, their relationship with God grows. Spivey compared the spiritual growth of groups of church members over a six-week period.[21] One group focused on outreach to the local community, while another engaged solely in spiritual disciplines. A third group combined the two. At the end of the time, it was clear that the group combining both mission and spiritual practices grew spiritually the most, as Spivey explains,

> The missional events gave the blended community a common experience of pushing themselves spiritually and missionally. The spiritual disciplines gave them new ways to reflect on these experiences and integrate them into their lives. The small group gathering provided a place for corporate reflection on both practice and service.[22]

Questions for discussion/reflection:

1. Is the culture of your church one where the leader does most of the work, or are members being encouraged and equipped to be missionaries in everyday life?

2. What is the focus of your small groups? How do they equip the members to be outward focused and provide support for them?

---

20. Greene, *The Great Divide*, 8.

21. Spivey, *Developing a Process for Missional Formation*.

22. Ibid., 84.

Exploring new ways of being church

For Christians who want to be missional, Frost poses the following important questions:

> What does the reign of God through Christ look like in my neighborhood? If the kingdom of God has come and is overlapping with the broken world in which I live, how can I alert people to it? . . . This is a far more legitimate and creative question to ask than the usual questions about how we can attract people to our church programs.[23]

For some people, this has led to expressions of church within subcultures that look very different to our preconceptions of church. They are often centered around community and belonging, before people are expected to believe or behave, which makes for very messy discipleship!

Peter Dhyr is pastor of the Gospel Fellowship in Denmark, a church birthed within Copenhagen's Gospel singing community.[24] While many churches in Denmark, and indeed Scandinavia, have a Gospel choir, the strategy has often been to start a Gospel choir in order to get the people into church, and convert them so they become part of the church. The Gospel Fellowship has a different vision. While it is under the umbrella of a local Lutheran Church, *Kobenhavns Frimenighed*, it began not as church having a gospel choir, but as gospel choirs becoming church in their own right.

Peter and the choir leaders, Hans Christian Jochimsen and Claes Wegener, sensed that God was already at work in the Gospel Choir community. People were being touched by the Holy Spirit through the power of the music and words, but they would not then automatically go to "church" because they viewed it negatively as an institution. "There isn't that much residual memory of faith in Danish culture," says Peter. "Not many of the people who attend the Gospel choir were confirmed or baptized. If they went through confirmation, they hated it. Maybe they have come to a Sunday service and found it boring and didn't connect with it—but this is where the Gospel music is so powerful. It is not charismatic, but it is highly inspirational and connects highly with their feelings."

---

23. Frost, *The Road to Missional*, 28.

24. The direct quotations in this section are from interviews with Peter Dhyr, conducted by the author in September 2010 and November 2013.

"In these choirs people are coming to faith without knowing it, who can't go anywhere with their faith because there hasn't been any system of discipleship or a path where people can walk to develop their faith. So we decided we would love to do a church that somehow could take these people to the place where they want to go."

Over the last four years, the team developed a structure of big celebrations, mid-size clusters, and now small groups within the Gospel Fellowship, in order to create this "path."

The celebrations take place twice a month on Sundays—one is a big choir and the other is a "meditation." They have Gospel music as their worship style, with everyone taking part, and the liturgy is adapted to suit the target audience. On another Sunday, the smaller cluster meets, with a brunch, singing, and group discussion. Newcomers are invited to hear more about the church. "They have to be part of the fellowship to see what it is," explains Peter. "They will have been to a celebration and experienced a cluster, and then we will tell them what it means."

The Fellowship also organizes four practical courses for people who want to be more intentional about their faith. Subjects include leading yourself, growing in spirituality, discovering your spiritual gifts, and a second level of leadership training.

Small groups are just beginning. "Some people will have already experienced a Church small group already, but it may have been a negative experience for them," says Peter. "Ours will be about teaching discipleship and values. Discipleship happens through conversation and experience. We need to be living examples that people copy and try to do themselves."

The path of discipleship displayed in the Gospel Fellowship is very much *"belong, believe, behave,"* rather than the process of *"believe, behave, belong,"* that is expected by some churches.

Belonging takes place as people feel they belong to the choir. As they attend, they are touched by the Holy Spirit, but are also given a language to explain what is happening, which, according to Peter, "is not just healing and good thoughts, but we need to say 'this is the Holy Spirit you are experiencing—this is the love of God.'"

They start to open their hearts and become believers—like the atheist who now says "I am an atheist, but I am starting to believe in God. I can see there is something going on in me, even though I don't think God exists." This is where it gets messy, however. Because they already have a strong sense of belonging, and are on a journey to belief, many people who are part of the church do not yet "behave." "We want them to behave not because of rules but because their hearts have been transformed by God," says Peter. "But negatively, we could be too accepting. It could be we have no ambition for people to be transformed."

"How much noise can we live with and how much do we expect people to have the same values? Do we accept the mess and try to play the right melody and hope that people pick up the tune as we go along?"

Questions for discussion/reflection:

1. Where does discipleship happen in your church?
2. Where is God at work in your context, and how can you join him there?
3. How much "noise" in terms of messy lives and the journey of discipleship are you prepared to put up with in your church context?

Building a missional identity

Being a disciple is challenging. We are called to lay down our lives for the sake of the Gospel. But we can only show love to others with the love we ourselves have received (1 John 4:19).

As church planters, you want to see things happen. I was part of a church plant for several years where we spent a lot of time "reflecting" and thinking about what to do. For a long time there were few visible results. The activist in me became incredibly frustrated.

If you are like me, thinking about "spirituality" can seem like a waste of time because we want to be out there seeing people become Christians, churches growing, and society changing.

It becomes very easy to shape our identity around our achievements. If we feel we are not achieving, we try to *do* more and more in order to make something—anything—visible happen. More often than not, burnout follows, accompanied by a sense that there must more out there but it is just out of reach. If we do not want this to happen then our doing must come out of our being. As always, Jesus is our example.

One of the key missional texts is John 20:21–22, where Jesus meets his disciples and says, "'Peace be with you! As the Father has sent me, I am sending you.' And with that he breathed on them and said, 'Receive the Holy Spirit.'"

We are sent into the world by Jesus. But throughout his ministry, Jesus drew attention to the source of his strength and power—a deep relationship with God as Father. "The words I say to you are not just my own. Rather, it is the Father, living in me, who is doing his work" (John 14:10). [I pray] ". . . that all of them may be one, Father, just as you are in me and I am in you. May they also be in us so that the world may believe that you have sent me" (John 17:21).

Jesus's identity was in God as Father, and we too are invited to experience the Father's love. "How great is the love the Father has lavished on us, that we should be called children of God! And that is what we are!" (1 John 3:1).

As we go, do we experience God as our Father? Do we know for sure that his love for us does not depend on our ability to perform or grow churches? If we had to stop everything we were doing, how would God feel about us?

When we experience the unconditional love of God as Father, we become free to be ourselves, to take risks, and to love others without being afraid of failure or rejection. We can encounter and minister to those who have nothing to give us in return, because God's love is giving us the sense of identity and security that we need. Yes, we are sent, but it is the Father who is sending us, and we go as children of the King.

In conclusion

Living a missional lifestyle is hard. We have to give up our natural tendency to focus on ourselves, and live for others. It is the love of God that motivates us—and especially the experience of his love in our lives. We must live out of our identity as children of the Father—who is also the King of Kings—if we are to be able to put the needs of others before ourselves. And this is a life-long journey of discipleship for each of us.

14

HOW CAN WE MEASURE THE EFFECTIVENESS OF CHURCH PLANTING?

Jim Memory

During my time as a church planter in southern Spain, specifically in the rural communities in the south of the Cordoba province where I worked for fourteen years, I often found myself asking two questions. First, how could I measure the effectiveness of what I was doing, and second, what was I to make of all the things that God was clearly doing in my community that had nothing to do with my strategies to build his Kingdom?

In some parts of the world, churches can be planted in a matter of weeks, and so church planters can easily evaluate their ministry. Church planting in many parts of Europe is slow and painstaking. How then can European church planters measure the effectiveness of their work? This is the fundamental question that this chapter seeks to explore.

The first part of this text presents the findings of primary research on church planting effectiveness conducted in 2011 among European church planters. The second part considers church planting effectiveness from a theological and missiological perspective and asks what this means for church planting if mission is firstly about the *missio Dei*. The third and final part makes use of the four marks of the church in the Nicene Creed to suggest how more useful effectiveness measures might be developed.

Part One: Church Planting Effectiveness in Europe

The following is a summary of my research that was first published in *Vista*, Redcliffe College's quarterly journal of research-based information on mission in Europe.[1]

Methodology and sampling issues

The research was conducted in early 2011 in collaboration with an open network of European church planters. The eurochurch.net database was used to contact respondents by email, and the results were gathered using a self-administered online questionnaire. (Eurochurch.net is an association which seeks to bring church planting practitioners and missional thinkers into an ongoing conversation about mission in Europe. This has involved developing a database of church planting networks which was used for this research.[2]) There were three principal research questions:

1. Do European church planters use specific tools to measure the effectiveness of their church planting approach, and if so, which ones?

2. Do European church planters use specific tools to measure their own personal effectiveness, and if so, which ones?

3. Do European church planters use specific tools to measure the impact or influence of their church plant on the local community?

In total, 125 church planters responded to the survey. Ninety percent of respondents were male, and their age distribution is reflected in Figure 1. They had on average twelve years of experience in church planting. The sample included nationals from eighteen different countries, but there was a distinct Anglo-bias with one in three respondents being of British origin, and one in six from the USA. There was a much greater diversity with respect to their location, with twenty-four different European countries mentioned.

---

1. Memory, *Vista*, 2011/1, 1–3.

2. www.eurochurch.net.

Age Distribution of the Church Planters

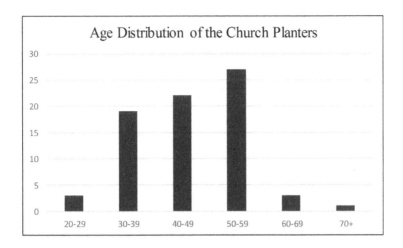

The question about affiliation revealed a significant diversity in the dataset with more than twenty different church denominations, twelve mission organizations, and over twenty local or international church planting networks. Nevertheless, it should be noted that twenty-four of the respondents said they were associated with the Baptist Church, and nineteen were missionaries with European Christian Mission (ECM).[3]

Findings

Almost half (58) of respondents said they used some sort of tool to evaluate the effectiveness of their church planting approach. The most popular tool was to count heads. One in six (20) used some simple quantitative measure; the number of church plants or groups established, leaders trained, attendance, conversions, disciples, financial data, and so on.

The second most popular tool (13) was peer evaluation. This might be a formal evaluation with colleagues or leaders, monthly ministry reports, participation in a learning community, or reflective practice. Other respondents (9) used qualitative measures to assess the spiritual health of the new Christian community; the quality of discipleship,

---

3. The bias in the sample reflects something of the dominant churchmanship of the eurochurch.net database, and also the fact that, as the lead researcher was a member of ECM, those belonging to that organization were more likely to return the questionnaire.

the development of leaders, or the spiritual health of participants. One asked: "Are authentic relationships being built? Is love encouraged and practiced?"

Two other tools were commonly used. Seven people said they used surveys or questionnaires to evaluate their work,[4] and seven others measured their church planting against objectives, purposes, or a vision statement, such as the strategic plan of the mission agency, or Rick Warren's five purposes.[5] Only one considered the community around the church as a valid way of measuring the effectiveness of their church planting approach.

The Effectiveness of Church Planting Strategy

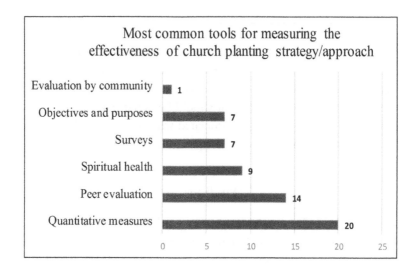

4. For example, the *Natural Church Development* (NCD) tool developed by Christian Schwartz.

5. Warren, *Purpose Driven Church*.

Personal Effectiveness of the Church Planter

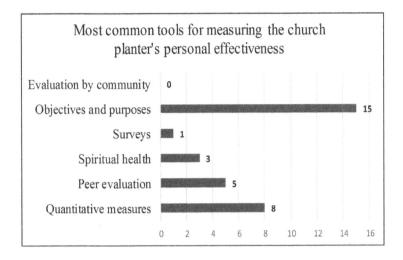

Only 37 percent (46) of the church planters in the survey said that they consciously evaluated their personal effectiveness. Their primary method was measuring themselves against the objectives, purposes, or vision statement of their mission or ministry (15). Several mentioned that this occurred during their appraisal by their leadership. Two even measured themselves against a timesheet!

Once again, quantitative measures were commonly mentioned. Eight church planters considered the number of attendees, converts, baptisms, cell groups, financial sustainability, and so on, to be a valid measure of their personal effectiveness. Only three saw the spiritual health of their congregation as an indicator of how well they were doing their work. Those who did, however, seemed to ask some valuable questions: "Am I praying for the community, for the church plant, and for all the relationships being established? Am I being bold and meeting new people regularly? What is my motivation when I meet people?"

Measuring impact or influence of the church on the community

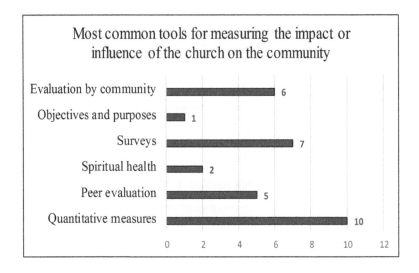

When it comes to evaluating the impact or influence that the church plant has on its community, only a third of respondents said they had some way of measuring this. Once again, most of the church planters (10) who suggested a specific measure focused on the numbers attending activities, the size of the congregation, the number of leaders, or the number of missional communities.

Seven respondents used a survey to evaluate the impact or influence they have on the local community, although three of these were internal church health surveys, like the aforementioned Natural Church Development (NCD) studies. Only six engaged more directly with the community to ask their evaluation of the church plant. The specific methods included listening and observation, dialogue with visitors, feedback forms, interviews with people outside the church, developing partnerships, and "finding out what people in town are saying about the church."

Surprisingly, five respondents looked to their peers as the best people to evaluate their impact on their community, and one further respondent saw the discipleship vision of their organization as the only legitimate measure of their impact.

Given the small sample size, gender, and nationality bias of the respondents, and the preponderance of Baptists and ECM missionaries, we cannot say that this is a representative sample of church planters in

Europe. Nevertheless, it does indicate some issues which might be addressed in future studies, or taken into account by mission agencies as they reflect on their own evaluation strategies.

Many church planters do not take time to evaluate what they do

Less than half of the church planters in this study made any attempt to evaluate their work, whether their church planting strategy, their own personal effectiveness, or their impact on the local community. That church planters are more interested in action than reflection is not surprising. That so few engage in any sort of evaluation of their ministry is striking. Further research would be necessary to ascertain the reasons for this reluctance.

Many church planters are focused on numbers

This research found that when church planters do stop to evaluate what they are doing, they appear to depend predominately on quantitative measures. For some this involves a simple head count of attendees, conversions, or leaders in training. For others it involves financial data, or the number of groups established in a certain timeframe. Given that the very mission of a church planter is to see new Christian communities formed, some degree of evaluation by numbers is useful. More worrying, however, was the significant number of church planters who judge their own personal effectiveness in this same way: *"If the church grows by a couple or more people becoming Christians every week, my work as a missionary has been effective."* Given the challenging context of mission in Europe, this way of thinking puts huge pressure on the missionary to produce results, and this may lead to frustration, or worse, if the expected results are not achieved.

Peer review is an important tool for the evaluation of church planting strategy

After raw numbers, this study found that the second most important tool for evaluating the church planting approach or strategy was some form of peer review. Church planters look to their colleagues to validate their work, to give them meaningful feedback, and thus evaluate the effectiveness of their approach. In some cases, this happens formally through regular team meetings, participation in a learning community, or by periodic coaching, supervision, and review. But however it happens, it is clear that a number of church planters do engage in reflective practice and look to their peers for honest appraisal of their work.

Quality is important to church planters

The spiritual health of the planted congregation was the third most popular measure for evaluating the effectiveness of their ministry—at least for the church planters in this study. Often this was done through self-questioning: "Is the church growing spiritually? How are the people doing in their personal growth in Jesus? How are they using their spiritual gifts?" Most church planters used either quantitative or qualitative measures. Only a small minority used both.

The personal effectiveness of church planters is principally measured against objectives

It is common for church planters, or their leadership/organization, to establish a vision, purposes, or objectives to orient and evaluate the development of a church planting initiative. What this research has shown, however, is that these objectives were not being used so much to evaluate the strategy or impact on the community, but rather as the principal means to evaluate the church planter's personal effectiveness. This might satisfy the requirements of the mission organization or sponsoring agency, but does a timesheet, the setting of goals, or an annual review by checklist satisfy the church planter's need for meaningful feedback on their effectiveness?

Church planters do use surveys to evaluate their work, but not always appropriately

Surveys are used by church planters to evaluate their work, especially the *Natural Church Development* (NCD) materials of Schwarz.[6] However,

6. Schwarz, *Natural Church Development*.

the NCD church profile focuses on the internal quality characteristics of the congregation, not the effectiveness of the planter, nor the impact on the local community. Yet several of the respondents said they used NCD to evaluate these things. Other surveys were used to evaluate the impact of the church on the community by some church planters, though no specifics were forthcoming.

Very few church planters ask the community to evaluate their work

Finally, church planters appear very reluctant to ask their community to evaluate their work. Even when the question specifically asks for the tools they use to measure the impact or influence of the congregation on their community, only six said they looked to the community to evaluate them.

Surely some degree of contextual research would give church planters valuable information and feedback on their impact in the locality where they work. The questions of one church planter in this regard might be asked by all those engaged in church planting in Europe today: "Is the church plant identifying with the community by fully being a part of the community? Is the church plant working towards a better future for the community and enabling transformation to happen?"

The working title for this chapter was "Effectively Ignorant," because that is the sorry situation of most European church planters. Too few give any time to evaluating the effectiveness of what they are doing. Too many use crude quantitative tools and draw inaccurate conclusions from them because they are measuring inappropriately.

Is there a way for church planters to escape the "quantitative obsession"? Too often we focus on the things that we can count easily (for example, the numbers attending a meeting), even when it blinds us to the more important transformative measures that correlate more closely with the biblical concepts of repentance and discipleship. Perhaps a way forward is to consider the effectiveness of church planting, and mission more generally, from the perspective of the *missio Dei*.

Part Two: Church Planting and the Missio Dei

Thinking on church and mission has been transformed over the last few decades by the concept of *missio Dei*—the realization that mission is not merely an activity of the church, but rather the result of God's initiative. Bosch summed up this new missional paradigm in the following way:

> Mission (is) understood as being derived from the very nature of God. It (is) thus put in the context of the doctrine of the Trinity, not of ecclesiology or soteriology. The classical doctrine of the *missio Dei* as God the Father sending the Son, and God the Father and the Son sending the Spirit (is) expanded to include yet another 'movement': Father, Son and Holy Spirit sending the church into the world.[7]

Jesus's words, "As the Father has sent me, I am sending you." (John 20:21) are a call to his disciples in every age to participate in this Trinitarian missional "movement" from God to the world, with the Spirit of God, rather than the church, as the chief protagonist. Through participating in what God is doing through his Spirit, the church fulfils its purpose in God's mission. Hence, the full breadth of mission may be understood as participation in the mission of God, or as Kim puts it, "joining in with the Spirit."[8]

But have church planters really internalized this concept of *missio Dei*? Do we demonstrate in our thinking, our words, and our actions that the planting of churches, the formation of new communities of Jesus followers is God's business in which we are privileged to participate, rather than something that we do on his behalf?

What follows here is a brief review of some of the key texts on church planting, church planting movements, and missional church viewed through the lens of *missio Dei*. It is by no means a thorough analysis, but rather an illustration of my core argument that church planters would benefit greatly from understanding their work more consciously as participation in the *missio Dei*. I am convinced that we must engage in a thorough critique of our church planting thinking if we are to break the "quantitative fallacy" which measures success by numbers rather than the transformative mission of God.

Traditional Church Planting Literature

Church planters tend to be activists and pragmatists. Consequently, they generally write "how to" manuals setting out the stages of the church

7. Bosch, *Transforming Mission*, 390.
8. Kim, *Joining in with the Spirit*.

planting process and the challenges that each phase presents. There are a few notable exceptions where theological considerations come to the fore,[9] but the vast majority of church planting books are analytical and practical.

Key considerations in the early stages tend to be the location of the church plant, the demographics of the community, and the methodology or model that is to be used. The authors typically then consider evangelism and the making of contacts, discipleship, developing leaders, the structure of the new congregation, and finally its reproduction. Even more recent treatments tend to follow this pattern.

In *Global Church Planting*,[10] the authors give a brief theological introduction and then quickly turn to strategic considerations and to a detailed treatment of the developmental phases, which takes up nearly half of the book. They are to be commended for the inclusion of many excellent global case studies, but the overall impression is of yet another "how to" manual. Is church planting, as the subtitle suggests, simply a matter of adopting "best practices for multiplication"? Or do we need a more radical re-appraisal of church and mission that relocates and redefines church planting as participating in a movement of the Spirit?

For many years, the Latin American theologian and missiologist, Samuel Escobar, has warned of the dangers of "managerial missiology."

> Missionary action is reduced to a linear task that is translated into logical steps to be followed in a process of management by objectives in the same way in which the evangelistic task is reduced to a process that can be carried on following marketing principles.[11]

Have the activist and pragmatist tendencies of church planters led to an unconscious assimilation of utilitarian business ideas that have little to do with *missio Dei* and much more to do with the idolatry of success that is the spirit of our age?

---

9. For example Shenk and Stutzman, *Creating Communities of the Kingdom*; Murray, *Church Planting*.

10. Ott and Wilson, *Global Church Planting*.

11. Escobar, *Evangelical Missiology*, 109.

Church Planting Movements

Over the last twenty years, missiologists in the West have become increasingly aware of indigenous church planting movements that can be found in many countries of the world. A movement that began in one restricted access country in Asia in November 2000 has resulted in 1.7 million baptisms and the planting of over 150,000 churches.[12]

David Garrison, director of the Global Research Department of the International Mission Board, established three criteria to assess Church Planting Movements (CPMs). To be recognized as a CPM there must be:

- A 25 percent annual growth rate in total churches for the past two years

- A 50 percent annual growth rate in new churches for the past two years

- Field-based affirmation that a CPM is emerging

Despite these very challenging criteria, Garrison's research had identified over 200 CPMs across the globe.[13]

It is, of course, hugely encouraging to read accounts of church planting movements occurring in the toughest of contexts. Books like *Miraculous Movements*[14] tell inspiring stories of thousands of churches planted among Muslim people groups around the world. Trousdale encourages us to believe in the vital power of the gospel to see new communities of Jesus followers established, even in the most hostile of environments, and for that he is to be thanked. Yet, like the aforementioned traditional church planting books, he cannot resist the temptation to suggest that anyone can facilitate the emergence of a church planting movement by following a few simple biblical principles. "God is doing all these things wherever these simple biblical principles are implemented."[15]

This reductionist thinking is even more evident in the case of Garrison, whose research led him to observe ten common features of CPMs which he suggested were ten universal elements:[16]

---

12. Garrison, "Church Planting Movement FAQs", 10.

13. Ibid.

14. Trousdale, *Miraculous Movements*.

15. Ibid., 187.

16. Garrison, *Church Planting Movements*, 33–36.

1. Prayer

2. Abundant gospel sowing

3. Intentional church planting

4. Scriptural authority

5. Local leadership

6. Lay leadership

7. Cell or house churches

8. Churches planting churches

9. Rapid reproduction

10. Healthy churches

Taken at face value, these common features of church planting movements are very instructive and there are echoes of the observations of previous generations of missiologists like Roland Allen.[17] Yet again, viewing this thinking through the lens of *missio Dei* causes us to ask a fundamental question: is it possible to reduce the work of God to a list of universal characteristics, much less a neat decimal formulation? Garrison clearly thought so, for he stated categorically, "Any missionary intent on seeing a Church Planting Movement should consider these 10 elements,"[18] adding later that the absence of some of these universal characteristics "may result in aborted movements."[19] In a later work he went even further, suggesting that the application of these universal characteristics was essential because they "are invaluable to anyone wishing to align themselves with the way God is at work."[20]

It is one thing to explore the phenomenon of CPMs to highlight the common features and suggest what we might learn from them, but it is quite another to suggest that church planting movements can be reduced down to ten universal characteristics, and that by intentionally facilitating these ten elements we can jump-start a church planting movement. Carlton lays bare the implications of Garrison's argument,

> These ten universal characteristics describe fully how God is at work through these church-planting movements, and the way

17. Allen, *Missionary Methods.*

18. Garrison, *Church Planting Movements*, 33.

19. Ibid., 53.

20. Garrison, *Church Planting Movements*, 172.

to align one's life and ministry with God is through the application of these characteristics. To do otherwise is to be misaligned with the way God is working.[21]

Church planting movements are movements of God's Spirit. We cannot reverse engineer what God is doing in one place so that we can bring it under our control and reproduce it elsewhere. It is God's mission.

Missional Church Literature

Our language of church planting has been transformed over the past fifteen years by the word "missional." The book, *Missional Church: A Vision for the Sending of the Church in North America,*[22] not only popularized the word missional, but also the broader concept of *missio Dei,* as many other authors picked up on missional language and its missiological basis.

Space will not permit me to engage in a broader study of missional literature, but I do want to ask the same questions as I have done about traditional church planting and CPMs. Are we planting churches or missional communities within a conscious framework of *missio Dei*? Or are we in danger of domesticating and reducing even the concept of *missio Dei* to manageable and reproducible principles?

For example, Alan Hirsch argues that the following six elements of missional DNA (mDNA) or Apostolic Genius are always present in Jesus movements.

1. Jesus is Lord

2. Disciple-making

3. Missional-incarnational impulse

4. Apostolic environment

5. Organic systems

6. *Communitas,* not community[23]

As with Garrison, the identification of common missional characteristics is helpful and instructive. However, Hirsch's missional DNA

21. Carlton, *Strategy Coordinator,* 190.

22. Guder and Barrett, *Missional Church.*

23. Hirsch, *The Forgotten Ways.*

also risks being misunderstood as, in essence, a new recipe for successful church growth; do this and you will have a missional church; do that and you will form an effective missional community; do all these and you will start a missional movement.

Given our tendency to measure effectiveness by counting heads, will we be able to resist the temptation to measure missional effectiveness in precisely the same way? If we do, then we are not truly operating in the light of *missio Dei*, but rather continuing to use a human metric to measure a divine reality.

The Mission of God cannot be domesticated. It cannot be classified and reduced to a set of principles, even missional ones. The movement of the Spirit cannot be bound—the wind blows where it wills (John 3:8).

Part Three: Towards some new measures of church planting effectiveness

In the light of *missio Dei,* should we even be trying to measure effectiveness at all? As Dunn puts it, if mission is defined as "finding out where the Holy Spirit is at work and joining in," then "discernment is the first act of mission."[24] An evaluation of church planting effectiveness can be part of that discernment. The problem is with the measures we tend to use and more specifically how we measure success.

Roxburgh has cautioned about what he calls the "ecclesiocentric obsession," where the success of our church (or church plant) becomes our focus rather than God's mission.[25] Clearly, as I have suggested above, this can even be a problem for missional church thinkers, unless we redefine what successful church planting looks like.

One author who has also observed this same problem and suggested a way forward is Bryan Stone. His thought-provoking work, *Evangelism after Christendom,* calls for a re-conceptualizing of evangelism as a constitutive Christian practice, aside from its apparent results or product, and hints at a fundamentally different set of effectiveness measures. In the introduction he asks,

> Is evangelism a *productive* activity, governed by the aims of reaching, conversion, or initiation, and thus the *making* of converts? If so, the skilled evangelist might employ whatever

24. Dunn, *The Christ and the Spirit,* 72.
25. Roxburgh, *Missional,* 48.

creative means will "work" to achieve that end. The practice of evangelism is then evaluated by an instrumental logic whereby the means and the end of the practice are *external* to one another. If, however the logic of evangelism is not primarily the logic of production but instead the logic of bearing witness, we find ourselves talking about evangelism differently. Now the "end" of evangelism is internal to its practice (as a quality of character and performance) rather than externalized in its "product." Martyrs rather than the pastors of megachurches might now become our evangelistic exemplars, and the "excellence" of evangelistic practice will be measurable not by numbers but rather by obedience to a crucified God.[26]

In the conclusion he hints at how effectiveness might be measured differently. "The 'success' of evangelism is to be found in directions quite other than the marks of success that characterize the prevailing consensus among evangelistic practitioners today. Cruciformity rather than triumph, growth and expansion will be among the primary marks of evangelism practiced well, and the virtuous evangelist will be identified not so much by her expertise as by her discipleship. The church's evangelistic effectiveness will have to be measured by the clarity, consistency and inhabitability of its testimony rather than its toleration by a world where value is measured in terms of utility."[27]

While Stone's work is essentially about evangelism, his argument holds true for church planting as well. As our research has shown, church planters in Europe continue to measure their effectiveness principally by numbers and in terms of utility.

Of course, we know all too well that quantitative growth in the short-term is no guarantee of long-term vitality; the parable of the sower tells us that (Luke 8:1–15). However, neither is the lack of immediate visible results an indication of an ineffective ministry. The "success" of today's church planters in Africa, Asia, and Latin America is due in large part to the faithful work of previous generations of evangelists and church planters, many of whom saw little fruit from their labors. Church planters must resist the temptation of assuming that growing churches provide generalizable models for growth elsewhere, and that the absence of apparent success in the present is a sign that God is not working. As I have argued throughout this chapter, we must not try to reduce the *missio Dei*

---

26. Stone, *Evangelism after Christendom*, 18.

27. Ibid., 315.

to universal principles of church growth. While we reflect on effectiveness, we must never forget that God's ways escape our comprehension. "As you do not know the path of the wind, or how the body is formed in a mother's womb, so you cannot understand the work of God, the Maker of all things." (Ecclesiastes 11:5)

Following Stone's lead, I would like to suggest four church planting effectiveness measures that might help us to discern what God is doing, but without falling into the quantitative trap. Space will only allow me to suggest possible ways forward. My starting point is the definition of the church that is found in the Niceno-Constantinopolitan Creed: "I believe . . . in one, holy, catholic and apostolic church."

While these have traditionally been considered as marks or static attributes of the church, Van Engen (building on the thinking of Jürgen Moltmann) has suggested that they have a dynamic quality that orients outward to the world in mission.

> Maybe it is time we begin to see the four words of Nicea not as adjectives which modify a thing we know as the Church, but as adverbs which describe the missionary action of the Church's essential life in the world.[28]

Not only does this give us a new way of conceiving the missionary nature of the church, but it suggests how we might measure the effectiveness of the church's activity in each of these four dimensions.

Relationality (Oneness)

In the research set out in Part One, we found that quality was an important measure for some church planters. This is hardly surprising since much of the New Testament is about relationality; i.e. the quality of our relationships with Christ, with each other, and with those around us. One could make a good case that it is the principal theme of the Epistles, but what is clear is that there is a particular emphasis on unity, on being one—one in Christ, but also one with each other. Any measure of church planting effectiveness must make a point of measuring relationality.

Michael Schluter[29] has argued convincingly that our modern globalized world has had a devastating impact on the quality of relationships.

28. Van Engen, *God's Missionary People*, 68.
29. Schluter, *The R Factor*.

The Relationships Foundation, which he founded, has developed tools for measuring relationality, or what Schluter calls "relational proximity." These tools may have an application to church planting.

What is clear is that relational health is one of the principal measures that we should be using to measure our effectiveness as church planters.

Fidelity (Holiness)

The church is holy because it has been set apart by God for his purposes—not for any empirical holiness of its own. God has invited us to be his people, and to participate in the life of the Trinity as we worship him in word, deed, and mission. So rather than suggesting that church planters can measure holiness *per se,* I think a *missio Dei* perspective would encourage us to focus on measuring fidelity. That is, how faithfully is our church plant reflecting the God we love and serve? The church is holy only as far as it reflects God's holiness as the body of Christ. Therefore, it seems right to question to what extent a given church plant is doing that.

Jesus's goal was to form faithful disciples rather than the gathering of a crowd. At the start of John chapter six, Jesus had over 5000 people following him. By the end of the chapter, there were just a few faithful disciples left. Faithfulness is the prime measure of a servant's effectiveness; ". . . well done, good and faithful servant!" (Matt 25:23). I think this is in part what Stone meant when he talked about cruciformity, the radical faithfulness to God's will that is even willing to die if that is what will bring life. If we were to measure church planting effectiveness in this way, would it not liberate us from the tyranny of the quantitative trap?

Catholicity

Of all the words in the creed, the word "catholic" is the most problematic due to its associations. Moreover, as Volf puts it, "The theological content given to the concept of catholicity obviously depends on the intended referent of the [Greek word] *holos* ('whole') contained in the term 'catholicity.'"[30] Catholics and Protestants alike have tended to emphasize the extensive aspects of catholicity, where notions of geographical expansion and continuity through time are at the fore. Yet there is another

---

30. Volf, *After our Likeness,* 264.

aspect to the meaning of catholicity: the intensive or qualitative sense in which catholicity is seen primarily as *fullness,* and only secondarily as universality. This eschatological aspect of catholicity anticipates the time when his entire people, and all creation, will come into full unity under Christ, such that God will be "all in all" (Eph 1:10, 1 Cor. 15:28).

When a local church declares, "I believe in the ... catholic ... church," it confesses that it exists in relationship to other local expressions of Christ's body and in anticipation of the complete wholeness we will experience as the eschatological people of God. As Volf has stated, "a local church can be catholic only by way of a connection with an ecclesiological whole transcending it."[31]

Jesus prayed "that all of them may be one, Father, just as you are in me and I am in you. May they also be in us so that the world may believe that you have sent me" (John 17:21). If our unity with other Christians is such a fundamental part of the impact we have on the world, should not catholicity be a measure of our missional effectiveness? As Beckett has put it, "the church cannot be faithful to a local/global missional mandate unless it is actively *living out* and *pursuing* its catholicity."[32]

Church planting in Europe almost always occurs in the context of other Christian churches. Our agency, our capacity, and authority to plant is a collective one that is not only dependent on our call from God or the authority of our sending church, but also the collective agency of the churches around us. My case study on a collaborative church planting platform in Spain illustrates precisely what catholicity means for church planting. I suggest that another essential measure of church planting effectiveness must be the degree to which we are collaborating with other churches as we seek to join in with God's Spirit in establishing new outposts of the Kingdom.

Contextuality (Apostolicity)

Apostolicity is a complex and contested concept. Yet perhaps all the debates about apostolic succession and right doctrine have distracted us from the essential and foundational aspect of apostolicity: that the apostolicity of the church is ultimately grounded in the *missio Dei,* God's mission to the world.

31. Ibid., 272.
32. Beckett, "Evangelical Catholicity", 134.

The church is sent into the world to participate in the mission of the Father and the Son in the power of the Holy Spirit. As God contextualized himself in the incarnation, so must the church be contextualized if it is to fully participate in this missional movement. A church must attend to its local context if it is to be effective. As Davies suggests, effectiveness in mission cannot be a matter "of simple pragmatism: the quickest and cheapest way of doing mission. For mission to be effective it must be both holistic and contextual."[33]

Hence, apostolicity is intrinsically linked to contextuality; the degree to which a church is effectively communicating the gospel message in ways that are understood and appropriated by the local people. Contextual church planting does not establish congregations that exist in isolation from culture. Rather, it seeks to plant churches among the people. In many ways the whole corpus of missional church literature wrestles with this precise issue—how can the church communicate the gospel within our dramatically changed Western context?

Sadly, as we saw in Part One, very few European church planters actually engage their local community in evaluating their effectiveness. Church planters must develop contextual effectiveness measures if they are to fulfill their apostolic mandate of communicating the good news of Jesus Christ.

Conclusion

This chapter began as a piece of research on church planting effectiveness, or more precisely, the degree to which church planters measure their effectiveness. Its principal finding was that many church planters are "effectively ignorant" of the real impact of their ministries. When they do measure their effectiveness, they rely more often than not on crude quantitative measures of "success."

A review of church planting and missional church literature found a worrying tendency to reductionism. This sits uneasily with an understanding of mission as *missio Dei*.

Although the last section only scratches the surface in developing alternative effectiveness measures, it does so, however, as a conscious attempt to break free of our reflex to measure "success" by numbers. By reframing the four marks of the church (one, holy, catholic, and apostolic)

---

33. Davies, *Faith Seeking Effectiveness*, 182.

as dimensions of dynamic engagement (relationality, fidelity, catholicity, and contextuality), we can begin to refocus on our church planting *practice* rather than the *product*. For as all church planters know, we may plant but it is God, and only God, that makes it grow (1 Cor 3:6–8).

Discussion highlights

The discussion following Memory's presentation focused on some of the categories he used to measure effectiveness. One participant suggested that the word "fidelity" should be changed to "fruitfulness," referencing an image used in passages such as John 15 where the plant is "a productive plant, not just a plant to be admired." Another asked why words such as "multiplication" or "transmission" were not included.

"With all these things you push a counterargument to see how far it will go," replied Memory. "In a sense, I am reacting to the focus on numbers and productivity as a measure of true effectiveness. There is going to be a point where you have to say you can't take the argument any further.

"The thing I wrestle with is not so much multiplication, but more that we are never in a position where we can objectively measure our fruitfulness. That is for God to do. Sometimes we say that we have only effectively discipled someone when they are making disciples who are also making disciples. Fruitfulness is not only a quantitative measure."

But disciple-making is also long-term and uncontrolled. "How many of us are living in a country different to the person who discipled us?" asked Memory. "That person may have no idea how effective their work in us has been, and is continuing to be in the lives of others who have followed on in Christ after us. Having a business-type approach that looks to numbers to say, 'yes, we have been effective,' is almost futile."

Participants agreed, with one commenting that we have to be aware of what effectiveness means in terms of the stage we are in. "Korea, for example, is in a harvesting stage where people are becoming Christians in large numbers," he said. "Europe is in a pioneering stage with slow growth, and that is where fidelity is so important. Are we being faithful?"

Several participants, however, felt numbers needed to be taken into account in several areas of church life. The first point being when Christians moved from an existing church to a newly planted one, giving an

unrealistic impression of growth in the new church—until they moved
to another church in a few years' time. Memory agreed, adding that we
need to look at where the numbers come from. "If you have a collaborative vision that is more about the growth of the Kingdom than of your
congregation, you will be prepared to tell someone who comes to your
church from another church, 'No, I think you should be back where you
came from.' How many of us have the boldness to do that? Justifying our
ministry in terms of growth is a big mistake."

The second area where participants felt numbers should play a part
is in deciding when to stop a ministry. "At what stage should we say to
one another that it is better to stop rather than [to continue to go] nowhere, [thus] losing all our joy, energy, and faith in what we are doing? Is
there a moment where we might be better used elsewhere?"

Memory answered that in churches we often downplay some aspects
of effectiveness and over-emphasize others. "The creedal focus doesn't allow you to pick and choose. Rather, you can look and see areas that may
need to be improved. Relationality, fidelity, catholicity, and contextuality
are the four essential marks of the church. You may have a church plant
which is displaying great fidelity in spite of low numbers, but what about
contextuality—are they really engaged in their community? Are there aspects of catholicity which need to be brought in to help them collaborate?
This helps them to make sure they are not focusing exclusively on one
area to the detriment of the others.

"I think the call of God on someone's life keeps people doing the impossible year after year in incredibly hostile situations. Take, for example,
the nineteenth century missionaries who went to their graves without
seeing anything of the fruitfulness that exists today because of their labors. So I wouldn't put myself in judgment over anyone who makes that
decision, but we need to give people the freedom to make that decision
under God."

A final comment turned the idea of measuring effectiveness on its
head, asking that if you did not have these things, could you guarantee
ineffectiveness?

"If you work your way down the list, if someone is not building
relationships (relationality) trust will break down," agreed Memory. "If
someone is not faithful and rooted in Jesus (fidelity) would we expect
their ministry to work? If they refuse to work with anyone else (catholicity) will they be as effective? And what if they say they will only do things

the way they are done back home (contextuality)? If we look at it that way, we can say, 'yes, if we get these things wrong, we are in bad shape,' which implies that the areas identified are good ones to be measuring."

15

CREATIVE CHURCH PLANTING INVOLVING LAY PEOPLE

Ron Anderson

WHAT IS CREATIVE CHURCH planting? The first thing to recognize is that this is a *process* through which credible, appropriate, growing church communities are established. By definition, the creative process does not force the use of any one model, but rather seeks to recognize what God is doing and move alongside him. The strength of this practice depends on the church planting team's ability to continually understand and craft together the reality of following three variables:

1. God's creative working
2. God's creativeness in preparing the context
3. God preparing a creative church

God's creative working

God is by nature a creative God. He declared to King David that he would build a house for himself, and later told the disciples, "I will build my church" (2 Sam 7:5–16, Matt 16:18). The reality is that God is the one designing, planting, and constructing the church, and there is no reason to believe that he would only have a "one model" system for church planting. In fact, it is even stranger to think that he would always use the same model.

The examples of God's inventiveness and originality are many. He made all things creatively in the beginning of time, and continues to cause all things to grow. He put a creative salvation plan into place for humanity. He changed water into wine, walked on water, let his friend Lazarus die so he could be resurrected, and stopped Saul in his tracks in a most unusual way. So why do we question when God does the same with us?

God's creativeness in preparing the context

God molds the context for church planting in a variety of ways. We should not think that God only arrived in a given situation when *we* first got there. In fact, we can be sure that he has been working on the preparation of the context long before a church planting team first arrives. We need to remember how he prepared the children of Israel for four hundred years to be freed, and Moses for eighty years to free them.

Creative church planting starts with detecting how God has molded the context (and people therein) in preparation for the church being established. Doing a good, thorough research in an area can show the church planter where God is already at work. Gaining an in-depth understanding of the culture, population structure, and history will highlight what God is doing and what he has done in the past. This information may yield important insight as to the way to proceed. Some questions to ask are: Are there other Christians in the area? What are some key values that determine the way the inhabitants here make their decisions? What are the valued needs of the community? What are the struggles they face?

Another approach is to look at the community through the thirty-six focus areas listed in the Cape Town Commitment. Seeing an area through those lenses might shed new light on a particular way that God may have already prepared the context for you to minister. Some of the main focus areas from that document are:

- Integrity and Anti-Corruption
- International Student Ministry
- Proclamation Evangelism
- Reconciliation
- Religious Liberty

- Scripture Engagement
- Strategic Evangelistic Partnerships
- Technology
- Arts
- Buddhism – Hinduism – Islam – Judaism
- Business as Mission/Marketplace Ministry/Tent making
- Care and Counsel as Mission
- Children at Risk
- Diasporas
- Disability Concerns
- Freedom and Justice[1]

In all these areas of consideration, the overriding key question is: How has God prepared the context you are working in?

God preparing a creative church

God has planned that all members of the Kingdom of God are participants in fulfilling his mission. Jesus's death on the cross not only redeemed us, it also broke down the barriers that existed in the old sacrificial system. All believers are now part of the royal priesthood.

When Jesus returned to heaven, he portioned out his own five-fold ministry to the believers (Eph 4:11). Alan Hirsch has placed the creativeness of the five ministries as an integral part of what he calls the missional DNA, or "m-DNA," in a list of six key elements that he identified as critical ingredients of a missional movement.[2]

God also uses each individual's personality, abilities, personal motivation, background, and gifting in the process of church planting. It is the work of the Holy Spirit that unites all the diverse parts into one creative force. The unity of the Church in the midst of diversity that Jesus prayed for in John 17 is of great value in God's inspired plan. Therefore, we need to have a good understanding of all who are part of the church

---

1. Lausanne Movement, *Cape Town Commitment.*
2. Hirsch, *The Forgotten Ways.*

and discover how the various creative gifts are to be used together. *The church planter engages the whole church!*

As one creative urban church planting team stated,

> We value courage, creativity and diversity as we try to discover relevant ways of being church in different contexts.[3]

Example of a creative church planting process

The Church of England has been working with a creative model that they call "Fresh Expressions," which they describe as,

> . . . relatively new worshipping and witnessing communities that are reaching those who may have been previously unreached by the Church.[4]

In order to be classified as a "fresh expression" of church, a group should meet a number of criteria:

- It is something Christian and communal, new and further; not an existing group that is to be modified
- It has tried to engage with non-church goers
- It meets at least once a month
- It has (or is seeking to have) a name giving it an identity
- There is an intention to be Church (not a bridge to bring people back to the "real church")
- It is welcomed by the Bishop as part of the diocesan family
- There is some form of leadership recognized within, and from outside
- The majority of members see it as their major expression of church
- There is an aspiration/aim to become "up/ holy, in/one, out/apostolic, of/catholic"
- There is an intention (where it is appropriate to the context) to become self-financing, self-governing, and self-reproducing

3. Urban Expression.
4. Church of England, *From Anecdote to Evidence.*

There is also recognition of multiple creative models.

> There is no single recipe for growth; there are no simple solu-
> tions to decline. The road to growth depends on the context, and
> what works in one place may not work in another. What seems
> crucial is that congregations are constantly engaged in reflec-
> tion; churches cannot soar on autopilot. Growth is a product of
> good leadership (lay and ordained) working with a willing set of
> churchgoers in a favorable environment.[5]

But while there is no single recipe for the church planting process,
researchers have concluded that there are common ingredients strongly
associated with growth in churches of any size, place, or context. These
shared elements are:

- Good leadership

- A clear mission and purpose

- Willingness to self-reflect, to change, and to adapt according to
  context

- Involvement of lay members

- Nurturing disciples

- Prioritizing growth

- Being intentional in the chosen style of worship

As the Fresh Expressions report continues, "Lay leadership is important and the research shows that good quality lay leadership is linked
to growth. There are high associations with growth and lay leadership
and rotation (when there is change and refreshing of roles, rather than
the same people always fulfilling the same roles)."[6]

Questions for reflection

Consider some examples of creative church planting.

1. What are some variables that make your chosen example creative?

2. Reflect on the three variables of creative church planting in the
   framework of your examples.

5. Ibid.
6. Ibid.

- How has the church plant team engaged their efforts in what God is doing?

- How have they understood and uniquely identified with their context?

- How have they effectively identified and engaged God's team?

3. What kinds of things can you do to make your own church plant more creative?

Unleashing the laity

When laity are not included in the process of church planting, they sense no real purpose in the mission of God. Often church structures are based on the Old Testament model of the tabernacle and priests, rather than that of the New Testament.[7] This perpetuates the misunderstanding that ministry is only for the "elite," and leadership development suffers. The result is that lay people cannot use the gifts that God has given them, they feel more of a spectator rather than a participant, and their initiative is killed. They become confused, disappointed, and apathetic.

However, including them in the process of church planting leads to incredible results. As "part owners" of the ministry, they become motivated according to their gifting. There is freedom for them to be more creative, which results in a fulfillment in their service to the Lord. It is then possible for them to see God working in and through them.

How can the laity be unleashed?

We can unleash the laity through the process of teaching and modeling to lay people and clergy that there is no divide when it comes to fulfilling the mission of God. Laity need to be encouraged to believe that they are a part of God's overall plan by giving them freedom, opportunities, and structures that encourage a *dynamic and interdependent freedom* within the Body of Christ. Let us examine this phrase a bit closer.

7. Pillai, "A study contrasting the traditional model and the house church model in Chennai, India."

- *Dynamic*: Changing as needed; not static in form and method. Attentive to the winds of the Spirit. Open for change. Ready to change direction as the Lord leads.

- *Interdependent freedom*: It is not freedom *from* something; rather, it is freedom to be interdependent one to another in the Community. It is a freedom that is only limited by the boundaries that all have agreed upon, which are outlined in the Scriptures. It is not curtailed by only one person's idea of what church should be like. Instead, it is open to what the Holy Spirit is saying to the whole group. It looks at the whole Body and the whole Scriptures to set boundaries for its freedom.

When we apply this concept to a church plant in the area of *worship* we can envision the following:

- Dynamic worship is more participative and less "show," but is at the same time biblical.

- It meaningfully connects one with God on a personal level, and is uplifting personally because it is owned personally.

- It is worship that reinforces the royal priesthood of all believers.

- It listens to one another in the process of worship, and encourages and exhorts others to ever meaningful praise and worship.

When laity is unleashed in the area of *loving the community* of believers, we can see the following characteristics:

- They learn the concept of "interdependent freedom" in the love and care of the community groups. Community by definition is best lived in smaller groups (10-20) where each person is a valuable participant.

- There is a mutual commitment to others to help "bear one another's burdens" (Gal 6:2).

- Each person is taught to take hold of his own spiritual growth, as well as help others in their journey. Basic preventative pastoral care is done by and for the laity by each other at this level.

When laity is unleashed in their expression of God's *love to the world,* we witness great diversity and ownership. The community group is often the easiest place to encourage laity to reproduce themselves by being missional in their own context and doing what God has put on their heart to do. They can work on projects together on the small scale. Their ministry projects tend to be more natural, down to earth, reproducible, and high impact at low cost, as opposed to the church driven programs requiring a great deal of resources that are often not available.

Involving the laity

It is important to include lay people in the church at *every* stage in their spiritual journey, and encourage them along as co-laborers, even if they have not formally accepted Jesus or been baptized. Involve them in the vision making and decision making process from the very start, and encourage them to be apprentices who are stakeholders of their own faith; "doers" instead of "consumers of discipleship." Do not stifle their initiatives as they grow in Christ; guide them by walking with them. Help them understand and know how to express what God is putting on their hearts to do within the boundaries of interdependent freedom. Teach them and be a model of the concept of interdependence instead of dependence, and help them develop into their personal fullness in Christ. Keep it dynamic and ensure growth, ownership, and involvement. This all starts with good discipleship models that teach people to become imitators of Christ in their own creative ways instead of followers of a system.

It is often the case that laity are difficult to recruit and involve in the church plant or a new project, and there are as many excuses given as there are people giving them. These can include the fact that they would rather be a consumer instead of a co-participant. A consumer tends to express his or her apathy in terms of lack of motivation, time, and energy. Some cannot seem to break free from the old wine-skin of the laity/clergy divide, and they claim to not have the experience, training, or ability to do anything of value in the church plant.

Example of the Camarma church

The *Comunidad Cristiana de Camarma* (CCC) is the only evangelical church in the village of Camarma, Spain, which has a population of 7000 residents, and is located thirty kilometers from the Madrid Airport. The main weekly service gathers between 150–200 people on a Sunday, and those who call CCC their church home come from a radius of thirty kilometers away. A strong part of the life of CCC is lived in the six house groups that meet throughout the region during the week. Recognized lay leaders, who also act as the official contact with the larger body of believers, lead these groups. In addition to these purposefully small gatherings, CCC has several programs for the whole church, including a social outreach ministry that seeks to meet the physical needs of local and area residents. This program revolves around food distribution, and also helps people find jobs, pay electricity bills, and so on. It is run in conjunction with the social worker from the local government, but this relationship does not limit the ministry in any way. Other programs in the church are the youth group and Sunday school, and in addition to the children's classes, the Sunday school program includes four different classes for adults. An additional class is called the "Discipleship Class," where new believers are taught the basics of the Christian life. An energetic time of extended prayer is held once a month as well. All of these programs are operated by laity who have a sense of "ownership" of the ministry as the place where they can express their God given gifting.

Several factors contributed to the innovative start of this church in Camarma seven years ago:

- Several local Christians had prayed for over twenty years that a church would be established in the village.

- An evangelical Christian Academy moved into town and established a good rapport with the villagers, especially since it provided a platform for learning English.

- American missionaries were accepted by the locals because the village had had a good experience with American Military personnel renting homes in the community some twenty years earlier.

- Two missionary couples were dedicated to the task of church planting in this village.

- Several independent house churches in the area were invited by the church planter to meet together for a larger one-time service.

The creative parts of this church plant included the liberal use of English, while still maintaining Spanish as the prime language. The core group crafted this "weakness" of too many Americans in the area into a strength that met the desire of local residents to better their English. The Lord used the good feeling that the US Military left years ago to open the door for the school to be built in the community, and then the Lord used the school to open the door to get a positive response from the village towards an Evangelical church. God had creatively prepared the context long before the church arrived.

The decision making process was shared from the start amongst the whole group, or at least anyone who wanted to take part was welcome to attend the organizational meetings. The once-a-month meeting became known as the "Core Team" or "Collaborators meeting." By including everyone who wanted to be a part of this team, an increased involvement in activities was seen; participation in taking responsibility, training in decision making, and a greater sense of ownership also became apparent. Everything was first thought about and considered, and decisions were made as to what practice would be more correct for our context (such as the content of services, the way of giving communion, and baptism). The establishment of house groups and participation in them was promoted, even if people did not come to Sunday worship. There was an intentional reduction of the perceived division between clergy and laity, and a high emphasis placed on promoting widespread participation in the preaching, teaching, leading, organizing, and worship roles, which used many more individuals' gifts and abilities. Flexible systems that fitted the needs of the moment were set in place, instead of the fixed structures that impaired growth. This openness to doing ministry in a very different way than what was considered "normal" or traditional church in Spain was possible because Creative God had prepared a creative team of believers who were now open to new ways because of bad experiences in the past.

Of course, problems have arisen. The once useful structure of flexible, inclusive leadership was challenged when the community was confronted with substantial growth. As the amount of participants grew, so did the number of issues needing to be dealt with, with a result of defaulting to the more well-known traditional leadership structure.

The initiatives of the laity were stifled by the church officially recognizing a pastor, elders, and deacons, who took it upon themselves to "police" all church activities, which in turn has stunted the natural growth and expression of the members in the pews. In hindsight, more thought should have been given to the matter of how to grow a missional, creative structure that could deal with the growth of the community, and in this way ensure that everyone continued to be actively involved. As soon as individuals were named as the ones responsible for a ministry, others began to take a back seat.

Conclusion

I believe that church planting can be seen as a creative art. From this perspective, the effective church planter sees themselves as a craftsman who understands how God has worked creatively in the area where the church is being planted. The many different models of church planting are then not seen as fixed procedures for producing churches, but rather as tools in the church planting craftsman's toolbox which equips them with appropriate ideas, enabling them come alongside what God is doing.

In addition, creative church planting is all about promoting the creative natural expression of Christ as seen in each Christian. It is the art of enabling Christians to becoming and *being* the visible manifestation of the Body of Christ. This expression is not limited to a few clergy, but includes the whole body of Christ—the laity as well. The art of church planting gives the opportunity to each Christian to express Christ in dynamic ways and learn to be interdependent in the process. Jesus said, "I will build my church," but he has equipped church planters to be master craftsmen to help him.

Questions for reflection

1. What challenges have you encountered in trying to engage laity in:
    - Worship?
    - Community?
    - Mission activity to the world?
2. Why do you think you have had these problems?
3. What could you do differently to encourage more engagement?
4. Consider an example of a time you curtailed (stifled, limited) the initiative of a "lay" person because you did not want to lose "control."
    - Why were you so restrictive?
    - What was the outcome?
    - What might you consider doing differently next time?
5. Consider an example of a time you felt that you gave laity too much responsibility too quickly.
    - What was the outcome?
    - What would you do differently next time?

16

WORKABLE WAYS TO START HEALTHY, REPRODUCING CHURCHES

Johan Lukasse

WE SEE MANY SMALL churches that never grow over the forty member mark, and one wonders why this is. Why is there no mentality of growth left? Why are they happy with the status quo? What are the reasons they get stuck in the process? Is there a future for them? Without going into all the answers to these questions, we hope that focusing on the positive topic of starting healthy, reproducible church just might help.

"Z-thinking" —beginning with the end result in view

Church planting requires serious preparation. When beginning the construction of a reliable building, the preparations and definitive plans are of crucial importance. The same principles apply to starting a new church, and the heavenly Architect must be prayerfully listened to. Mutual consultation ensures that all the participants have understood the plan, agree with it, and are in unanimous approval concerning its end result.

We should have the end result in view right from the beginning. This seems so obvious, but in spiritual work it is often assumed that God will guide the project as it goes along and we just have to wait and see how it turns out. It is not necessary to waste so much time in meetings; we like to let God surprise us. Unfortunately, this attitude causes many problems which could easily be avoided. Beginning with the end-result in view is sometimes called "Z-thinking." The leaders of *The Alliance for Saturation Church Planting* (SCP) state emphatically,

> There are things we must do in ministry so that "Z"may happen. If we think about the end result and work backwards towards "A" (where we are today), the intermediate steps become clearer. We need to outline, from the last step to the first step, each of the things that needs to happen to take us from where we are now to where we will be when "Z" is reached.[1]

In the process of "Z" planning, and through prayer, we should realize that there is not only a need for preparation, but also for finalizing the goal. What is the end product in our minds? When can we say we have arrived? For a missionary enterprise, this is very important. There needs to be a "closing point" in the best sense of the word. A church planter is a missionary, not a pastor, although he might have pastoral gifts as well. If the whole plan includes a closing formula, he and his family know when it is time to move on and hand the church over to the local or national leaders. Donovan writes,

> All these practicalities derive from the very important distinction between missionary and pastoral work. Pastoral work, the tending of a Christian flock, by its very nature and definition will never be finished. But the work of evangelization (the biblical definition of missionary work) in a particular area by its very nature must be *finish-able*, that is, it must be planned and carried out in such a way that it is finish-able in the shortest possible time. Not in some vague future, but *now*.[2]

This is what we mean by *A to Z* planning. While we should know how to start in the best possible way, it is equally important to know when the goal is reached; when the time comes to hand the leadership reins over to local leaders who perhaps you yourself have trained and prepared.

Also included in the description of the "finished product" should be a plan to start another church, so the work and prayer are focused toward a movement of church planting. As there are no perfect local churches on earth, and it is always possible to improve, our final goal should not be

---

1. DAWN (Disciple A Whole Nation).

2. Donovan, *Christianity Rediscovered,* 39.

to look for perfection in a church plant, but for the potential of ongoing growth and development.

Plan in prayer

It is apparent that major practical and spiritual differences exist between a normal building plan and a project to start a new church. As was stated above, the Architect is the Lord. He will build his church (Matt 16:10). For this reason it is an absolute necessity to seek the Lord in prayer. In practice, we have the tendency to spend more time speaking *about* prayer than we do actually praying. Church planters are usually practical people; more "doers" than contemplative thinkers. We should emphasize that our plans must be born out of consultation with God through prayer. It is interesting to read the story about Paul and his team in Acts 16. As they were traveling, the Holy Spirit kept them from preaching the word in the province of Asia, and did not allow them to enter Bithynia. "So they passed by Mysia and went down to Troas" (v8 It was there that Paul had the famous vision of the Macedonian man who called, "Come over . . . and help us." We can easily conclude that prayer and the seeking of God's will was high on their agenda, even in the middle of their missionary journey, as they were redirected twice in a row. God spoke to them and was clear about where He was already at work and where He wanted His "personnel" to go.

In recent literature on church planting and the missional church it is repeatedly mentioned that what we are involved in is all about the *missio Dei*; God's mission. But how are we to find out where God is at work and how He wants us to take part in it, if not by listening to him in prayer? God speaks even today, if we take time to hear His voice. So let us plan, present those plans to God, share them with other trustworthy Christian men and women, and pray again. We must allow God to stop or redirect us, or even cause us to abandon a plan altogether if He does not confirm it—and then start over again. All church planters should be "prayer-planners." Vision is great if it comes from the right source and grows into a passion shared and understood by more than one person.

Planning and prayer go hand in hand. Dutch pastor Wigle Tamboer told me that when he and his wife Judith felt called to plant a church in Hoofddorp, close to Amsterdam, they took more than a year to visit evangelical churches and Christian leaders in the wider area to share their vision. Wigle believed that Jesus wanted to make this a growing and fruitful church plant; a beacon at sea and a light in the night. By God's grace it happened, and in September 2014, the church celebrated their 30th anniversary.

What kind of church?

When asking what kind of church we want to start, three basic tenets should be kept in mind.

1. *Scriptural Foundation.* God is eternal and unchanging. The truth that comes from God through the divinely inspired Scriptures is absolute; it cannot be diffracted. We must submit to it, and if we do, we receive the blessings he promises.

2. *Cultural relevance.* There are different options as to how things should be put in practice without harming the truth. In an Arabic church in Belgium, the singing is in keeping with the North African cultural background of the people who meet in that church, although I have difficulty recognizing a tune. Many things in a church can be adapted to the region or country where you are working so that the church is attractive. You need to remain within God's boundaries, of course, but you must be open, through God's love, to the people who are seeking him. A church or fellowship must be flexible in the manner in which the unchanging truth about God is translated so that the message is understandable in today's world. The motto of a dying church is: "We always did it this way!"

3. *Social connection.* People today communicate more quickly than ever, and they can search for absolutely anything on the internet. International interchange is also much easier, and networking is the key. We can no longer be an isolated church. Expression of God's concern for the whole man and the society he lives in is another element of this, and it has been developed by other authors in this book.

How do we get there?

How do we get from our "A" to where we want to be, our "Z"? This question might have a variety of answers depending on all manner of variables. There are, however, certain guidelines to consider.

Research

To be well informed about the point of departure makes a lot of sense, does it not? That is why we need to be informed—not just about a country in general, but also about a specific place within the land. Every area has its own special characteristics that the local people are usually very proud of. Who are the people living there? What is, in general, their occupation? Is it a rather high or lower economic class area? Would there be receptiveness to the gospel? Are there spiritual needs which are not met by any existing church? Have there been earlier attempts to get a Christian group going? If so, how did that work out? The more you know about your target area the better. Other things to take into consideration are: Will there be opposition? What kind of resistance would that be? What can we do about it? How can we be prepared to have an answer for that in love?

When we set out to start a church in the Park of the Nations in Lisbon a few years ago, we knew very well that it was going to be tough job. The people in this neighborhood were rather well to do, highly educated professionals, living in expensive apartments. It was a challenge to such a degree that Dr. Fabiano Fernandes, director of the Portuguese Bible Institute, said, "If a church plant succeeds here, it will be possible in all of Portugal." With a seven-year plan, and a lot of prayer and effort, God performed a miracle, and today there is a church in the Park of the Nations. This church is now planning to start another church, which will be in a rather different social area, where a different approach will be necessary.

Form a church planting team

One reason small churches have little potential for growth could be by way of a false start. This can happen if the project is begun with only one person or couple. They might make an effort with all good intentions, but if they are missing the support and insight of others, they are like a soldier going to war on his own. If this person or couple is from another area or county, there is an extra cultural difficulty to overcome, and what they try to do is considered very foreign.

Most missions and church organizations have come to the realization that a new church plant is best done by a group of people. The best way is to compose a team is in cooperation with a nearby, healthy church. In the case that the church planter is a missionary or does not belong to that church already, he (and his family) need to join that church, become members, and serve as well as they can. They will then become known—not just by the leaders, but by the people as well, who will enjoy their ministry and gain an appreciation for their vision to start a new church. In a constant and growing relationship of trust with the leadership, they can share their dream of the church plant. This plan might be re-discussed and redefined by the church leaders. At a given point, the enterprising couple makes a proposal as to who they want to be a part of the project. This is always an interesting time, because the mother church should give their best members to serve, and they are not always willing or ready to let them go. The selection process is a vital element for the success of the plan. Some years ago, two families were willing to move to Rostock in Germany to start a new church in that city, but once they arrived it became clear that they had different motives and expectations. It took a little longer than they had hoped before the work there really started to flourish.

Team training

Training the team is a necessary aspect of the process, and is of great value. When a group of motivated people come together to be part of a new church plant, there might be as many opinions as there are people involved. Everyone has his or her own idea as to what is the best way of working. The team situation calls for times of fellowship, planning, and lots of discussion. Do not consider this as lost time. It is a matter of choice—you deal with the potential problems now or later. The time together should first of all have an element of fellowship. It is good to come to appreciate one another, as well as to learn to express thoughts and insights in the group. There is then the need to build unity—not just being nice and open to one another, but real unity in purpose. What do we want? How are we going to achieve this? What is the plan? These things need to be mulled over and stated plainly so everyone understands and is on the same page.

There must also be unity on basic theological convictions. That seems obvious, of course, but it is not always so. It needs to be openly restated, as it has a great deal to do with what kind of church we hope to see as the end product of the collective effort. Finally, there should be a timeline of operation clearly set out. When should the team members leave the mother church? The elders of that church will have to have a say in this as well. The whole group together—mother church, the church planter, and the team—should grow together towards a crescendo moment, culminating in a special service where the team members are commended to the Lord as in Act 13:3, "So after they had fasted and prayed, they placed their hands on them and sent them off." The church planter operates as the team leader, and he should guide this whole process while developing and maintaining the unity of the team.

Develop ongoing cooperation with the mother church

One of the major advantages of church planting from within a mother church is that there is almost always a limited geographic distance. This allows for ongoing cooperation in certain areas where the new church plant is, in its early stages, still very weak. One of those important areas would be the youth. Young people like to hang out together, and when the number is too small, the group is not very interesting for them. They want to do things together for fun, but also for the church (music, singing, art, drama sketches, etc). It is essential that they are involved, otherwise you might lose them. One idea is that they rotate between the church plant and the mother church and have a joint youth group and program together with the two churches.

Another element of importance is music. If the best musicians leave with the church planting team, the mother church will then suffer. On the other hand, if there is not enough musical talent in the new team, it takes away from the attractiveness of the effort. I recently observed a church that planted two daughter churches at the same time. They took a long time to prepare for the projects, and once they started, arrangements had to be made to distribute talents equally to all three groups. As this was not effectively possible, they came up with the solution to rotate the musicians among the different groups.

An ongoing relationship between the leaders of the mother church and those in the new effort is important. They need to stay in contact, exchange information, and plan for certain events together. In the initial planning stage, before the group is sent off under God's blessing, it is essential that they decide who has the final say in the new church plant. The question to be answered is whether the leaders of the mother church are going to be the overseers of the church plant or not. In many situations, this has been a point of friction, causing disagreements and quarrels, even to the point that it becomes dangerous for the ongoing ministry. Whatever decision is taken (staying under the leadership of the mother church for a while, or having local leadership in the new church plant from the beginning, with perhaps the leaders of the mother church having an advisory role), one thing is certain: this question must be dealt with *before* the start of the project.

A pioneer church plant with a team

Another way to start is with a qualified visionary church planter. The apostle Paul might be our example here. Although Paul was unique in his ministry, and none of us claims to be equally qualified with him, we need to proceed with all caution so as not to fall into the trap of acting solo. Consultation is required, and the plan should be shared. Trusted local Christian organizations or churches should have the opportunity to question the plan. There is also the consideration of where and how to find the right co-workers to join the effort. Be aware that, when starting from scratch, it is not a good idea that all team members be full-timers. This gives an unhealthy impression, and it is much better that the co-workers are students or have a job of some sort. The composition of the team and their occupations is of major importance since they will form a frontline battalion to break into foreign territory and make a bridgehead for God in that place. My experience of working with mature young people for a mid-term period of time in such a situation has been a blessing in many ways. A setting like this gives the team leader/church planter the opportunity to train and disciple those young people and to encourage them through the experience of planting a church. This approach also helps the missionary to "break into society" in a variety of effective ways. As the young people become members of local clubs, humanitarian organizations, and volunteer in the community, there is no end to what they can do while being agents for Christ. Of course, this implies a serious and very thoughtful selection process, because as much as they could further the work, they could equally cause damage to the effort. The plan and overall objective should be repeated, re-discussed, and even rehearsed here as well.

How do we get started and develop a new church?

After these considerations as to how we might prepare for church planting and how to get started, we move on now from the preliminary planning to the work of reaching out to people and seeing our plan go from A to Z. Let us look at the eight stages in the process of church planting, as this is the line along which the progression takes place.

From making contact to multiplication

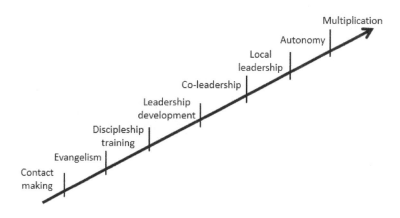

Making contacts

In the past, people were invited to events with flyers, advertisements, etc. Some came, others did not, but there was some response which made this way of working acceptable. If we invite people to events this way today, no one comes, except for a handful of church members who do not want to be unfaithful to the pastor. Those who need to hear the Gospel certainly do not come. So we need to go about things in a different way through participating in public life and seeking people where they are.

Where do we find the openings?

"The Gospel flies the best on the wings of relationships."[3] When we look to the early church in the Acts of the Apostles, we discover what we could call "oikos evangelism." (*Oikos* is Greek for "house.") Relationships were built in various houses —there was contact making and evangelism. The notion of "house" is not limited to a building. It is more about the network of who knows who, and who talks to whom. Take Cornelius for example (Acts 10). Three things can be noted:

1. Cornelius lived in a big house—not an apartment sized dwelling, because when Peter arrived he found "a large gathering of people" (v 27). It appears obvious that Peter, and the brothers who traveled with him, were able to enter as well.

2. Cornelius was a man with a wide circle of acquaintances. In verse 24 it says that "Cornelius was expecting them and had called together his relatives and close friends." This would be the circle of people he related to and talked to from time to time. They knew him and he knew them.

3. Cornelius had talked to them about God before. They knew where he stood; his insight on spiritual matters had already had an effect on his friends and family. We read that he said, "Now we are all here in the presence of God to listen to everything the Lord has commanded you to tell us" (v 33). Peter preached and God blessed in a remarkable way. This is "oikos evangelism."

We find another very intriguing example in Paul's letter to the Philippians. He writes that he is imprisoned in the courtyard of Caesar (1:12–13). Although some people are negative and give him a hard time, he was a witness there. At the end of this letter he writes, "All the saints send you greetings, *especially those who belong to Caesar's household*" (4:22).

Jesus used the principle of the house and connected it to "the person of peace" principle. He said, "When you enter a house, first say, 'Peace

3. Cole, *Organic Church.*

to this house.' If a man of peace is there, your peace will rest on him; if not, it will return to you" (Luke 10:5–6). This means that by making the right contacts and building relationships, the Gospel will make fast and effective inroads. "People of peace" are those people seeking after God and looking for answers in their lives; people who are prepared by God, so to speak. They have relationships and influence; they are people with a reputation, good or bad. If something happens to them, it will be noticed. Lydia apparently had a good reputation, but the lady from John 4 had a different story. In both cases, this was the person who opened the door wide for the Gospel. So did the possessed man in Mark 5, and if you read the following chapter, you will see the results.

I have experienced similar situations as I came in contact with those who have an effect on quite a number of others. I call them "opinion makers." If they start taking an interest in football, half a year later there will be a whole group of those who are interested in football. Recently we saw this working in the church plant in the Park of Nations in Lisbon. We had a great and long struggle to "get into society," but once we knew (and were known by) certain people who lived there—people who knew others—the process sped up.

We must take time to prayerfully seek God and ask him to lead us to the right people, especially at the beginning of a new church plant. This is also an encouragement to not be afraid of approaching people with a reputation—good or bad.

Evangelism

Planting a new church begins with evangelism—perhaps with the exception of an existing (mother) church starting a daughter church. But even then, it will not be long before they start evangelizing in order to add people to the new group. If this does not happen, an inward looking vision takes hold, and this, in time, means "death in the pot." Whatever form of church planting we choose, we must always evangelize as soon as possible in the process. We want to present Jesus Christ to people by communicating with them in such a way that they understand the Gospel, are converted, and receive forgiveness of sin and eternal life. They can then develop fully, and God's purpose for their life will be fulfilled, by and through their adherence to a local church.

Making disciples

The logical next step on our line of progress is discipleship, which encompasses a great deal. You *become* a disciple when you understand God's call and surrender obediently. God acquires sovereignty over your life, but you discover simultaneously that He loves you very much. *Being* a disciple means that you follow Jesus and are taught by him your whole life. A definition of a disciple is:

> Disciples of Jesus have come to love Him so much and are so convinced that He is God's Son that they desire to give up their previous lifestyle in order to imitate Him, to learn from Him, and to strive for His objectives, thereby sharing in His destiny, both in earthly suffering and in His celestial exaltation.[4]

Another definition, which is perhaps simpler and easier to remember, is:

> A disciple is a lifelong student who has a personal relationship with his Master, for the purpose of learning from him and becoming like him.[5]

Following this explanation of discipleship, we return to our church planting process. We have taken the first step, met and gotten to know people, and built relationships in which we are able to tell others of our faith in Jesus Christ. Hopefully some have reacted positively. We must now help these people to become disciples of Jesus. We should not pluck those who have become Christians, or who are almost Christians, out of their situation, except if they are in an extremely sinful position or are being abused. It is better for them to learn to take their steps of faith in their own surroundings. We must help them in this respect with good advice, but primarily by walking with them and being a part of their life.

On the line of progress, this element of making disciples is of vital importance. First of all, new converts are the best at winning others to Christ in the enthusiasm of their new-found faith. Second, this is the

---

4. Lukasse and Kamp, *Divide and Multiply,* 109.

5. Ibid.

basis to grow into service and leadership, which is the next phase. Alan Hirsh writes about this, saying,

> The quality of church leadership is directly proportional to the quality of discipleship. If we fail in the area of making disciples we should not be surprised if we fail in the area of leadership development.[6]

The vital spot

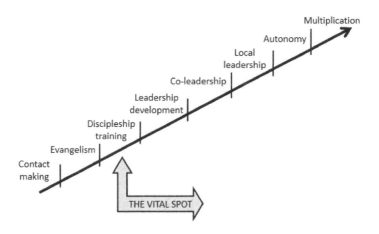

Appointing leaders

Missionaries who want to start a church must plan from the outset to pass on their tasks and responsibilities. They are the first to put this principle into practice. But it is far from easy to pass something on to others that has taken an enormous amount of effort and difficulty to build up. Watchman Nee is reported to have said, "An elder is always at home, and an apostle is always on the road." Church planting is an apostolic ministry. The founder and his team are just passing through, and they must complete their task as quickly as possible and then move on. They are called a "bridgehead" in military terms. They have to penetrate enemy territory and set up advance posts that will be used by the troops who are following. This is why we must talk about and consider potential local leaders right from the start—look for them, encourage them, and appoint them. While this is a good outlook for the new people that God gives

6. Hirsch, *The Forgotten Ways,* 119.

us, it is also of particular import for the workers who are there from the beginning, who can then remind themselves of their ongoing commission. This naturally begs all manner of practical questions, such as: When should we start training local elders? When should they be appointed? Who is suitable? Can young Christians bear such responsibility? Should they get a theological education first, or at least take a course of Bible Study?

Recruiting from the harvest

The elders of a church once asked a preacher who was getting old, "Where will good preachers come from in the future?" His answer surprised the whole church board. "Oh, that is very simple," he said. "They are still sitting in the pubs. We must preach the Gospel to them. Jesus will save and cleanse them and equip them by giving them His Spirit. That is where the preachers will come from." The man was right.

Starting new churches is missionary work, and new leaders come from among new believers. As we evangelize and make disciples, our vision is to win not only souls but also people who are going to serve God. Every person we meet has the potential to become a future fellow-worker in the Kingdom of God. God is already working in their hearts before we meet them, and he has given these people personality, character, talents, and, when they are converted, gifts of the Holy Spirit as well. If you keep the principle in mind that discipleship leads to following Jesus and becoming like him, you will meet future leaders. This happened in the Bible, too.

In the relationship between Barnabas and Paul, between Paul and Timothy, and between Elijah and Elisha, we can see that new leaders arise from apostolic and prophetic ministries, particularly because spiritual fathers beget spiritual sons and daughters. Paul writes to the Galatians, "My dear children, for whom I am again in the pains of childbirth until Christ is formed in you . . . I am perplexed about you!" (Gal 4:19-20). Paul does not address the Galatians as students or pupils, but as children. This is a hallmark of the New Testament apostles; they are almost constantly enduring spiritual birth pains. Christian maturity is achieved when spiritual sons and daughters have spiritual fathers and mothers in Christ.

The pain experienced by Paul was particularly felt because of the need for spiritual growth and the taking on of responsibilities in these churches in the correct way.

Training just in time

When looking for leaders in a new situation we need to ask ourselves who is suitable. This is always a challenge, and it is much more difficult in a church that has come to a standstill. I have often been asked to come and help, like a sort of doctor, in churches where people no longer knew what to do. Problems often arise when there is no renewal or rejuvenation of the leadership team. When I ask which of the young people could be trained as a new leader, I am told there are no suitable candidates. I give them a rather direct reply, saying, "I refuse to believe that there is no one suitable in a church of 100 people; that is impossible. You have not carried out your duties as you should, because you have not trained people and have not taught them to bear responsibility. Why did you not take someone along with you when you were ministering? Then you could have given him on-the-job training, just like Jesus did."

This is the how it should be done; training people on the job. You can explain swimming strokes on land, but if you want to teach people to actually swim you will have to get in the water with them. This is how we must train the people who should eventually take over the leadership of a church from the church planter. George Paterson has given a remarkable example from his work in Honduras. These two simple drawings illustrate what he meant and put into practice.

Teacher—passive student, the negative example

TEACHER   PASSIVE STUDENT

Teacher—student worker, the positive example

TEACHER   **STUDENT-WORKER**

During Paterson's ministry, he taught new converts to get involved in the church from the start. He gave them enough information to carry out their duties, and trained them step-by-step.[7]

If the new believers that God gives us are put to work very quickly, people will start to long for more. Those who make a physical effort become hungry and thirsty, and this is equally true in the spiritual realm. Give young Christians tasks from the start and they will ask for training and guidance. We must first explain the task and indicate what has to be done. They can then experiment and try it out as they go. Finally, an evaluation follows: how can we improve? This is the best way to teach something. It flies in the face of the normal way of doing whereby we only dare to deploy people or entrust them with duties in the church after they have followed a whole series of Bible Studies. That method breeds "excess spiritual fat" instead of trained spiritual muscles. Just-in-time training is a tremendous way to grow spiritually, and is applicable practically within a short time.

Two women were converted in a local church and were very enthusiastic in their desire to tell their family and friends what they had discovered. But how were they to go about it? They discovered the Alpha course, read the books, attended a training weekend and decided to organize a course themselves. When they announced this in their church,

---

7. Hawthorn, *Perspectives on the World Christian Movement*, 606-7.

there were immediately negative reactions, because these women were not yet deemed capable of teaching such a course. However, after a while it was decided that they could go ahead with the course and that a few older Christians would support them. They initially thought of using the DVDs, but then decided to study and give the lessons themselves. It was a great adventure with very fine, touching moments, but also with struggle and discouragement. They themselves were blessed the most in the end. They learned and discovered so much, and grew enormously spiritually.

Expansion

The church grows explosively when good working procedures are developed with self-multiplying small groups. This looks like Wolfgang Simons' idea for house churches, which starts with a small group that meets regularly. The participants talk about it with friends and colleagues, and there is soon a colleague who wants to come but he lives 15 miles away. The group offers to come to him, if he wishes, or they can hold the next evening at the home of one of the other members who lives in his neighborhood. And so a new group is started, with the expectation that it will grow and that it will eventually split once again and multiply.

Each of these new groups can grow into a new church. A beautiful dream? Yes, of course, but on the Day of Pentecost, Peter said that Joel had prophesied that "old men will dream dreams." God's Spirit gives these dreams and ensures that they are fulfilled. I know of several places where this vision is being put into practice.

Multiplication—a concrete example

The Baptist Church in the center of Zagreb numbers about three hundred people. Recently, they had plans to expand and become a megachurch. The church building became too small and a solution needed to be found. Stephen and Tabita Bell of European Christian Mission and John and Lynn Lehn of Greater European Mission and their families joined the church and talked with the pastor, Peter MacKenzie, and the elders about an alternative plan that would perhaps bring more people to Christ. They wanted the central Radiceva Baptist Church to plant several new churches.

Stephen, who is the strategist, drew up a plan with different possibilities. The vision was shared, they prayed, the plan was discussed again, adjusted, and finally accepted. It was then presented to the church so that not only the leaders would be involved, but the church as a whole could also devote itself enthusiastically to carrying out the plan. As a result, a group of twenty-five church members started a daughter church in Dubrava, one of the suburbs of Zagreb. This new church is growing and flourishing, evangelizing and proclaiming the Gospel with much more energy than the mother church had expected.

The leaders and church members of the Radiceva Baptist Church regularly come to help their brothers and sisters in Dubrava, and as a result they themselves are being stimulated and are encouraging the mother church to act. Encouraged by the blessing of the Lord, further ideas have been shared with the aim and real potential to plant five to seven new churches around the city, following the same procedure. This could be achieved, among other things, when the daughter church becomes a mother church that starts new churches, possibly with the help of the church in Radiceva, which would thus become the grandmother church. This plan has now also been developed in Dugo Selo, fifteen kilometers from Zagreb. A new church plant is underway there, with the help of a Brazilian pastor and a lot of enthusiastic support from the Dubrava church.

Conclusion

As we look through the New Testament, we see groups of church planters traveling around from one place to another. We see Paul always taking new people with him who were part of the results of his own missionary work. A good example is Timothy, whom he most certainly met during his first mission trip. On his second journey, he takes Timothy with him, and he writes about this young man to the church in Philippi, "I have no one else like him, who takes a genuine interest in your welfare" (Phil 2:20).

So, Paul has evangelized, recruited leaders from the harvest, and trained them along the way for the ministry of mobilization and planting new churches. As we move forward in faith, let us look for the potential in the believers around us, and include them in our calling. That is about the only hope to see a next generation of workers stand firm and lead on.

IV

CASE STUDIES

17

EXPERIMENTAL CHURCH PLANTING IN BELGIUM

Joanne Appleton
with Eric Zander

"It all began with a deep personal crisis," shares church planter, Eric Zander. "I was director of a Belgian church planting mission, but felt deeply frustrated at not seeing the work of the Gospel and church planting moving on. We were trying to duplicate a certain model of church as if it was the only one available, and I had a growing sense that something was missing.

"I felt like the disciples in the boat when Jesus sent them to the other side, who were not moving because the wind was against them (Mark 6:48). The disciples were professional fishermen, just like we are professional church planters. They knew what they were doing; it was their lake. It was home, but still they were putting in all this effort and they were not moving. I felt like 'this is me.'"

God used this time of questioning however to change Eric's vision of the world and the church.

"I realized that there is a separation between culture 'out there,' and 'church culture,'" he explains. "Imagine it is a Saturday evening and your non-Christian friends ring your doorbell. When you answer they tell you that they want to come to church with you the next day. They've never been to church before. What is your reaction? For most Christians, it is panic. You think things like, 'let me see who is preaching,' or 'I'm not sure that service is suitable.'"

"But then imagine that at the end of next Sunday's service, your pastor announces that the church is closing and this is their last service. How would your neighbors react, or the authorities, or people in the community? Most of them wouldn't notice. At best they would be sad because one option for Sundays would be missing, but that's all, which shows the lack of impact between the church and the world around."

Through this process of reflection, Eric felt that his only hope was to go back into church-planting ministry where he could work out a fresh vision of church; a re-imagination of the model. He wanted two things: to be connected to the outward world, and to develop a "different way of being church together."

"The whole strategic process of church planting had to be reversed," he says. "Instead of the typical 'Z' thinking leading the way, we had to experiment and go through cycles of observation and analysis, reflection and intuition, leading to more experimentation."

A new adventure

With the blessing of his mission, Eric and his family embarked on this new adventure. For the first season[1] they met monthly with about fifteen young Christian adults who shared the same frustrations about church. Eric also spent time visiting other projects and experimental church plants in Europe and the US, gathering ideas which he fed back into the group.

"We analyzed what type of group we were," he states. "I am a French speaking Belgian, which means I am Latin. Latin people meet around tables, and we talk—usually everyone at the same time! There should be space for this. So we experimented.

"I also visited different churches in Belgium, Switzerland, the Netherlands, the UK, and the US—anyone I could find who was trying to do different ways of being church connected to our culture. As I reflected, I would try it out on this little group and they would react and feed the process."

Another important aspect of the reflection process was to evaluate their resources, as this would affect the kind of ministry they could fulfill.

---

1. "Season" being the ten months between September and June. So far there have been six seasons.

In the beginning, the resources were limited to those of Eric's immediate family.

While the first season was a time-limited experiment, the group had generated lots of ideas for Eric and his family to take into the future. But they first needed to define who they wanted to reach.

"We live in a small town in the middle of nowhere, surrounded with a network of fifteen villages. It is a mix of rural people and commuters to Brussels. This is where we have our house, where our kids go to school. We were already living there but not really being incarnated," he says. "I had to learn to intentionally be part of this social space, rather than living there but being a Christian in a solely Christian space."

So a second process of analysis and reflection began, where Eric and his wife made lists of all the people they knew, as well as those with any kind of social responsibility in the area.

"I visited all of these people on the list, which took months," said Eric. "If they were part of our friendship network, I would tell them, 'I have just been through a hard time in my life; I've been working in church for a long time and I got discouraged and wanted to quit because church does not work.' Most people would say, 'oh yes!' so I would tell them about my dream of a community that would really connect with culture and ask them what they thought about this. Everyone, even our non-believing friends, had plenty of ideas and a lot to say, including some very accurate and troubling remarks.

"I also went to the key administrators and community leaders in the town. I would ask them about their work, and tell them, 'I am here to say thank you for what you are doing because it is what the Good News of Jesus asks us to do.' I would explain about my dream of a church community that would connect and ask them what they thought. Did they have any advice, and if I started something was there any way that they would be interested in collaborating or connecting?

"Many people were interested, and told us to let them know if we did start something. Out of this process we realized that having our own building wouldn't work—we needed to be part of the social network and meet in a social space."

Again, Eric considered their resources, which at this point were still just him and his family. They felt they could afford to rent a hall and provide coffee and croissants once a month from September to June. They decided to call it a "Christian Community" ("Communauté" in French, litt. "fellowship") rather than "church," and distributed invitations to all their contacts.

"We started once a month for ten months," says Eric. "God brought exactly the same number of people that we had put chairs out for. We were amazed. People came who we didn't expect, some we didn't even know.

"We were family gathering together around tables, with food and interactive activities. Sometimes I would talk, and we tried visual, multi-sensory, and physical things to do. People would give us feedback—too long, too short, or too loud, which also fed our process."

New opportunities

After that first year, the community began meeting twice a month. During the second year, Eric received a phone call from a retirement home director who had been told about the church and their desire to integrate into society by the (non-Christian) town mayor. Despite there being no evangelical believers living in the home, the director felt it would be good to have "some kind of Gospel gathering" in their building.

Again, the process of analysis, reflection, intuition, and resources helped. "They needed relationships, so we brought in families. We visited with the residents in their rooms which helped us understand their context. Regarding resources, my kids play good classical music, which was more appropriate for [the retirees] than pop-rock. They wanted us to come once a week, but we couldn't resource that. So we decided to try it for one year once a month."

The community now has a group of 15-20 elderly people who are coming to the service each month. Most of them are from a Catholic background, says Eric, and it has been a joy to see them grow in the knowledge of Jesus and learn to pray, share and thank God. At Christmas and Easter they hold a celebration in this, and another, retirement home.

A further sub-culture within the larger one is that of bikers. "The motorcycle is a social connector; it creates communities," Eric explains. "I wondered whether there would be room for attempts to have a community of Jesus emerge within the big community of bikers." For the last three years, Eric has met monthly with ten to fifteen bikers from across Belgium, to "do church on the road, open our Bibles, and discuss." Eric goes on to say that while ten to twelve people is the right size for this kind of close fellowship, a family (community) gathering works best with between twenty-five to fifty people. "The type of fellowship you want dictates the numbers you have."

A danger with new church plants is that it is common for Christians to visit from further afield who want to join the new venture because they are disillusioned with their own situation. However, the incarnational approach of being embedded in the *local* community does not happen if you live outside a certain radius. Eric has tried to discourage people from other towns joining the community—with one exception.

"A family who lived in another town started visiting. They said they dreamt of a community in their area, and we could see they shared our vision and values. They became part of our leadership team and learned alongside us for a couple of years. Last year [in the] summer we decided to go with them for a season, once a month. We've now had ten months there and the development is so positive. There are now some 30 to 40 adults plus children. We are going to evaluate, redefine their social space and go for another season."

Practical considerations

Not everyone who comes to the group connects with it or attends regularly. When asked to give reasons why there is a high turnover, Eric explains that sometimes people simply are not ready to commit.

"Our gathering of being church together is that of journeying together with Jesus. If someone comes and he is not wanting to journey together with Jesus, then he will eventually leave. And that's alright. Each time we gather we talk on a particular text and topic, and it always leads to a form of response. You don't need to be a Christian to respond, but you can say 'I am ready to take that step.'

"But while we may lose people because that is a step too far, I believe you should never lose the friendship. All of these people are still great friends, and they will be the ones who will send their friends to us as well."

Eric aims for the administration of the church to be as "low maintenance" as possible, with "no big budgets, buildings, or salaries." The ongoing vision is shared informally as part of the gathering, rather than at a specific "vision evening," and there is a box at the back where people can contribute financially to the church, and also to mission projects.

"Every time we meet we put the figures on the screen. For example, last month our activities cost us 'so much,'" explains Eric. "Two months ago we had no money left, so I said, 'next time, no croissants . . .'"

Connecting to the community

While the gatherings have had the most attention in this case study so far, they are not the sole focus of the community's ministry. In addition to asking, "how are we being church together," Eric also asks, "how are we connecting with the world?"

"We deliberately keep the gatherings to a minimum—just at weekends—so that we can be in the world. We chose not to start any new activities, but to integrate with what was already going on in the world—to bring real life into their service, to bring Christ within their work. There is so much social work going on and it is easy as they all have needs.

"I need to set an example, so I am 'Eric the driver' on Fridays. I drive a truck and I take furniture and food for the poor. I'm 'Eric the teacher' on Tuesdays, doing after-school education.

"As people join the community they also get involved. And once a year the Red Cross comes to our church gathering and UNICEF also comes annually to share a project."

Eric is also involved in a network of social and cultural leaders in the area. "They say, 'we don't have any priests or pastors or religious guys who come—you're not really religious are you? You are a community that is here for the good of the people,'" says Eric. "I am now part of the leadership of this group, and next week they are coming to my house for a BBQ where we are going to reflect on the future of social health in our region."

What is success?

When starting a new initiative, it is important to know how you will evaluate what you are doing. Eric decided on three criteria.

1. *People within the community are being changed to the image of Jesus.* "I can look at their lives two or three years ago and their lives today with God and see a difference. People are changing."

2. *The world around is changed and being changed because of us.* "Last year, the mayor visited our gathering and I asked him to share what

he thought about us over the five years we had been in existence. He said he was thankful, and told us, 'Everywhere I go in this city I hear about the good things you do for us. Your community radiates in our city.' Praise God!"

3. *The community multiplies.* New people are added and communities themselves multiply.

What are the challenges?

While Eric and his family are supported financially by other Christians, the leaders of the newly planted community in another town both have full time jobs. "We need to find a model that works with the people and their circumstances," says Eric. "Sometimes I think that if our model is so 'idealistic' or 'beautiful,' we will never be able to achieve it. So we need to be realistic."

Supporting children and young people also requires flexibility. At times everyone meets together, but there are also times when they have separate groups, depending on the topic.

"I always thought church should be church for everybody together," admits Eric. "It is amazing to see the teenagers invite their teachers to the group because they have fun and want to share it. But I've come to realize that teenagers need their own social space as well. So we have started a regional teenagers gathering, which is growing.

"Leadership and stability are also challenges, but at the same time, this is so passionate. I feel like how I imagine Peter felt in the boat because he was struggling and the winds were against him. He could not move on, and Jesus said, 'leave the boat and walk upon water.' That was a risk.

"We feel that by taking the risk of starting a new kind of church, God has shown us a key to our Western situation. I am passionate about it, but at the same time it is scary because I don't know where it is going. But that is OK. If Jesus is going to build his church, he *will* build it."

18

COLLABORATIVE CHURCH
PLANTING IN CORDOBA, SPAIN

Jim Memory

MOST OF THE STORIES that we hear about successful church planting involve a single congregation or denomination. They are often stories of churches planted in thriving cities or among a particular cultural sub-group. In many cases, these churches grow not as a result of new conversions but through transfer growth from other churches. For this reason many church leaders have very negative perceptions of church planting, seeing it as divisive and inherently imperialistic.

Yet there is one church planting strategy that stands apart from the rest. This strategy does not seek out either receptive target groups, or the reproduction of a given church model or denomination; it does not try to impose a common methodology on the churches who adopt it; and it specifically takes a stand against "sheep stealing." This is the strategy of collaborative church planting.

Murray has provided a very helpful definition of collaborative church planting:

> What is envisaged by collaborative church planting is that local church leaders, denominational or regional church leaders, and representatives of mission agencies meet together to consider the needs and opportunities of their region or city. Their task is the identification of under-churched communities (geographical and cultural); the selection of appropriate models and methods to respond to the challenge of planting churches in these communities; the discovery of the personnel and resources

available; and the development of a strategic initiative which is owned by participating agencies.[1]

The following case study tells the story of how the evangelical churches in one Spanish province did precisely that.

The story of the churches of Córdoba

Córdoba is an interior province of the Autonomous Region of Andalucía. The province had 804,498 inhabitants as of January 2012, with 328,841 of those living in the provincial capital of Córdoba.[2] At the beginning of the sixties, there was just one Protestant church in the capital city, and Andalucia was recognized as one of the least evangelized provinces in the whole country. During the sixties and seventies, a handful of new churches emerged (Baptist, Independent, Pentecostal, Apostolic), and one of these churches, the *Iglesia Bautista de Córdoba*, approached the European Christian Mission (ECM) to see if they could send missionaries to work with them. The first ECM missionaries arrived in 1979.

During the '80s, further missionaries arrived and began working in a number of the un-evangelized towns in the province, establishing churches in five locations in the area. At the same time the pastors of the city churches began to meet to pray, and in time they formed the *Fraternidad Ministerial Evangélica de Córdoba* (FRAMEC). Though focused on prayer, the fraternity also enabled inter-church issues to be discussed and occasional united events to be held. There was little common vision for mission, however, until 1992, when the Expo in Sevilla was held.

The missionaries from the province had started to become involved in the fraternity meetings and their presence encouraged the pastors towards a more provincial vision for mission. The fraternity decided to take advantage of the Expo to hold a series of united evangelistic events, and to distribute a piece of literature to every home in the province of Cordoba, more than 160,000 dwellings at that time.[3] This proved to be a huge undertaking, but it had the effect of uniting the churches in a concerted mission initiative for the first time.

---

1. Murray, *Church Planting*, 287.

2. Instituto Nacional de Estadística, *Municipal Register: 1 January 2012*.

3. Ibid.

Vision 2015

During the late eighties and early nineties, the ECM missionaries had been working toward a vision called 2000/30, the planting of thirty congregations in the province of Córdoba by the year 2000. As the year 2000 approached, the number of ECM-planted congregations remained in single figures, yet remarkably, when the all the provincial churches and mission points that were in existence were counted up, the total did come to thirty, a fact celebrated by a united meeting of the Córdoba churches in October 2000.[4]

Rather than congratulating themselves, the FRAMEC adopted a new vision that there would be a church established in every town and city district of more than five thousand inhabitants by 2015. They took the decision to organize a first Missionary Conference of Córdoba in June 2002, with a view to stimulating the churches to new church planting, and a group called the *Plataforma Misionera* was formed to organize the event.

As part of the conference it was felt that a more thorough demographic study of the evangelical presence in the city and province was necessary, and this study proved to be one of the principal outcomes.[5] After its presentation in the conference, churches were encouraged to consider planting in one of the unreached towns. New churches were planted, but many of the smaller churches (including many of those planted by ECM missionaries) simply felt unable to do this on their own.

The Covenant for the Evangelization of Córdoba

As one of ECM's missionary church planters in Córdoba at that time, I became increasingly convinced that ECM's strategy of church planting with teams of foreign missionaries had ceased to be effective. We were planting churches that, more often than not, displayed a chronic dependency on the missionaries. At the same time I saw huge potential for developing collaborative relationships with the strong national churches in the city of Córdoba that might be mutually beneficial. In light of this, I decided to investigate this topic for my master's thesis.[6]

---

4. Clark, *Sharing Christ's Love in Europe*, 29.

5. Memory, *El estado actual de las Iglesias de Córdoba*.

6. Memory, "The Church Planting Strategy of the European Christian Mission in Córdoba, Spain."

The thesis presented me with the opportunity of engaging all the pastors and missionaries in the research so that they saw it as their own. They were involved in every phase of the study, from its design to the interpretation of the results. Nearly every pastor and missionary in the province was interviewed and their opinions sought on the strategy of ECM and the possibilities and potential pitfalls of church planting through collaboration. It produced some very interesting findings, but more importantly it prepared the way for the reconvening of the *Plataforma Misionera* and the organization of the 2a Conferencia Misionera de Córdoba in November 2010.

This second conference had three significant outcomes. First, there was a much more explicit commitment to plant, with specific towns being prioritized by certain churches, and others highlighted more generally for concerted prayer. Second, and perhaps even more noteworthy, the pastors signed a covenant, which was an agreement to not compete against each other for growth, but rather to work together in reaching the province with the gospel. A framed copy of this document, the *Pacto por la Evangelización de Córdoba*, hangs on the wall of many churches in Córdoba as a permanent reminder of the commitment to work together in mission.

Pacto por la Evangelizacion de Córdoba

Third, the *Plataforma Misionera* ceased being merely an organizing committee for the conference, and became a permanent commission of the FRAMEC with the focus to encourage and facilitate this initiative.

Present and future

The *Plataforma Misionera* continues to meet on an almost monthly basis in pursuit of the following stated objectives:[7]

- Promote the Córdoba 2015 vision such that all the towns and city districts of Córdoba of more than 5000 inhabitants might be reached by the gospel.

- Act as a nexus for all those taking part in that vision, whether churches of the FRAMEC, mission agencies, denominations, or international agencies.

- Foster a missionary culture so that, where possible, the churches also collaborate in world mission.

- Conduct research studies that might help to evaluate and visualize the spiritual situation in the province of Córdoba.

- Organize missionary conferences that reflect on the Great Commission, promote missionary vocations, and establish common objectives.

- Stimulate the churches to prayer and reciprocal assistance in pursuit of our common "Kingdom vision."

- Facilitate these objectives in whatever way possible, offering consultancy to churches that seek it and information to those who request it.

Perhaps the most significant statement that can be made regarding the churches of Córdoba is that their commitment to a common vision for mission continues and deepens. A more recent development is the interest of engaging in common reflection on thinking regarding Missional Church and what that would mean for the relatively traditional churches of a province like Córdoba. And the *Plataforma Misionera* is now thinking about holding another conference, both to celebrate what has been

---

7. *Conclusiones y Delimitaciones de los objetivos de la Plataforma Misionera,* FRAMEC, 2013 (unpublished).

achieved and to stimulate a final push towards the goals that were set at the turn of the millennium.

Collaborative Church Planting—a model for Europe

Collaborative church planting is not a common approach in Spain. Nevertheless, it appears that the pastors and missionaries of Córdoba would agree with Murray in saying, "The church planting needed in rural and urban areas will not be achieved by individual churches operating independently."[8]

However, a more critical assessment of the experience of the Córdoba churches would highlight the strengths and weaknesses of the approach. In fact, during the aforementioned field research prior to the *Seconda Conferencia Misionera*, all the pastors were specifically asked what they would see as the advantages and disadvantages of church planting through collaboration.[9] The pastors and missionaries of Córdoba all agreed that collaborative church planting would have many advantages. It would contribute to the unity of the churches, release human and material resources for the evangelization of the province, and be mutually enriching. The missionaries also felt that it would help to ensure the full identification of the church plants with the Spanish culture; it would clarify the role of the missionary, and also give new training opportunities for young leaders. In addition, it would help to resolve many of the dependency issues that were affecting the churches that the missionaries had established.

An honest assessment of the disadvantages of collaboration highlighted that the main disadvantage of closer partnership between churches, and between the churches and ECM would be denominational or doctrinal issues. Though theological differences were raised as a potential problem, they have rarely proved to be so. Addicott's observation would seem to be the key,

> In the area of differences in ecclesiology, church-planters run into practical difficulties as our ecclesiology defines the nature of the churches we seek to plant. Can a Pentecostal cooperate with a Conservative Baptist to bring a church into being? The

8. Murray, *Church Planting,* 286.

9. Memory, "The Church Planting Strategy of the European Christian Mission in Córdoba, Spain," 49–50.

answer is "Yes." There are many examples of where this is happening, but in every case it requires a high level of mutual trust and understanding as well as grace of God to enable them to recognize the appropriate nature of the church in the host culture in which it is being planted.[10]

There was a general recognition that, though doctrinal differences may emerge from time to time, given the respect that exists between the pastors and missionaries, there is a good foundation for building consensus and working arrangements. Fundamental to building this trust is time for prayer and honest dialogue about the realities of collaboration. Prior discussion of all aspects of the collaborative effort must take place if conflict is to be avoided, as others have also found.[11] Additionally, the research found the pastors and missionaries in Córdoba considered that it was essential to build a Kingdom vision in the churches through preaching and teaching on the essential unity of the body of Christ. This has been fostered through the annual church united meetings and as one of the stated objectives of the *Plataforma Misionera*.

While pastors and missionaries were candid about the challenges of collaboration, there was a sense of expectation, which is perhaps best reflected by the words of one of the young Spanish pastors, who said, "If this works, it is because God is behind it. It would be spectacle, a spectacle for the glory of God that would bless the whole country."

Could the example of collaborative church planting in Córdoba inspire other European cities and provinces to consider the strategic benefits of collaboration for the greater glory of God? My prayer is that it might.

Discussion highlights

After the presentation, the audience discussed the following questions in small groups, then shared their observations with the whole group. The questions included:

---

10. Addicott, *Body Matters*, 137.

11. Rickett, "7 Mistakes Partners Make and How to Avoid them," 309. Taylor, *Kingdom Partnerships for Synergy in Missions*, 21.

- The pastors and missionaries in Córdoba were asked what they saw as the advantages and disadvantages of collaborative church planting. What would you say they are in your particular context?

- What were the most significant moments in the story of how the churches in Córdoba began to work together?

- What is your instinctive reaction to the possibility of engaging in collaborative church planting?

The small groups could see many advantages of working together in church planting, including sharing of gifts to create a good team, sharing experiences, praying together, and sharing contacts and networks, including knowledge of who is not being reached by existing churches and where church plants could begin.

Memory related the story of a united choir and subsequent youth choir, which both contained members from across the range of churches: "My eldest daughter would go off to Córdoba each week for the gathering of this youth choir. It gave a massive boost for the youth to mix together not only for social purposes. There was a missional agenda as well, because they were preparing to do outreach using music and drama. When you start to work together and build trust, unexpected things happen. This was one of them."

Whilst having a fraternity of leaders meeting together to pray and come up with a common vision was seen as significant moment in the Córdoba church planting story, several of the groups expressed uncertainty as to what collaborative church planting would look like in their context. This was particularly where churches have their own certain history and identity, or a history of competition or disagreement.

Again, prayer and building trust is key, said Memory. "For years the group just met to pray, then they started talking about things of common interest. For example, 'what are we going to do with this brother who came to my church but now wants to become a member in another church when he hasn't resigned his membership at my church?' Rather than fighting over it, they came up with a protocol with dealing with that situation. Over time they built trust and then started to organize joint events and common platforms like the choir."

From Memory's perspective, the role of a missionary can help to facilitate the process. "Missionaries can be the glue that works between churches. In my case I think I have been able to encourage the churches to collaborate more because I am not perceived as a threat. I have no denominational powerbase that I can apply, and the church leaders know that I spent fourteen years working in a tiny town, which has built a certain amount of respect and credibility. A lot of missionaries have a similar back story that could give them the credibility to enable this kind of process."

But as Memory emphasized, collaboration does not happen overnight; it is a slow process. "How great to be part of something where you cannot say, 'That was down to me.' You do it with such a long-term Kingdom perspective that you know the benefit of your work will only be apparent in maybe twenty years' time, but you do it right now because you believe in it 100 percent."

19

THE BALKAN PROJECT

JOANNE APPLETON
WITH STEPHEN BELL

MISSION REQUIRES PARTNERSHIP, AND has done so since Paul and Barnabas were sent out by the church in Antioch to reach the Gentile world. Once again, Europe is a missionary destination. But in today's increasingly globalized world, partnership happens in all directions and across greater distances than ever before.

Stephen Bell is the Balkan Coordinator for European Christian Mission (ECM), with 29 years' experience working in Kosovo, Albania, and now Croatia. Since 2010, he has facilitated "The Balkan Project," a cross-cultural church planting project involving Brazilians and Ukrainians working alongside local Balkan pastors.

The context

"Evangelical churches, pastors, and congregations in the Balkans are isolated and discouraged," explains Bell. "Revival is a foreign word. There is a sense of inferiority and a feeling that even though they want to church plant they can't do it, it is too difficult. They compare their struggling congregations with large Roman Catholic churches which have overflowing car parks every day of the week and they give up even before they begin."

This attitude shocked Bell when he first encountered it, having just come from a "semi-revival" situation in Albania. "I believe God wants to do something through the wonderful Christians in the Balkan countries if only they knew how gifted they are. But they need help."

The birth of the Balkan Project

In 2010, Bell organized a missionary prayer week in Central Croatia, with Ron (ECM Field Ministries Leader) and Brenda Anderson as the main speakers. "All the missionaries we worked with were unable to attend the central meetings, so we decided to visit them one-by-one in their locations," says Bell. "After 600km of the 2000km round trip, Ron had tears in his eyes because he had met these isolated pastors. 'Could you use 12 Brazilians?', he asked. And with his question, the Balkan Project was born."

As they discussed the idea, the vision, task, and timeframe were identified as follows:

- *Vision:* To enable keen local pastors to plant churches in clusters across their regions.
- *Task:* This means, first, to seek out keen visionary churches in the Balkans and develop partnership, and second, to envision and recruit numerous missionaries from revival countries.
- *Timeframe:* To establish bridgeheads of effective church planting teams in four Balkan countries by 2014.

Brazil and the Ukraine were identified as "revival countries," where large numbers of churches have been planted in a short period of time. "Because they have seen it happen already, they have the expectation that it can happen again," explained Bell. "We have not experienced this in the Balkans, so we need help from our brothers and sisters who are used to seeing it in order to raise our expectations."

Various names for the project were also discussed. The first, "Church planting in simultaneous cluster zones," described the desire for a model of a mother church that would plant several satellite churches with shared oversight and local lay leadership. This was modified to "A vision for radically accelerated church growth" and "Revival in the Balkans."

"The end result must be a major blessing for the lost peoples of the Balkans, and hopefully with many, many conversions along the way," Bell said. "So the challenge is to reach the lost, and raise numerous teams of four Brazilians and two Ukrainians coming in two-year terms, repeated over a longer period to help us reach that goal."

But before they began, Bell admits he had to undergo "revival" himself. "I was faced with a radical personal choice. I had to count the cost of what this project would take in order to succeed. I would have to explain this 'wacky' idea to our Field Ministries team, as well as convince Brazilian and Ukrainian church leaders to send their people to Europe. But in October 2010, I decided that the project would not fail because of me. I would do all that was needed. God would have to deal with the rest."

The task

Bell identified two parts of the task. The first was to "seek out keen visionary churches in the Balkans and develop partnerships." He called these "two and five talent churches," after the parable of the talents in Matthew 25:14–30. "If we are sending valuable missionaries, we do not want to waste them in churches without a vision for accelerated planting. If you put them in such a church, you get frustration and problems. You frustrate the church, who doesn't want to do anything, and you frustrate the missionary, who wants to start two churches in the first year, but quickly discovers it is not going to happen.

"I consider one of the first churches to receive a team to be a five talent church. They came to one of our church planting seminars with a vision to plant six churches in their region of twenty thousand people. I was cautious at first and asked them to send me a written plan. By the time I got home they had already emailed it to me, so I realized they were serious! Now with the help of the Brazilian team, they have planted two churches, and recently had baptisms of eight new converts."

The second part of the task involves envisioning and recruiting missionaries from revival countries, currently Brazil and Ukraine. The first step is prayer. "We realized a need for prayer on an unprecedented scale," says Bell. "Why has God not brought great growth to the Balkan region in the way he did in Albania? Probably because of lack of prayer. So we started asking him for ten thousand serious prayer partners, and developed the 'Revival in the Balkans' website[1] to facilitate prayer."

Bell asked the local churches to contribute materials and vision plans. Alongside videos, they prepared "pastor-friendly" resources to

---

1. www.revivalinthebalkans.org.

enable busy church leaders to lead a three-hour—or all-night—prayer meeting. And with the target audience in mind, the information has been translated into Ukrainian and Portuguese in addition to English.

As well as sustained prayer, relationships with Brazilian and Ukrainian churches needed to be built. Existing ECM contacts in both countries helped this process. Between the beginning of the project and now (2014), Bell has visited Brazil five times and the Ukraine four times, speaking at churches and presenting both the need and the vision.

"In Brazil we have held many mass meetings where people have been inspired to help us in Croatia and Bosnia. Almost a third of Brazilians are evangelicals, so they cannot conceive an area like the Balkans where there are less than 1 percent evangelical Christians. We would present the challenge and make an appeal at the end of every meeting for missionaries to come forward to volunteer. We would also challenge churches to pray and to give financially and sacrificially for the Balkan Lost. At one church, the teenagers had tears in their eyes as they prayed for the need in the Balkans. At another, even before the service ended, the elders were discussing how they could help us!"

So far, nine missionaries in three teams from Brazil have partnered with churches in the Balkans. While no Ukrainian missionaries have been able to join the teams to date, leaders from the Ukrainian *Bible Education by Extension* regularly hold training seminars and conferences for local Balkan pastors and church planters. "They are also the eyes and ears of the wider Ukrainian church, reporting back and raising much prayer support for the lost peoples of the Balkans," says Bell.

Seeing the context is an important part of raising awareness. Every October a large group of Brazilian pastors and businessmen, along with leaders from Ukraine and other areas, travel around 2,700 km through the Balkan countries over a period of eleven days, visiting pastors and "envisioning together." A major benefit of these tours is that the local pastors and churches are encouraged and begin to hope, knowing that help is on its way.

The Timeframe

The initial timeframe was to establish bridgeheads of effective church planting teams in four Balkan countries by 2014. That process is ongoing. "Since the first three missionaries arrived some 18 months ago, perhaps twelve people in the various churches have become Christians," Bell shared. "Six of the missionaries have still not completed their first year. And in the Zagreb area, a new church is forming which would almost certainly never have started but for the Brazilian missionary couple opening their home and leading it."

But this is just the start. In order to "not lose momentum from the beginning," Bell has identified three phases. The first, with teams of missionaries in each of four locations is underway.

"But what if twenty people respond to our appeals? We would not want to flood our existing teams with too many missionaries, so we need to prepare for an overflow of resource," he explained. "We should be flexible enough to [be able to] place the next wave of missionaries. This leads us to the second phase of finding churches that are committed to the cause of evangelism by church planting, and where we can locate the next teams of missionaries.

"At first, we can visit these churches to encourage them or hold an evangelistic weekend. Even better, we can include them in the vision trips where twenty or thirty mobilizers from Ukraine and Brazil are exposed to their needs and potential. Our motto is, 'what we plan and prepare for today could come into being in two years' time,' and we want to be prepared in faith for what might happen. We do not make any promises, but say that we will 'try our hardest,' and we include them on the prayer list so that prayer is happening."

To date, Bell has identified churches in Slovenia, Croatia, Hungary, and Serbia where missionaries could be placed, but he has told them to "wait" as they first need to see movement in mobilization. Even so, the vision of church planting and revival throughout the Balkan region remains. And this will require the third phase of expansion and consolidation.

"If this vision is of God, then it is multipliable," says Bell. "The whole Balkan region needs radical revival, and we are committed to following the Godly visions of the local national Christian leaders. There are potential missionaries in abundance in Brazil and Ukraine. Making every area of this vision concept workable and fruitful is a great challenge, but if the structure can be effective and function, then the sky is the limit! I believe an integral part of the project is learning much from our brethren in these two great nations."

Difficulties faced

When undertaking a project of such breadth of vision there will, of course, be problems. One of the biggest is doubt from Balkan Christians and leaders who are more used to maintaining what they have in the face of many challenges, rather than expanding through church planting. However, as they observe the growth brought about through the current Brazilian missionaries, more pastors are beginning to catch the vision.

A second issue is the lack of finance, both for the missionaries and the receiving churches. "Even though we set a very simple budget, most of the member care conversations I have with the missionaries are about finance," says Bell. "Ukrainian missionaries have been prevented from coming largely because they just can't raise the money they need. One of our biggest lessons learned is that missionaries need to come with 100 or even 110 percent of their support already in place."

And the cross-cultural aspect of the vision can also create problems with communication and cultural distance. "Communication with leaders and mobilizers is often through translation—or Google Translate," explains Bell. "I stand in awe at the mutual trust between the various leaders in this project—it really is a miracle!"

And while in many ways the project is still in its infancy, with many challenges to overcome and a lot of hard work ahead, Bell is adamant that "no-one involved in the Balkan Project would ever turn the clock back."

LIST OF CONTRIBUTORS

Evert VAN DE POLL (editor), Professor of Religious Studies and Missiology at the Evangelical Theological Faculty in Leuven (Belgium), and pastor of the *Fédération des Églises Évangéliques Baptistes de France*, based in Nîmes.

Joanne APPLETON (co-editor), Writer and researcher with a particular interest in mission in Europe, co-editor of *Vista, Communicating research and innovation in mission in Europe*, former Communications Manager for Redcliffe College, and a trustee of ECM Britain.

Ron ANDERSON, Church planting consultant and trainer with European Christian Mission, Senior Associate for Church Planting for the Lausanne Movement.

Stephen BELL, Director of the *Balkan Project*, and church planter in Zagreb, Croatia with European Christian Mission.

David BROWN, Church planter and pastor with France-Mission, and GBU (French student movement).

Jeff FOUNTAIN, Director of the *Schuman Centre for European Studies*, Heerde, NL.

Ishak GHATAS, Founding pastor of *The Arabic Church* in Brussels, as well as two sister churches.

JOHAN LUKASSE, Church planting consultant, related to European Christian Mission, and founder and leader of European Church Planting Consultation.

JIM MEMORY, Postgraduate lecturer in European Mission at Redcliffe College in Gloucester, UK, and church planter with European Christian Mission.

BORIS PASCHKE, Postdoctoral researcher in New Testament Studies at the ETF in Leuven, Belgium.

ANDRE POWNALL, Pastor of the *Union of French Evangelical Free Churches*, member of the church planting commission of the French National Council of Evangelicals, and former lecturer in practical theology at the Bible Institute of Nogent-sur-Marne, France.

JOHANNES REIMER, Professor of Missiology at the University of South Africa and the Theologische Hochschule Ewersbach, Germany.

DIETRICH SCHINDLER, Europe-wide church planting consultant for the Evangelical Free Church of Germany.

CHRIS WIGRAM, International Director of European Christian Mission.

ERIC ZANDER, Church planter with the Belgian Evangelical Mission, based in Gembloux, Belgium.

BIBLIOGRAPHY

This bibliography comprises the titles mentioned in the footnotes, plus a number of additional publications that we would recommend for further reflection on the subjects dealt with in this book.

Addicott, Ernie. *Body Matters: A Guide to Partnership in Christian Mission.* Edmonds: InterDev Partnership Associates, 2005.

Ahrweiler, Maurice Aymard, ed. *Les Européens.* Paris: Hermann, éditeurs des sciences et des arts, 2000.

Allen, Roland. *Missionary Methods: St Paul's or Ours.* Cambridge: World Dominion, 1962.

―――. *The Spontaneous Expansion of the Church.* Cambridge: Lutterworth, 2006.

Appleton, Joanne. "The Missional Lifestyle of European Generation Y: An Analysis of Influences and Perception." MA Thesis, Redcliffe College, 2012.

Bakke, Pownall, et al. *Espoir pour la ville, Dieu dans la cité.* Québec: La Clairière, 1994.

Barna, George. *The Second Coming of the Church.* Nashville: Word, 1998.

Barna Org. "Five Reasons Millennials Stay Connected to Church." 2013. https://www.barna.org/barna-update/millennials/635-5-reasons-millennials-stay-connected-to-church#.Upc1k9J7Iuc.

Barrett, C.K. *A Critical and Exegetical Commentary on the Acts of the Apostles.* Edinburgh: T & T Clark, 1994.

Bauckham, Richard. "Prayer in the Book of Revelation." In *Into God's Presence: Prayer in the New Testament,* edited by Richard N. Longenecker. Grand Rapids: Eerdmans, 2001.

Beckett, J. "Evangelical Catholicity – A Possible Foundation for Exploring Relational Responsibility in a Global Community?." In *Evangelical Review of Theology.* 2010 34/2.

Berger, Davie, et al. *Religious America, Secular Europe? A Theme and Variations.* Farnham: Ashgate, 2008.

Beyerhaus, Peter. "Zur Theologie der Religionen im Protestantismus." In *Kerygma und Dogma* 15, 1969.

Billings, Alan. *Secular Lives Sacred Hearts: The Role of the Church in a Time of No Religion.* London: SPCK, 2004.

Bjork, David E. *Unfamiliar Paths: the Challenge of Recognising the Work of Christ in Strange Clothing.* Pasadena: William Carey Library, 1997.

Bock, Darrell L. *Luke, vol. 2, 9:51–24:52* (Baker Exegetical Commentary on the NT). Grand Rapids: Baker, 1996.

———. *Acts* (Baker Exegetical Commentary on the NT). Grand Rapids: Baker Academic, 2007.

Bosch, David J. *Transforming Mission.* New York: Orbis, 1991.

Breen, Mike. "Why the Missional Movement Will Fail." Verge Network, 2011. http://www.vergenetwork.org/2011/09/14/mike-breen-why-the-missional-movement-will-fail/.

Broomhall, Marshall. *Hudson Taylor's Legacy: A Series of Meditations.* London, CIM, 1931.

Brown, David. *L'implantation d'une Église racontée à mon stagiaire.* Lyon: Clé, 2013.

———. *Passerelles: entre l'évangile et nos contemporains.* Marne-la-Vallée: Éditions Farel, 2005.

———. *Servir à nos Français: Le défi de l'Église émergente.* Marne-la-Vallée: Farel, 2009.

Bruce, F.F. *The Acts of the Apostles.* Leicester: Apollos, third and enlarged edition, 1990.

Carlton, R. Bruce. *Strategy Coordinator: Changing the Course of Southern Baptist Missions.* Eugene: Wipf and Stock, 2010.

Carson, Donald A. *Christ & Culture Revisited.* Grand Rapids: Eerdmans 2008.

Carter, Craig A. "The Legacy of an Inadequate Christology: Yoder's Critique of Niebuhr's Christ and Culture." In *Mennonite Quarterly Review.* July 2003. http://www.goshen.edu/mqr/pastissues/july03carter.html.

Chester, Tim, and Steve Timmis. *Everyday Church: Mission by Being Good Neighbours.* Nottingham: IVP, 2011.

Chopin, Jamet, et al. *L'Europe d'après: en finir avec le pessimisme.* Paris: Lignes de repères, 2012.

Church of England. "From Anecdote to Evidence: Findings from the Church Growth Research Programme 2011-2013." www.churchgrowthresearch.org.uk.

Clapp, Rodney. *A Peculiar People: The Church as Culture in a Post-Christian Society.* Downers Grove: IVP, 1996.

Clark, David B. "Sharing Christ's Love in Europe." ECM, 2004.

Clay, Graham. *Disciples and Citizens.* Nottingham: IVP, 2007.

Clément, Raphael, and Edouard Husson. *Robert Schuman: homme d'État, citoyen du Ciel.* Paris: François-Xavier de Guibert, 2006.

Cole, Neil. *Organic Church.* San Francisco: Jossey-Bass, 2005.

Conn, Harvey M. *Planting and Growing Urban Churches: From Dream to Reality.* Grand Rapids: Baker, 1997.

Corvi, Bigi, et al. *The European Millennials Versus the US Millennials: Similarities and Differences.* Rome: Quarto Convegno Annuale della Societa Italiana Marketing, 2007.

Cullmann, Oscar. *Prayer in the New Testament, Overtures to Biblical Theology.* Minneapolis: Fortress, 1994.

———. "La prière selon les Epîtres pauliniennes," *Theologisches Zeitschrift* 35/2, 1979.

Dahl, Stephan. "Einführung in die Interkulturelle Kommunikation!." 2002. http://www.intercultural-network.de/einfuerung/.

Daily Mail. *The Disunited States of Europe.* http://www.dailymail.co.uk/travel/article-2598319/The-disunited-states-Europe-How-continent-look-divided-coffee-drinking-love-potatoes-beer-weather.html.

Daniel, Robin. *Missionary Strategies Then and Now.* Chester, UK: Tamarisk Publications, 2012.

Davie and Heelas, Linda Woodhead, ed. *Predicting Religion: Christian, Secular and Alternative Futures.* Farnham: Ashgate Publishing Limited, 2003.

Davie, Grace. *Europe: the Exceptional Case: Parameters of Faith in the Modern World.* London: Darton, Longman & Todd, 2007.

Davies, Norman. *Europe: A History.* Oxford University Press, 1996.

Davies, Paul J. *Faith Seeking Effectiveness: The Missionary Theology of José Míguez Bonino.* Zoetermeer, Boekencentrum, 2006.

DAWN (Disciple A Whole Nation). www.dawneurope.net.

Dawson, Christopher. *Understanding Europe.* London: Sheed & Ward, 1952.

de Beauvoir, Simone. *Le Deuxième Sexe,* Paris : Gallimard, 1949

Donovan, Vincent. *Christianity Rediscovered: An Epistle from the Masai.* London: SCM, 2003.

Driscoll, Mark. *Confessions of a Reformissioned Reverend.* Grand Rapids: Zondervan.

DuBose, Francis M. *How Churches Grow in an Urban World.* Nashville: Broadman, 1978.

Dunn, James D. G. *The Christ and the Spirit: Collected Essays Vol. 2: Pneumatology.* Edinburgh: T & T Clark, 1998.

Escobar, Samuel. "Evangelical Missiology: Peering Into the Future at the Turn of the Century." In *Global Missiology for the 21st Century,* edited by W. Taylor. Grand Rapids: Baker Academic, 2000.

European Commission. *The Young Europeans in 2001.* Special Barometer, European Commission, 2001. http://ec.europa.eu/public_opinion/archives/ebs/ebs_151_summ_en.pdf.

Eurostat. *News Release 173/2013.* 20 November 2013.

Faix, Tobias, "Unsicher Zwischen Tradition & Aufbruch Was Christliche Jugendliche Von Ihrer Spiritualität Erwarten Ergebnisse Einer Umfrage Unter Jungen Erwachsenen." Opinion Survey, 2007. http://institut-empirica.de/uploads/1193406873-885768.pdf.

Faix, Tobias, and Johannes Reimer. *Die Welt verstehen. Kontextanalyse als Sehhilfe für die Gemeinde. Transformationsstudien Bd. 3.* Marburg: Francke Verlag, 2013.

Ferraro, Gary P. *Cultural Anthropology: An Applied Perspective. 3rd edition.* Wadsworth, 1998.

Ferry, Luc. *La révolution de l'amour: pour une spiritualité laïque. Paris: Plon, 2010.*

Fountain, Jeff. *Living as a People of Hope: Faith, Hope & Vision for 21st Century Europe.* Rotterdam: Initial Media, 2004.

———. *Deeply Rooted: The Forgotten Legacy of Robert Schuman.* Heerde: Schuman Institute for European Studies, 2010.

FRAMEC. *Conclusiones y Delimitaciones de los objetivos de la Plataforma Misionera,* 2013, (unpublished).

Fresh Expressions. www.freshexpressions.org.uk.

Friesen, Duane K. *Artists, Citizens, Philosophers: Seeking the Peace of the City: An Anabaptist Theology of Culture.* Waterloo, ON: Herald, 2000.

Frost, Michael. *Exiles: Living Missionally in a Post-Christian Culture.* Peabody, MA: Hendrickson, 2006.

———. *The Road to Missional: Journey to the Center of the Church.* Grand Rapids: Baker, 2011.

Frost, Michael, and Alan Hirsch. *Shaping of Things to Come: Innovation and Mission for the 21st-Century Church*. Peabody, MA: Hendrickson, 2003.

Gantenbein, Hansjörg. *Mission en Europe: Une étude socio-missiologique pour le 21ème siècle*. Strasbourg: Faculté de théologie protestante de l'Université de Strasbourg, 2010.

Garrison, David. *Church Planting Movements*. Richmond: International Missions Board, 1999.

————. *Church Planting Movements: How God is Redeeming a Lost World*. Monument: Wigtake Resources, 2004.

————. "Church Planting Movement FAQS." In *Mission Frontiers*, 33/2, 2011.

Gebauer, Roland. *Das Gebet bei Paulus: Forschungsgeschichtliche und exegetische Studien*. Gießen: Brunnen, 1989.

Giles Kevin. *What on Earth is the Church? An Exploration in the New Testament Theology*. Downers Grove: IVP, 1995.

Gnilka, Joachim. *Der Kolosserbrief* (Herders Theologischer Kommentar zum NT). Freiburg: Herder, 1980.

Green, Joel B. "Persevering Together in Prayer: The Significance of Prayer in the Acts of the Apostles." In *Into God's Presence: Prayer in the New Testament*, edited by Richard N. Longenecker. Grand Rapids: Eerdmans, 2001.

Greene, Mark. *The Great Divide*. London: LICC, 2010.

Grimm, Harold J. *Luther's Works, Volume 3.1, Career of the Reformer I*. Philadelphia: Muhlenberg, 1957.

Guder, Darrell L., and Lois Barrett. *Missional Church: A Vision for the Sending of the Church in North America*. Grand Rapids: Eerdmans, 1998.

Guenther, Bruce L. "The Enduring Problem of Christ and Culture." In *Direction*, 34/2, Fall 2005.

Guillebaud, Jean-Claude. *La refondation du monde*. Paris: Seuil, 1999.

Guinness, Os, and David Wells. "Global Gospel, global Era; Christian Discipleship and Mission in the Age of Globalization." http://conversation.lausanne.org/en/conversations/detail/10566#.U6P7BP229do.

Habermas, Jürgen. *Time of Transitions*. New York: Polity, 2006.

Habermas, Jürgen, and Joseph Ratzinger. *The Dialectics of Secularisation*. San Francisco: Ignatius, 2006.

Hamman, Adalbert Gautier. *La prière, vol. 1, Le Nouveau Testament* (Bibliothèque de Théologie). Tournai: Desclée & Cie, 1959.

Hanges, James C. *Paul, Founder of Churches: A Study in Light of the Evidence for the Role of 'Founder-Figures' in the Hellenistic-Roman Period* (Wissenschaftliche Untersuchungen zum NT 292). Tübingen: Mohr Siebeck, 2012.

Hansen, Randall. *A Superabundance of Contradictions: The European Union's post-Amsterdam Policies on migrant 'Integration', Labour Immigration, Asylum, and Illegal Immigration* (Occasional Paper nr. 28). Centre for Ethnic and Urban Studies, 2005.

————. *Migration to Europe: Its History and its Lessons*. The Political Quarterly Publishing Co. Ltd, 2003.

Harris, Murray J., *The Second Epistle to the Corinthians* (The New International Greek Testament Commentary). Grand Rapids: Erdemans, 2013.

Helland, Roger, and Leonard Hjalmarson. *Missional Spirituality: Embodying God's Love from the Inside Out*. Downers Grove: IVP, 2011.

Hengel, Martin. *Saint Peter: The Underestimated Apostle.* Grand Rapids: Eerdmans, 2010.

Herbst, Michael. *Und sie dreht sich doch: Wie sich die Kirche im 21. Jahrhundert ändern kann und muss.* Asslar: Gerth Medien, 2001.

Hervieu-Léger, Danièle. *Le pèlerin et le converti: la religion en mouvement.* Paris: Flammarion, 1999.

Hesselgrave, David J. *Planting Churches Cross-Culturally: A Guide for Home and Foreign Missions.* Grand Rapids: Baker, 2000.

Hirsch, Alan. *The Forgotten Way: Reactivating the Missional Church.* Grand Rapids: Baker, 2006.

———. *What is a Missional Church?.* Verge Network, 2012. http://www.vergenetwork.org/2012/04/03/alan-hirsch-what-is-a-missional-church/.

Hirsch, Alan, and Debra Hirsch. *Untamed: Reactivating a Missional Form of Discipleship.* Grand Rapids: Baker, 2010.

Hunter III, George G. *Church for the Unchurched.* Nashville: Abingdon, 1996.

Hunter, Shireen T., ed. *Islam, Europe's Second Religion.* Praeger/CSIS, 2002.

Instituto Nacional de Estadística, *Municipal Register: 1 January 2012.*

Jacques, Francis, ed. *Les racines culturelles et spirituelles de l'Europe: trois questions sur la place de la source chrétienne.* Paris: Parole et Silence, 2008.

Jenkins, Philip. *God's Continent: Christianity, Islam, and Europe's Religious Crisis.* Oxford: Oxford University Press, 2007.

Jervell, Jacob. *Die Apostelgeschichte: Übersetzt und erklärt* (Kritisch-exegetischer Kommentar über das Neue Testament 3). Göttingen: Vandenhoeck & Ruprecht, 1998.

Johnson, Luke T. *Living Jesus: Learning the Heart of the Gospel.* New York: Harper One, 1999.

Käser, Lothar. *Fremde Kulturen. Eine Einführung in die Ethnologie für Entwicklungshelfer und kirchliche Mitarbeiter in Übersee.* Erlangen und Bad Liebenzell, 1997.

Kelley, Dean M. *Why Conservative Churches are Growing.* New York: Harper & Row, 1972.

Kettani, Houssain, "Muslim Population in Europe: 1950 – 2020." *International Journal of Environmental Science and Development,* 1/2, June 2010.

Kim, Kirsteen. *Joining in with the Spirit.* London: SCM, 2012.

Kritzinger, JNJ. "Who do they say I am?." In *An African Person in the Making,* edited by Willem Saayman. Pretoria: Unisa, 2001.

Kirk, Andrew. *What is Mission? Theological Explorations.* London: Darton, Longman & Todd, 1999.

Landman, N. Islam in the Benelux Countries in *Islam in the West: Critical Concepts in Islamic Studies* edited by Westerlund and Svanberg. London: Routledge, 2011.

Lausanne Committee for World Evangelization. *The Lausanne Covenant* [online] http://www.lausanne.org/content/covenant/lausanne-covenant

———. *Report of the Willowbank Consultation on the Gospel and Culture.* 1979.

———. *Manilla Manifesto.* 1989.

———. *Cape Town Commitment.* 2010.

Law, Eric H. F. *The Bush Was Blazing But Not Consumed: Developing a Multicultural Community through Dialogue and Liturgy.* St. Louis, MO: Chalice, 1996.

Lingenscheid, Rainer, and Gerhard Wegner. *Aktivierende Gemeinwesenarbeit.* Stuttgart: Kohlhammer, 1990.

Lloyd-Jones, Martyn. "Heresies." www.the-highway.com/heresies_Lloyd-Jones.html.

Logan, Robert E. *Be Fruitful and Multiply: Embracing God's Heart for Church Multiplication*. St. Charles, IL: Church Smart Resources, 2006.

Lukasse, Johan. *Churches with Roots: Planting Churches in Post-Christian Europe.* Eastbourne: Monarch, 1990.

Lukasse, Johan and Stephanie Shackelford. *Effective Short Term Missions.* Hasselt, BE: European Church Planting Consultation, 2012.

Lukasse, Johan and Teo Kamp. *Divide and Multiply: A Vision and a Way to Go for Self-multiplying Churches.* Hasselt, BE: European Church Planting Consultation, 2010.

———. *Growth Scenario: A Practical Manual to See Christian Groups and Churches Grow and Multiply.* Hasselt, BE: European Church Planting Consultation, 2014.

Luzbetak, Louis J. *The Church and Cultures.* Pasadena: WCL, 1970.

Maggay, Melba. *Transforming Society.* Oxford: Regnum Lynx, 1994.

Mandryk, Jason. *Operation World: The Definitive Prayer Guide to Every Nation.* Leicester: IVP, 2010.

Marshall, I. Howard. *The Gospel of Luke: A Commentary on the Greek Text* (The New International Greek Testament Commentary). Grand Rapids: Eerdmans, 1978.

Mayers, Marvin K. *Christianity Confronts Culture: A Strategy for Cross-cultural Evangelism.* Grand Rapids: Zondervan, 1987.

McGavran, Donald A. *Understanding Church Growth.* Grand Rapids: Eerdmans, 1985.

Memory, Jim. *El estado actual de las Iglesias de Córdoba.* FRAMEC, 2002.

———. "The Church Planting Strategy of the European Christian Mission in Cordoba, Spain, and an investigation of the potential for collaborative church planting." Masters thesis, Redcliffe College, 2009.

———. "Effective Church Planting in Europe." In *Vista*, Issue 6, 2011.

———. "The Spiritual Values of European Young People." in Vista, Issue 6, 2011.

Minatrea, Milfred. *Shaped by God's Heart: the Passion and Practice of Missional Churches.* San Fransisco: John Wiley & Sons, 2004.

Möller, Christian. "Gemeindeaufbau." *Religion in Geschichte und Gegenwart.* 4th ed, vol 3, 2000.

Müller, Faix, et al. "Tat. Ort. Glaube. 21. Inspirierende Praxisbeispiele zwischen Gemeinde und Gesellschaft." *Transformationsstudien Bd. 6.* Marburg: Francke Verlag, 2013.

Müller, Klaus W., ed. *Mission im postmodernen Europa: Referate der Jahrestagung 2008 des Arbeitskreises für evangelikale Missiologie.* Gießen: Edition Afem, 2008.

Murray, Stuart. *Church Planting: Laying Foundations.* Carlisle: Paternoster, 1998.

———. *Planting Churches: A Framework for Practitioners.* Exeter: Paternoster, 2008.

———. *Post Christendom: Church Mission in a Strange New World.* Milton Keynes: Paternoster, 2005.

Newbigin, Lesslie. *Foolishness to the Greeks: The Gospel and Western Culture.* Grand Rapids: Eerdmans, 1986.

———. *The Gospel in a Pluralist Society.* London: SPCK, 1989.

———. *The Open Secret: An Introduction to the Theology of Mission.* Grand Rapids: Eerdmans, revised edition, 1995.

———. *Proper Confidence: Faith, Doubt, and Certainty in Christian Discipleship.* London: SPCK, 1995.

New York Times, The "Mission from Africa" [online] http://www.nytimes.com/2009/04/12/magazine/12churches-t.html?pagewanted=all

Niebuhr, Richard. *Christ and Culture.* San Francisco: HarperCollins, 1951.

Noort, Paas, et al. *Als een kerk opnieuw begint: Handboek voor missionaire gemeenschapsvorming.* Zoetermeer: Boekencentrum, 2008.

Nyquist, J. Paul. *There is No Time: A Parable . . . to make a difference in time for eternity by rapidly planting churches where none exist.* Portaga: Fidler Doubleday, 2000.

Oak, John. *Healthy Christians Make a Healthy Church.* Fearn Rosshire: Christian Focus Publications, 2003.

Ogden, Greg. *Transforming Discipleship: Making Disciples a Few at a Time.* Downers Grove: IVP, 2003.

Olofinjaja, Israel. *Reverse in Ministry & Missions: Africans in the Dark Continent of Europe, an Historical Study of African Churches in Europe.* Milton Keynes: Author House, 2010.

Orr, Graham. *Not So Secret: Being Contemporary Agents for Mission.* Nottingham: IVP, 2012.

Ostmeyer, Karl-Heinrich. *Kommunikation mit Gott und Christus: Sprache und Theologie des Gebetes im Neuen Testament* (Wissenschaftliche Untersuchungen zum Neuen Testament 197). Tübingen: Mohr Siebeck, 2006.

Ott, Craig, and Gene Wilson. *Global Church Planting.* Grand Rapids: Baker Academic, 2011.

Padilla, Rene. *Mission Between Times. Essays on the Kingdom.* Grand Rapids: Eerdmans, 1985.

Pagden, Anthony, ed. *The Idea of Europe: From Antiquity to the European Union.* Cambridge: Cambridge University Press, 2002.

Paschke, Boris. "Prayer to Jesus in the Canonical and in the Apocryphal Acts of the Apostles." *Ephemerides Theologicae Lovanienses* 89/1, 2013.

———. "Praying to the Holy Spirit in Early Christianity." *Tyndale Bulletin* 64/2, 2013.

Pillai, Joshua. "A study contrasting the traditional model and the house church model in Chennai, India." Research project.

Prugl, Elisabeth, and Markus Thiel. *Diversity in the European Union.* Palgrave: Macmillan, 2009.

Quadrant, "June 2002 Christian Research." www.christian-research.org/publications/quadrant/quadrant-index.

Rainer, Thom S. *Breakout Churches.* Grand Rapids: Zondervan, 2005.

Ratzinger, Joseph. *Europe, Today and Tomorrow.* San Francisco: Ignatius, 2007.

Reimer, Johannes. "Die Zur Verantwortung für die Welt gerufene Gemeinde." In *Die Welt verändern. Grundfragen einer Theologie der Transformation. Transformationsstudien Bd. 2,* edited by Faix, Reimer, et al. Marburg: Francke Verlag, 2009.

———. *Die Welt umarmen: Theologie des gesellschaftsrelevanten Gemeindebau.* Marburg: Francke, 2009.

———. "Common Ground oder doch nur Anknüpfungspunkt? Zur Frage der hochspektralen Kontextualisierung am Beispiel des Islam." In *Theologie im Kontext von Biographie und Weltbild* (GBFE Jahrbuch), edited by Faix, Wünch, et al. Marburg: Francke, 2011-2012.

———.Der Missionale Aufbruch. Paradigmenwechsel im Gemeindedenken". In "Die verändernde Kraft des Evangeliums. Beiträge zu den Marburger Transformationsstudien." *Transformationsstudien Bd. 4,* edited by Tobias Faix and Tobias Künkler. Marburg: Francke, 2011-2012.

————. *Hereinspaziert. Willkommenskultur und Evangelisation.* Schwarzenfeld: Neufeld Verlag, 2013.

————. *Leben-Rufen-Verändern. Chance und Herausforderungen gesellschaftstransformierender Evangelisation heute* (Transformationsstudien, 5). Marburg: Fracke, 2013.

Rhodes, Stephen A. *Where the Nations Meet, The Church in a Multicultural World.* Downers Grove: IVP, 1998.

Rickett, Daniel. "7 Mistakes Partners Make and How to Avoid Them." *Evangelical Missions Quarterly*, 37/3, 2001.

Rifkin, Jeremy. *The European Dream: How Europe's Vision of the Future is Quietly Eclipsing the American Dream.* New York: Jeremy Tarcher/Penguin, 2004.

Robinson, Martin. *A World Apart: Creating a Church for the Unchurched.* Tunbridge Wells, UK: Monarch, 1992.

Robinson, Martin, and Christine Stuart. *Planting Tomorrows Churches Today.* Eastbourne: Monarch, 1992.

Roxburgh, Alan J. *Missional: Joining God in the Neighborhood.* Grand Rapids: Baker, 2011.

Schindler, Dietrich. *The Jesus Model: Planting Churches the Jesus Way.* Carlisle: Piquant, 2013.

Schluter, Michael, and David Lee. *The "R" Factor.* London: Hodder & Stoughton, 1993.

Schneider, Gerhard. *Die Apostelgeschichte, 2. Teil* (Herders Theologischer Kommentar zum Neuen Testament). Herder Verlag, 2002.

Schnelle, Udo. *The History and Theology of the New Testament Writings.* London: SCM, 1998.

Schuman Centre for European Studies. www.schumancentre.eu.

Schwartz, Christian. *Natural Church Development.* Saint Charles: ChurchSmart Resources, 1996.

Schweizer, Eduard. *Gemeinde und Gemeindeordnung im Neuen Testament.* Zürich: TVZ 1959.

Schweyer, Stephan. "Sie hielten alle einmütig fest am Gebet: Zum Stellenwert des gemeinsamen Gebets für den Gemeindeaufbau." *European Journal of Theology* 21/1, 2011.

Shenk, David W., and Ervin R. Stutzman. *Creating Communities of the Kingdom: New Testament Models of Church Planting.* Scottdale, PA: Herald, 1988.

Shenk, Wilbert. *Exploring Church Growth.* Grand Rapids: Eerdmans 1973.

Smith, David. *Mission After Christendom.* London: Darton, Longman & Todd, 2003.

Søgaard, Viggo. *Media in Church and Mission: Communicating the Gospel.* Pasadena, California: William Carey Library, 1993.

Spivey, Eric T. "Developing a Process for Missional Formation: A Ministry Project in the Baptist Church of Beaufort, SC." PhD Thesis, Gardner-Webb University, 2011.

Stackhouse, Ian. *The Gospel-Driven Church: Retrieving Classical Ministries for Contemporary Revivalism.* Milton Keynes: Paternoster, 2005.

Stetzer, Ed. *Planting New Churches in a Postmodern Age.* Nashville: Broadman & Hollman, 2003.

Stetzer, Ed, and Thom S. Reiner. *Transformational Church.* Nashville: Broadman & Hollman, 2010.

Stone, Bryan. *Evangelism After Christendom.* Grand Rapids: Brazos, 2006.

Stott, John. *The Contemporary Christian: An Urgent Plea for Double Listening.* Leicester: IVP, 1992.

———. *God's New Society*. In "The Paul We Think We Know," quoted by Timothy Gombis. Christianity Today, July 2011.

Taylor, Charles. *A Secular Age*. New York: Harvard University Press, 2007.

Taylor, Ed. *Kingdom Partnerships for Synergy in Missions*. Pasadena: William Carey Library, 1994.

Triandafyllidou, Anna. *Addressing Cultural, Ethnic, Religious Diversity Challenges in Europe*. European University Institute: Robert Schuman Centre for Advanced Studies, 2012.

———. *Integration, Transnational Mobility and Human, Social and Economic Capital*. European University Institute: The Robert Schuman Centre for Advanced Studies, 2014.

Triandafyllidou, Anna, and Rudy Gropas. *European Immigration: A Sourcebook*. London: Ashgate Publishing, 2007.

Trousdale, Jerry. *Miraculous Movements*. Nashville: Thomas Nelson, 2012.

Tylor, Edward B. *Primitive Culture: Researches into the Development of Mythology, Philosophy, Religion, Art and Custom*. London: John Murray, 1871.

Urban Expression. http://www.urbanexpression.org.uk/our-values.

Van de Poll, Evert. *Europe and the Gospel: Past Influences, Current Developments, Mission Challenges*. London: De Gruyter Academic, 2013.

Van de Poll, Evert, ed. *Vivre la diversité: multiculturalité dans l'Église et la société*. Paris: Croire Publications, 2011.

———. *Église locale et mission interculturelle: communiquer l'Évangile au près et au loin*. Charols: Excelsis, 2014.

Van Engen, Charles. *God's Missionary People*. Grand Rapids: Baker, 1991.

Van Gelder, Craig, and Dwight J. Zschiele. *The Missional Church in Perspective: Mapping Trends and Shaping the Conversation*. Grand Rapids: Baker Academic, 2011.

Viggo, Sogaard. *Media in Church and Mission: Communicating Christ*. Pasadena: WCL, 2000.

Volf, Miroslav. *After Our Likeness: The Church as the Image of the Trinity*. Grand Rapids: Eerdmans, 1998.

Wagner, Peter. *Your Church Can Grow*. Pasadena, CA: Regal, 1976.

Währisch-Oblau, Claudia. "Mission in Reverse: Whose Image in the Mirror?."*Anvil*, 18/4, 2001.

Walldorf, Friedemann. *Die Neuevangelisierung Europas. Missionstheologien im europäischen Kontext*. Gießen: TGV Brunnen, 2002.

Warren, Rick. *Purpose Driven Church*. Grand Rapids: Zondervan, 2002.

Watling, Marlin. *Start: Gemeinde gründen–von der Vision zur Wirklichkeit*. Witten: SCM Brockhaus, 2011.

Watson, David. *Gemeindegründungsbewegungen. Eine Momentaufnahme*. 2. Auflage. Schwelm: DIM, 2011.

Weigel, George. *The Cube and the Cathedral: Europe, America, and Politics Without God*. New York: Basic, 2005.

Wells, David. *No Place for Truth: or Whatever Happened to Evangelical Theology?*. Nottingham: IVP, 1994.

Wilkinson, Bruce, and Kenneth Boa. *Talk Thru the Bible*. Tennessee: Thomas Nelson, 1983.

Willaime, Jean-Paul. *Europe et religions: les enjeux du XXIᵉ siècle*. Paris: Fayard, 2009.

Winter, Steven C. Hawthorn, ed. *Perspectives on the World Christian Movement: A Reader.* Pasadena: William Carey Library, 1983.

Yoder, John Howard. "How H. Richard Niebuh Reasoned: A critique of Christ and Culture." In *Authentic Transformation. A New Vision of Christ and Culture,* edited by Stassen, Yeager, et al. Nashville: Abingdon, 1996.

Zscheile, Dwight. *Cultivating Sent Communities: Missional Spiritual Formation (Missional Church).* Grand Rapids: Eerdmans, 2011.

Zulehner, Paul M. *Mystik und Politik: In Gott eintauchen, bei den Menschen auftauchen.* from a speech in Benediktbeuern, Germany, 19.11.2007.

'K Ltd.

16

005B/282/P